ANCIENT ARMAMENTS:
THE FRANK ZAPPA SINGLES PROJECT

GREG RUSSO

CREDITS

"Ancient Armaments: The Frank Zappa Singles Project" was completed on May 20, 2019. Version 1.1 was completed on March 1, 2020. Version 1.2 was completed on November 15, 2021.

Copyright © 2019, 2020, 2021 Crossfire Publications. Special thanks to Ron Furmanek and John Blair.

All rights reserved. Published in the US.

No part of this book may be used or reproduced in any manner whatsoever without written permission of Crossfire Publications.

Bibliography

In addition to my record company and Musician's Union files, record collection and "Cosmik Debris," this book would not be possible without these essential reference sources:

Ulrich, Charles. (2018). The Big Note. Vancouver, BC, Canada: New Star Books Ltd.

Albertos, Román García (ed.). (2019). http://www.donlope.net/fz/lyrics/index.html

Various (ed.). (2019). http://Zappateers.com

Herheim, Bjørn Olav. (2019). http://Zappafrenzy.com

Photos of nearly everything listed here can be found at Zappafrenzy.com.

Also available from Crossfire Publications:

Cosmik Debris: The Collected History And Improvisations Of Frank Zappa (The Return Of The Son Of Revised[2] Edition) by Greg Russo

My Brother Was A Mother: Take 4 by Patrice "Candy" Zappa

Flying Colours: The Jethro Tull Reference Manual (5th Edition) by Greg Russo

Yardbirds: The Ultimate Rave-Up (7th Edition) by Greg Russo

Time Of The Season: The Zombies Collector's Guide (5th Edition) by Greg Russo

Mannerisms: The Five Phases Of Manfred Mann (4th Edition) by Greg Russo

If I Could Only Be Sure: The Life Of Nolan Porter by Patrice "Candy" Zappa

http://www.crossfirepublications.com
email: crossfirepublications@gmail.com
Crossfire Publications, 54 Chester Avenue, Stewart Manor, New York 11530 USA.

ISBN-13: 978-0-9983550-7-8

TABLE OF CONTENTS

Introduction 7

The Early Years (1961-1965)
THE MASTERS: Sixteen Tons/ Breaktime 9
THE HOLLYWOOD TORNADOES: Moon Dawg/ The Inebriated Surfer 10
THE PENGUINS: Memories Of El Monte/ Be Mine 12
BABY RAY AND THE FERNS: How's Your Bird/ The World's Greatest Sinner ... 13
BOB GUY: Dear Jeepers/ Letter From Jeepers 15
THE HEARTBREAKERS: Everytime I See You/ Cradle Rock 16
BRIAN LORD AND THE MIDNIGHTERS: The Big Surfer/ THE MIDNIGHTERS: Not Another One! ... 17
NED & NELDA: Hey Nelda/ Surf Along With Ned & Nelda 18
THE (HOLLYWOOD) PERSUADERS: Tijuana (Surf)/ Grunion Run (both single listings) ... 19
MR. CLEAN: Mr. Clean/ Jessie Lee 20
RON ROMAN: Tell Me/ Love Of My Life 21
THE RHYTHM SURFERS: 502 (Like Getting Pinched On A 502)/ Big City Surfer ... 22
THE TORNADOES: Phantom Surfer/ Shootin' Beavers 23
CONRAD AND THE HURRICANE STRINGS (HURRICANES): Hurricane/ Sweet Love ... 24
THE CORDELLS: Happy Time/ I Love How You Love Me 25
THE DECADES: Lonely Drummer/ The Phantom Strikes Back 26
THE WOODY WAGGERS: The Sahara Hop/ FRANK AND THE WOODY WAGGERS: Three Guns ... 27
THE DECADES: Dance Forever More/ Louie De Loop 27

Honorable Mentions From The Early Years (1961-1965)
THE VELVETEENS: Dog Patch Creeper/ Johnny's Jump 28
THE ROTATIONS: Heavies/ The Cruncher 29

Frank Zappa, Mothers Of Invention & Sessions (1966-1993)
BOBBY JAMESON: Reconsider Baby/ Lowdown Funky Blues 30
THE MOTHERS OF INVENTION: How Could I Be Such A Fool/ Help I'm A Rock 3rd Movement: It Can't Happen Here ... 31
BOBBY JAMESON: Gotta' Find My Roogalator/ Lowdown Funky Blues 33
THE MOTHERS OF INVENTION: Trouble Comin' Every Day/ Who Are The Brain Police? ... 34
BURT WARD: Boy Wonder I Love You/ Orange Colored Sky 36
BARRY GOLDBERG: Carry On/ Ronnie Siegel From Avenue L 38
THE MOTHERS OF INVENTION: Why Don't You Do Me Right/ Big Leg Emma ... 38
THE KNACK: Softly, Softly/ The Spell 40
FRANK ZAPPA: Sink Trap/ Gypsy Airs 40
ERIC BURDON & THE ANIMALS: It's All Meat/ The Other Side Of This Life ... 42
VARIOUS ARTISTS: MGM, Verve, Verve/Forecast Radio Commercials 43
TOMMY FLANDERS: Friday Night City/ Reputation 45
THE MOTHERS OF INVENTION: Lonely Little Girl/ Mother People 46
THE MOTHERS OF INVENTION: Mother People – Flower Punk/ Nasal Retentive Calliope Music – Absolutely Free ... 49
WILD MAN FISCHER: The Circle/ Merry-Go-Round 50
RUBEN AND THE JETS: Anyway The Wind Blows/ Jelly Roll Gum Drop 52
RUBEN (REUBEN) AND THE JETS: Deseri/ Jelly Roll Gum Drop 54

THE MOTHERS OF INVENTION: Radio Spots For Bizarre/Reprise Album – The Mothers Of Invention – Uncle Meat	54
THE MOTHERS OF INVENTION: My Guitar/ Dog Breath	56
FRANK ZAPPA: Radio Spots For Bizarre Reprise Album "Hot Rats"	59
FRANK ZAPPA: Radio Spots For Reprise Album 6356 - Frank Zappa - Hot Rats	60
FRANK ZAPPA: Peaches En Regalia/ Little Umbrellas	61
THE MOTHERS OF INVENTION: WPLJ/ My Guitar	63
FRANK ZAPPA: Sharleena/ Bognor Regis	65
THE MOTHERS OF INVENTION: Radio Spot For Mothers Of Invention – Weasels Ripped My Flesh – Reprise Album MS 2028	66
FRANK ZAPPA: Radio Spots For Frank Zappa "Chunga's Revenge" Reprise Album MS 2030	68
FRANK ZAPPA: Tell Me You Love Me/ Will You Go All The Way For The U.S.A.?	68
JUNIER MINTZ: Tears Began To Fall/ JUNIER MINTZ FEATURING BILLY DEXTER ON GUITAR: Junier Mintz Boogie (first US issue)	70
MOTHERS OF INVENTION: Tears Began To Fall/ Junier Mintz Boogie (UK issue)	71
FRANK ZAPPA: Special Radio Spot Commercial – Frank Zappa's "200 Motels"	72
(NO ARTIST LISTED): "200 Motels"	72
FRANK ZAPPA: What Will This Evening Bring Me This Morning/ Daddy, Daddy, Daddy	74
FRANK ZAPPA AND THE MOTHERS OF INVENTION: Tears Began To Fall/ Junier Mintz Boogie (second US issue)	75
FRANK ZAPPA: Magic Fingers/ Daddy, Daddy, Daddy	76
THE MOTHERS: Cletus Awreetus-Awrightus/ Eat That Question	77
RUBEN AND THE JETS: If I Could Be Your Love Again/ Wedding Bells	79
RUBEN AND THE JETS: Charlena/ Mah Man Flash	81
THE MOTHERS: I'm The Slime/ Montana	82
FRANK ZAPPA: Cosmik Debris/ Uncle Remus	85
FRANK ZAPPA: Don't Eat The Yellow Snow/ Cosmik Debris	87
GRAND FUNK RAILROAD: Can You Do It/ 1976	89
GRAND FUNK RAILROAD: Just Couldn't Wait/ Out To Get You	90
FRANK ZAPPA: Find Her Finer/ Zoot Allures	92
FRANK ZAPPA: Disco Boy/ Ms. Pinky	94
FRANK ZAPPA: Sheik Yerbouti "Clean Cuts" (aka "Limited Zappa Edition")	97
FRANK ZAPPA: Dancin' Fool/ Baby Snakes	102
FRANK ZAPPA: Bobby Brown/ Baby Snakes (Dutch release)	104
FRANK ZAPPA: Joe's Garage/ Central Scrutinizer (US release)	105
L. SHANKAR: Dead Girls Of London/ Dead Girls Of London	108
FRANK ZAPPA: Joe's Garage (sampler)	109
FRANK ZAPPA: Joe's Garage/ Catholic Girls (UK release)	113
FRANK ZAPPA: Bobby Brown/ Stick It Out (German release)	114
FRANK ZAPPA: Stick It Out/ Why Does It Hurt When I Pee?	116
FRANK ZAPPA: I Don't Wanna Get Drafted/ Ancient Armaments	116
FRANK ZAPPA: Tinsel Town Rebellion – Special Clean Cuts Edition	118
FRANK ZAPPA: Love Of My Life/ For The Young Sophisticate	121
FRANK ZAPPA: Special Clean Cuts Edition – You Are What You Is	122
FRANK ZAPPA: Goblin Girl/ Pink Napkins	127
FRANK ZAPPA: Harder Than Your Husband/ Dumb All Over	128
FRANK ZAPPA: You Are What You Is/ Harder Than Your Husband	129

FRANK ZAPPA: You Are What You Is – Pink Napkins/ Harder Than Your Husband – Soup 'N Old Clothes	129
FRANK ZAPPA: The Frank Zappa E.P.	130
FRANK ZAPPA: Valley Girl/ No Not Now (Dutch release)	132
FRANK ZAPPA: Valley Girl/ FRANK ZAPPA: Teenage Prostitute (UK release)	133
FRANK & MOON ZAPPA: Valley Girl/ FRANK ZAPPA: You Are What You Is (US release)	134
FRANK ZAPPA: Shut Up 'N Play Yer Guitar Sampler	135
FRANK ZAPPA: The Man From Utopia Sampler	136
FRANK ZAPPA: Barking Pumpkin Goes Digital	140
FRANK ZAPPA: The Man From Utopia Meets Mary Lou (Medley)/ Sex	143
FRANK ZAPPA: Cocaine Decisions/ Sex	143
FRANK ZAPPA & THE BARKING PUMPKIN DIGITAL GRATIFICATION CONSORT: The Girl In The Magnesium Dress/ Outside Now, Again	144
FRANK ZAPPA: Baby, Take Your Teeth Out/ Stevie's Spanking	145
FRANK ZAPPA: True Glove	146
FRANK ZAPPA: Thing-Fish/ Them Or Us	148
DWEEZIL ZAPPA: Let's Talk About It/ Electric Hoedown	150
FRANK ZAPPA/ DWEEZIL ZAPPA: Sharleena/ MICHAEL SCIUTO: Grand Prize Stun Solo	151
FRANK ZAPPA: Black Page No. 1/ EVA-TONE INC.: Hear For Yourself How Sound Sells	151
FRANK ZAPPA: Peaches En Regalia – I'm Not Satisfied – Lucille Has Messed My Mind Up	152
FRANK ZAPPA: Sexual Harassment In The Workplace – Watermelon In Easter Hay	153
FRANK ZAPPA: Zomby Woof – You Didn't Try To Call Me	154
FRANK ZAPPA: Montana (Whipping Floss) – Cheepnis	154
FRANK ZAPPA: Stairway To Heaven/ Bolero	155
FRANK ZAPPA: Bobby Brown/ I Have Been In You – Dancin' Fool	156
FRANK ZAPPA: Valley Girl/ You Are What You Is (1993 UK reissue)	158

Posthumous Singles

FRANK ZAPPA: Bobby Brown – Valley Girl/ The Torture Never Stops	158
FRANK ZAPPA: I Don't Wanna Get Drafted – Dinah-Moe Humm – My Guitar Wants To Kill Your Mama	160
THE TORNADOES: The Swag/ Raw-Hide	161
FRANK ZAPPA: Lumpy Money OMORP	162
FRANK ZAPPA: Penguin In Bondage/ The Little Known History Of The Mothers Of Invention	166
FRANK ZAPPA & THE MOTHERS OF INVENTION: Help I'm A Rock – It Can't Happen Here/ Who Are The Brain Police? – Who Are The Brain Police? (Basic Tracks)	167
FRANK ZAPPA: Don't Eat The Yellow Snow/ Down In De Dew	167
FRANK ZAPPA: Zoot Allures (1982)/ Cosmik Debris (1973)	168
ESA-PEKKA SALONEN, CONDUCTOR – L.A. PHILHARMONIC: Overture (200 Motels)/ FRANK ZAPPA – THE ROYAL PHILHARMONIC ORCHESTRA – ELGAR HOWARTH, CONDUCTOR: What's The Name Of Your Group?	169
FRANK ZAPPA: Pick Me, I'm Clean	169
FRANK ZAPPA: Rollo/ Portland Improvisation	170
FRANK ZAPPA: Lumpy Gravy Primordial (Side One)/ Lumpy Gravy Primordial (Side Two)	171
FRANK ZAPPA: Peaches En Regalia (1969 Rhythm Track Mix) – Little Umbrellas (1969 Rhythm Track Mix)/ Peaches En Regalia (1969 Mono Single Master) – Little Umbrellas (1969 Mono Single Master)	173

FRANK ZAPPA: The Zappa Movie Official Soundtrack EP! - Exclusive Backer Reward Edition 174
FRANK ZAPPA: A Very Zappa Birthday 175

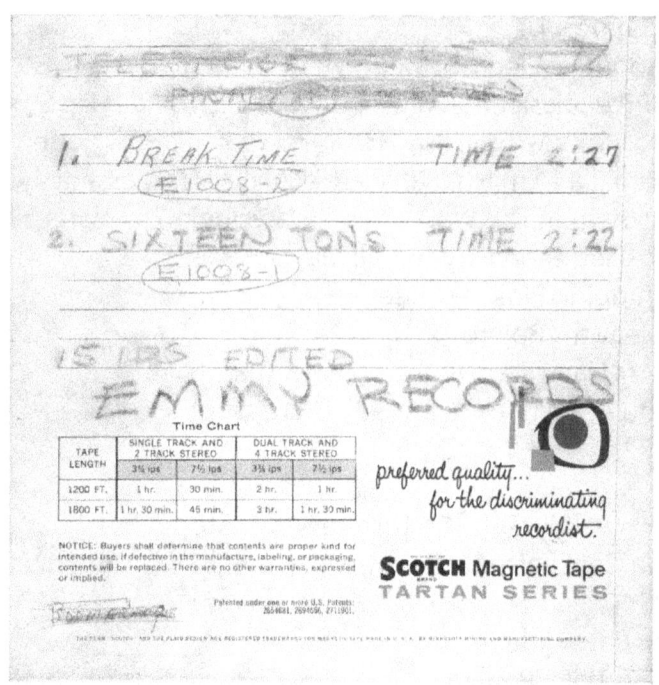

INTRODUCTION

Many fine works have been written about Frank Zappa's albums and the conceptual continuity of the recordings on those releases. However, an extensive discussion of how Zappa's singles relate to his project/object has never been presented. That is the aim of this work, which is an adjunct to my book "Cosmik Debris."

We have quite a bit of evidence which proves that Frank Zappa had enormous contempt for the way radio stations did their business – what they played, what they didn't play, what radio programmers did to ensure that only certain records were heard, and how slick DJs spoke to their audiences. Frank discovered as a child that the music he found most enjoyable was not on the airwaves. Despite all of this, Zappa found radio to be a necessary evil: the communicative power of that medium could not be denied. The process that took Frank from a pre-teen musical novice to an effective and extremely convincing multifaceted communicator took place concurrently with his musical and artistic pursuits.

The first nationwide glimpse of what we could expect from Frank Zappa took place on "The Steve Allen Show," a Westinghouse Broadcasting syndicated program that first aired on March 27, 1963. The sight and sound of Zappa and Allen creating sounds with bicycles over orchestration and backing tapes would form an early template for how Frank would present his work in public. At the end of the next year, Zappa's two installments of "The Uncle Frankie Show" for Pomona College's radio station KSPC in Claremont, CA promoted the ill-fated "I Was A Teen-age Malt Shop" project and described some equally absurd follow-ups.

The best example of Frank's early contempt of radio can be heard on an MGM promotional disc from September 1967: "MGM, Verve, Verve/Forecast Radio Commercials." That record included three Zappa-led mono promotional radio spots for Mothers Of Invention albums on side two – one for "Freak Out!," one for "Absolutely Free," and one for both albums. Despite his contempt, Zappa felt it necessary to regularly present sarcastic sales pitches such as these MGM promos in case some people were open-minded enough to be converted.

Since 1958, Frank Zappa had been dabbling with informal recording. Frank initially stepped into Paul Buff's Pal Recording Studio in Cucamonga, CA near the end of 1960. At that time, the music business could not have been more polarized – large record labels such as Capitol had their own recording studios and in-house business operations, while a vast number of small, start-up record labels released tracks recorded at makeshift studios and fought for attention. Paul Buff was one of those maverick independent studio/record label owners, having created in-house record productions since 1957.

Buff's method of operation was to create numerous short-term record labels to accomplish various goals. Those labels responded to current musical trends by offering audio replicas and/or satires of popular records of the time. In Zappa, Buff finally had a co-conspirator to create records that would make people take notice. Armed with his previous art and music training and research, Zappa's mission was to subvert all forms of media and replace their messages with his own.

Some of the early Pal sessions were very instructive for Frank, while others simply paid the bills. From this moment on, the 45 rpm single became Frank's primary method of communication until the creation of The Mothers Of Invention. When the emphasis in the 1960s marketplace changed from singles to albums, so did the requirements of buyers of those formats. Long-playing albums (LPs) were a real luxury at the time for most people, and if you happened to create a stereo edition of an album for your record company, you charged an extra dollar for it.

Frank Zappa knew that singles consumers and radio programmers were different breeds when compared to album buyers. That is precisely why he very rarely extracted album tracks "as is" for single release. Instead, Frank used different mixes, edits and/or performances to present these miniatures on 45 rpm records and later formats. Fads like novelty records and three-chord instrumentals (surf and otherwise) came and went, but their long-term influences on Zappa would become clear once his own style incorporated everything to which he was exposed.

So, what's here and what's not here? As an American artist, Frank Zappa's US retail singles and special singles releases for radio programmers are the main concentration. If a non-US release offers something unique in its content or reception, it is mentioned here. Singles that were planned but not released are also featured. Radio shows, interviews, and public service commercials are also discussed. All releases listed use their originally released titles, such as "Trouble Comin' Every Day" rather than "Trouble Every Day." And so, we're now ready to discover how these singles – whether Zappa's own or those to which he contributed – work into his entire project/object.

* * *

Here is the format used for each single release…

ARTIST NAME: Titles (BOLD TITLES HAVE FRANK ZAPPA INVOLVEMENT) (Format)
Original Release Date, Record Label and Release Number

<u>A-side, B-side (or Track #)</u>
Title (Original Track Timing) (Songwriter) • Master # • MONO or STEREO
Recording Date and Location
Personnel
Producer
Engineer

For releases that are not two-sided or only have partial Frank Zappa involvement, relevant individual tracks are listed in order with the same data.

Commentary about conceptual continuity and any other important information.

Current availability of the singles mixes for the release.

* * *

The turntable has been fired up at 45 rpm and the adaptor is firmly in place, so let's take a fascinating trip through the singles as they happened.

Greg Russo
May 20, 2019

THE EARLY YEARS (1961-1965)

THE MASTERS: Sixteen Tons/ **Breaktime** (7" 45 rpm single)
Original Release: June 1961 as Emmy E-1008-1 (A-side)/ E-1008-2 (B-side)

B-side
Breaktime (2:27) (Ronald Williams – Paul Conrad Buff – Frank Zappa) • Master #: E 1008-2 Re • MONO
Recorded: May 1961 at Pal Recording Studio, Cucamonga, CA
Personnel: Frank Zappa (lead guitar, rhythm guitar); Paul Buff (piano); Ronnie Williams (drums, bass)
Producer: Paul Buff
Engineer: Paul Buff

Zappa got underway with recording at Pal almost immediately. His first jazz recordings ("Take Your Clothes Off When You Dance" and "High Steppin'") were made in January 1961. Neither was released at the time. The latter track was sped up for release on the Verve edition of "Lumpy Gravy" in 1968, while the former was first released on "The Lost Episodes" in 1996.

Meanwhile, Paul Buff had been recording instrumentals on his Emmy label as The Masters with lead guitarist Ronnie Williams and rhythm guitarist Johnny Fisher. Williams came to Pal Recording Studio during the summer of 1960 and brought Frank Zappa along a few months later. The Masters' debut single "T Bone"/ "Sunday Blues" first appeared in October 1960. Billboard magazine was very impressed by the record.

Guitarist Duane Eddy had been banging out instrumental hits by playing melodies and solos on the bass strings of his instrument. Buff and Williams decided to apply the Duane Eddy treatment to the "Tennessee" Ernie Ford hit "Sixteen Tons," which amazingly had not been recorded by Eddy. Ronnie Williams was well versed in playing what we currently call "American roots," so nailing down the Duane Eddy guitar style was no problem at all. Johnny Fisher wanted to record vocal tracks like his 1960 Emmy single "Tell Me Yes"/ "Dream Tonight" while developing relationships with radio station personnel, so he removed himself from The Masters.

Paul Buff and Ronnie Williams didn't have a B-side. They asked Zappa to write one. Frank came up with the structure of the instrumental "Breaktime." Since Buff and Williams' contributions would be made up on the spot, Zappa agreed to share writer credit with them. Ronnie Williams could also play drums and he had a better feel for the rhythm that Frank wanted from the song. Just for this track, Ronnie would be drumming instead of Paul Buff. The recording was made in three stages on Buff's homemade five-track recorder. The first stage consisted of Ronnie Williams playing drums on one track with Paul Buff's piano and Zappa's rhythm guitar on a second track. Paul Buff then went to the recording booth while Williams overdubbed bass on the third track, and then Zappa recorded guitar overdubs on the fourth and fifth tracks to complete the master recording.

The fact that the song was eventually called "Breaktime" was not a coincidence. "Boomerang" was the original title, as evidenced on the tape box. Zappa, Williams and Buff each had solo breaks within the track to produce an exuberant instrumental out of a typical three-chord (I-IV-V) structure. Like many instrumental sections of later Zappa works, a basic framework was used for improvisation. Initial test pressings for both sides of this single were rejected and the successful second pressing incorporated the designation "Re" for both master recordings.

The record has a "Supervised By Gary Price" credit on both labels. Gary Price was an evening DJ at California radio station KFXM, which covered the San Bernardino and Riverside areas. Price was not at Pal when this single was made. The supervision credit was the result of a backroom deal made between Johnny Fisher and Gary Price to have Gary's name on the label in exchange for a #43 weekly record survey listing for Fisher's year-old single "Tell Me Yes." Despite this deal, "Sixteen Tons"/ "Breaktime" did not appear on KFXM's weekly survey. Instead, "Breaktime" ended up receiving airplay on Los Angeles' KRLA as lead-in music for news reports.

"Breaktime," Zappa's first released recording, was first officially reissued in the first volume of the "Paul Buff Presents The Pal And Original Sound Studio Archives" download series in 2010 before its inclusion on the 5-CD set "Paul Buff Presents Highlights From The Pal And Original Sound Studio Archives" two years later. Since many of the early singles listed in this section were captured on that boxed set, the set will be subsequently referred to as the "Buff box" for short.

After this record, Zappa concentrated on live gigs with various musicians while working on writing and recording new compositions. Buff and Williams did a final Masters record without Zappa: "Under The Earth"/ "Rolling Blues" (Emmy E-1009; August 1961).

* * *

THE HOLLYWOOD TORNADOES: Moon Dawg/ The Inebriated Surfer (7" 45 rpm single)
Released February 1, 1963 as Aertaun 102

A-side
Moon Dawg (2:14) (Derry Weaver) • Master #: GDF-1018 • MONO
Recorded: January 1963 at Pal Recording Studio, Cucamonga, CA
Personnel: Gerald Sanders (bass, dog howls, backing vocals); Jack Sessums (dog howls); James Norman "Roly" Sanders (lead guitar, backing vocals); Jesse Sanders (rhythm guitar, backing vocals); Leonard Delaney (drums); Dave Aerni (arranger, conductor)
Producer: Dave Aerni for Aertaun Enterprises
Engineer: Frank Zappa

B-side
The Inebriated Surfer (2:30) (James Norman Sanders) • Master #: GDF-1019 • MONO
Recorded: January 1963 at Pal Recording Studio, Cucamonga, CA
Personnel: Gerald Sanders (bass); James Norman "Roly" Sanders (lead guitar); Jesse Sanders (rhythm guitar); George White (sax); Leonard Delaney (drums); Dave Aerni (arranger, conductor)
Producer: Dave Aerni for Aertaun Enterprises
Engineer: Frank Zappa

Dave Aerni presented himself as an entrepreneur to Paul Buff as he was generating a lot of buzz with The Tornadoes' debut single "Bustin' Surfboards." Aerni and his Aertaun Enterprises partner George Taunton sponsored local concerts while managing the instrumental group The Tornadoes, and Dave also proved that he could play guitar in the then-popular surf style. Paul Buff and Dave Aerni did some recording as The Rotations along with sax player Mike Dineri, who played with Frank Zappa in Joe Perrino's group The Mellotones.

The Tornadoes recorded their first two singles ("Bustin' Surfboards" and the two-part "The Gremmie") at William Locy Sound Company in Riverside, CA. That studio was adequate, but "The Gremmie" was roundly ignored. The main problem was that the British group The Tornados (without an "e") had just scored an enormous British and American hit with "Telstar," and Dave Aerni credited "The Gremmie" to The Hollywood Tornadoes to distinguish his client from the "Telstar" band. Aerni brought The Tornadoes into Pal Recording Studio to regain the momentum of their debut. When Dave Aerni was convinced that the British group would be unable to produce a strong follow-up to their hit, Dave would again promote his group as The Tornadoes in the spring of 1963.

To develop a rapport at Pal, Dave Aerni asked Frank Zappa to engineer The Tornadoes' output in December 1962. The first two tracks that Zappa engineered were "The Swag" and "Raw-Hide," both of which were popularized by Link Wray. Those were not released until much later, but The Tornadoes greatly appreciated Frank's creative approach in recording their music. The single release of those recordings is shown in the "Posthumous Releases" section.

The third Tornadoes A-side, "Moon Dawg," was worked up in surf instrumental style before the band hit the studio. It became something completely different once Frank Zappa put his own stamp on the band's performance. The Tornadoes were a bunch of pleasure seekers who would do anything to create great records and have fun at the same time. On this occasion, the band's friend Jack Sessums was on hand at Pal to see how the group would record "Moon Dawg." As it turned out, Jack would be part of the action. Zappa suggested that Tornadoes leader Gerald Sanders and Jack Sessums should assume a doggie stance on the floor and bark like dogs at appropriate points of the song. Sanders and Sessums were up for the idea and followed Frank's suggestion. That small but essential addition to the arrangement would separate The Tornadoes' version from the original. Roly Sanders' rapid guitar picking captured the essential melodic components and descending chord changes.

The lineage of "Moon Dawg" is quite interesting, as it involves three people that Zappa would work with later: studio session producer Nick Venet (producer of the original "Lumpy Gravy"), future Mothers Of Invention rhythm guitarist Elliot Ingber, and jazz record producer Richard Bock (producer of violinist Jean-Luc Ponty's "King Kong" album). Lead guitarist Derry Weaver wrote "Moon Dawg" and recorded it with the studio-based group The Gamblers in late 1959. In addition to Weaver and Ingber, the other Gamblers were keyboardist Bruce Johnston (later of The Beach Boys, who incidentally recorded the song prior to his joining), future Canned Heat bassist Larry Taylor (bass guitar), and "Teen Beat" drummer Sandy Nelson. Richard Bock was looking to buy finished master tapes to release on the World Pacific label. Bock specialized in jazz, but he employed Nick Venet to produce masters such as The Gamblers' single. On October 6-7, 1969, Richard Bock produced the Whitney Studios sessions for Ponty's album for World Pacific in Glendale, CA. Released on May 25, 1970, the album consisted of five Frank Zappa works and the Ponty-composed "How Would You Like to Have a Head Like That" with FZ on guitar. Frank also served as Ponty's album arranger and conductor.

The B-side, "The Inebriated Surfer," took a comical approach to the surf instrumental format with tumbling Leonard Delaney drums, brief sax bursts by George White, and Duane Eddy-style riffing by Roly Sanders along with Roly's own soloing ability. Part of the engineering work by Zappa on this side involved some light phasing on the drums, which contributed to the feel of the title. This was the first recorded appearance of George White, who was in the band for a few months but was not used on previous sessions for "The Swag," "Raw-Hide," or "Moon Dawg."

Dog references in later Frank Zappa material could fill a book, but it is important to note that dog barking can be found as part of the intro of "Andy" on "One Size Fits All" in 1975. Both sides of this single would be released on The Tornadoes' album "Bustin' Surfboards" (Josie JOZ 4005; released July 26, 1963). However, the phasing on "The Inebriated Surfer" was not included on the album mix. The first reissue of both original single masters took place on The Tornadoes' "Now And Then" CD (Crossfire Publications 9501-2; issued October 27, 2005).

The regional success of this single was greatly appreciated by The Tornadoes, who would return to Pal and Zappa in June 1963 to record six Dave Aerni-produced tracks to complete their Josie album: "Vaquero" (by George Tomsco and Norman Petty), "The Tornado" (a Leonard Delaney drum showcase written by Aerni), Chuck Berry's "Johnny B. Goode," "Bumble Bee Stomp" (a band arrangement of Nikolai Rimsky-Korsakov's "Flight Of The Bumblebee" from "The Tale Of Tsar Saltan"), "Malagueña" (actually a combination of Ernesto Lecuona's work of that title with the Russian traditional "Dark Eyes"), and Gerald Sanders' notorious "Shootin' Beavers." The latter track would also appear on a single at the end of 1963, and will be discussed a bit later.

* * *

THE PENGUINS: Memories Of El Monte/ Be Mine (7" 45 rpm single)
Released February 20, 1963 as Original Sound OS-27

<u>A-side</u>
Memories Of El Monte (2:36) (Frank Zappa – Raymond Eugene Collins) • Master #: or-060 • MONO
Recorded: January 1963 at Original Sound Recording Studios, Hollywood, CA
Personnel: members of The Penguins – Cleve Duncan (lead vocal); Walter Saulsberry (backing vocals); members of The Viceroys – James Conwell (backing vocals); Andrew "Jack" White (backing vocals); Charles Jones (backing vocals); Oliver Williams (backing vocals); Herbert White (backing vocals); Frank Zappa (vibes); other personnel unknown
Producer: Art Laboe
Engineer: Paul Buff

Deejay and Original Sound Records owner Art Laboe (born Arthur Egnoian) was a big fan of doo-wop and rhythm and blues vocal records. Since 1957, Laboe had been promoting dances at the Legion Stadium in El Monte, CA, where ordinances banning those under 18 from attending dances without Board of Education sponsorship did not exist. Art Laboe started licensing recent local and national R&B and doo-wop hits for the first two volumes of his "Oldies But Goodies" album series for Original Sound in 1959. Licensing of such recordings was in its infancy, as rights owners placed low values on their masters due to their feeling that no one would want those records after the singles stopped selling in large quantities.

Laboe followed up his "Oldies But Goodies" compilations with another that recalled those El Monte shows and the artists that appeared at them – "Art Laboe's Memories Of El Monte (The Best Of L.A.'s Rock And Roll)." The back cover of that LP, this time released on his Starla offshoot label, promoted both "Oldies But Goodies" releases. Future Mothers Of Invention vocalist Ray Collins had recorded "I Remember Linda" with Little Julian Herrera for a Starla single. It was one of two in-house tracks on the El Monte album ("Handsome" Jim Balcom's Starla single "Corrido Rock" was the other.). Collins had participated in those El Monte Legion Stadium concerts with Little Julian Herrera and with Chuck Higgins, the tenor saxophonist known for "Pachuko Hop." (The B-side of "Pachuko Hop" was "Motor Head Baby," the nickname source of another MOI alum – Jim "Motorhead" Sherwood. Over the years, Frank Zappa performed live versions/ quotes of four tracks from the El Monte album: "Pachuko Hop," "Corrido Rock," The Shields' "You Cheated," and Gene & Eunice's "This Is My Story.")

Both Frank Zappa and Paul Buff had met Art Laboe by this time, but they needed to come up with a way to get Art interested in what they were doing. While Zappa was living at 314 West G Street in Ontario, CA, he and Ray Collins worked on what became "Memories Of El Monte." After running the idea past Art Laboe, Art suggested that Zappa and Collins work in song quotes of doo-wop groups. Zappa and Collins signed a publishing agreement with Laboe's publishing arm Drive-In Music Co., Inc. on August 23, 1962.

Penguins lead vocalist Cleve Duncan, the lead voice of "Earth Angel," was asked to vocalize "Memories Of El Monte." The defunct Penguins were revived in another incarnation featuring tenor vocalist Walter Saulsberry and five backing vocalists from Original Sound vocal group The Viceroys. In March 1961, The Viceroys and Chuck Higgins' band released the single "Dreamy Eyes"/ "Ball N' Chain." Frank Zappa played vibes on "Memories Of El Monte," but there is no documentation for the other players.

Song quotes, which became regular parts of Zappa's output, actually turn up quite often during "Memories Of El Monte." Cleve Duncan sang The Five Satins' "In The Still Of The Night," The Shields' "You Cheated," The Heartbeats' "A Thousand Miles Away," The Medallions' "The Letter," Tony Allen & The Chimes' "Nite Owl" (actually credited to The Champs), and "Earth Angel" by Cleve Duncan's group The Penguins. The B-side "Be Mine" did not feature Zappa, but included the other vocalists on the A-side. Duncan would officially revive The Penguins after its release and they continued until his death in 2012.

Despite Art Laboe's promotion for this nostalgic single, "Memories Of El Monte" did not generate national interest. It did, however, become a sizable local hit. The record strengthened the relationship between Laboe, Buff, and Zappa. Laboe would keep "Memories Of El Monte" in print for a very long time, and it appeared on numerous singles, LPs and CDs over the years. Most recently, "Memories Of El Monte" appeared on Volume 7 of the Paul Buff download series and on the Buff box. A slightly longer stereo mix was first released on the CD "Spotlite On Original Sound Records" (Collectables COL CD 6045) on January 25, 2000. The Mothers Of Invention performed a live version of "Memories Of El Monte" at the Whisky a Go Go on July 23, 1968. It was released in late 2020 on "The Zappa Movie Official Soundtrack Album! - Exclusive Backer Reward Edition" and "Zappa - Original Motion Picture Soundtrack."

* * *

BABY RAY AND THE FERNS: How's Your Bird/ The World's Greatest Sinner (7" 45 rpm single)
Released April 8, 1963 as Donna 1378

A-side
How's Your Bird (2:10) (Frank Zappa) • Master #: DF-363-526 • MONO
Recorded: March 1963 at Pal Recording Studio, Cucamonga, CA
Personnel: Frank Zappa (lead guitar, rhythm guitar, drums, percussion); Paul Buff (bass, snorks); Ray Collins (lead vocal, backing vocals)
Producer: Paul Buff
Engineer: Paul Buff

B-side
The World's Greatest Sinner (2:25) (Frank Zappa) • Master #: DF-363-527 • MONO
Recorded: November 1961 at Pal Recording Studio, Cucamonga, CA

Personnel: Frank Zappa (lead guitar, rhythm guitar, backing vocals); Paul Buff (bass, drums, saxophones); Ray Collins (lead vocal, backing vocals)
Producer: Paul Buff
Engineer: Paul Buff

The very busy year of 1963 continued with Zappa, Buff and Collins going off into a satirical direction that would permeate nearly all of their records that year. Inside jokes and references abounded. Frank Zappa had been tasked with providing the soundtrack for Timothy Carey's self-financed film "The World's Greatest Sinner" in June 1961. That summer, Frank regularly rehearsed and played with numerous musicians. Different permutations of Ronnie Williams (guitar), Rex Jakabosky (guitar, harmonica, vocals), Joe Perrino (piano), Dwight Bement (tenor saxophone) and Al Surratt (drums) joined Zappa during a three-month stint at The Sportsman Tavern, 1055 East Holt Avenue in Pomona, CA. Zappa expanded this lineup to create The Blackouts when performing at "Battle Of The Bands" competitions. It was at The Sportsman bar that a somewhat inebriated Ray Collins joined Zappa's core band on Hank Ballard & The Midnighters' "Work With Me, Annie," among others.

After the Sportsman gig was over, band and orchestral recording for "The World's Greatest Sinner" took place in November and December 1961 at Chaffey Junior College, Alta Loma, CA, while the film title song was laid down at Pal in November. Frank's guitar playing sounds very much like it did on "Breaktime" recorded six months before. Clearly, Zappa was listening to the "chee poppa doodly woppa" backing vocals on Huey "Piano" Smith And His Clowns' "Well I'll Be John Brown" (Ace 553; released November 1958) when he repurposed them on "The World's Greatest Sinner" and the later "Plastic People" on "Joe's Corsage."

Over about 19 seconds of a black film screen, Timothy Carey left space for a starting fragment of Zappa's recording with Collins and Buff to serve as the title theme. This is how the song and the film "The World's Greatest Sinner" were originally presented at the movie's premiere in June 1962. Absolute Films aired the film again in 1964 with the first 52 seconds of Zappa's recording instead of the original 19-second edit. The full recording would not be heard until about 16 months later.

Ray Collins and Frank Zappa had a shared love for the comic brilliance of Steve Allen and his Westinghouse TV-syndicated show. Allen's guest booker Jerry Hopkins entertained Frank's proposal of "blowing bicycle" – that is, creating music from a bicycle. Money was essential, so Frank was interested in the $235 that he would receive after appearing on this program. On March 14, 1963, Zappa filmed his appearance on "The Steve Allen Show" at The Steve Allen Playhouse on 1228 North Vine Street in Hollywood, CA. Allen was known for his repeated uses of catchphrases like "How's your fern?," "rat fink," and various others. Tapping into this madness, Zappa put together "How's Your Bird" (no question mark) with essential contributions by Ray Collins and Paul Buff. This was the first usage of snorks in a Zappa work. Despite Paul Buff's five-track recording capability, the massive overdubbing involved in creating the final master led to somewhat diminished sound quality. Zappa played drums on "How's Your Bird" rather than Buff, who was on the earlier B-side. The group name Baby Ray And The Ferns was also an obvious nod to Steve Allen.

Right at the end of his interview with Steve Allen, Frank Zappa mentioned the impending release of this record. The word "fink" is mentioned four times on "How's Your Bird" and it also asked "How's your grunion?," which would presage the name of the instrumental "Grunion Run" (listed later). The rhyming of the words fanny and granny would later be used on the "Bongo Fury" track "Debra Kadabra." Steve Allen was so inspired by his meeting with Zappa that he created the song "How's Your Sister" for release as a Dot single in 1964 and as part of the LP "Songs From The Steve Allen TV Show." "How's your fern?" was the only common lyric line for the Baby Ray and Steve Allen singles.

This was not a record for the strait-laced Art Laboe and his Original Sound label. Buff and Zappa negotiated a master licensing deal for "How's Your Bird"/"The World's Greatest Sinner" with Bob Keane of Donna Records in March 1963. The master numbers were given according to the label's tape receipt date rather than the original recording dates.

Both sides were reissued many times over the years, but the Buff downloads and the Buff box present the tracks in the best possible quality.

* * *

BOB GUY: Dear Jeepers/ Letter From Jeepers (7" 45 rpm single)
Released April 22, 1963 as Donna 1380

A-side
Dear Jeepers (2:25) (Frank Zappa) • Master #: DF-463-540 • MONO
Recorded: April 1963 at Pal Recording Studio, Cucamonga, CA
Personnel: Bob Guy (lead vocal); Frank Zappa (guitar, drums, sped up vocals); Paul Buff (bass, snorks, sped up vocals, sound effects)
Producer: Paul Buff
Engineer: Paul Buff

B-side
Letter From Jeepers (2:20) (Frank Zappa) • Master #: DF-463-541 • MONO
Recorded: April 1963 at Pal Recording Studio, Cucamonga, CA
Personnel: Bob Guy (lead vocal); Frank Zappa (guitar, drums, sped up vocals); Paul Buff (bass, piano, snorks, sped up vocals, sound effects)
Producer: Paul Buff
Engineer: Paul Buff

The next project was another step in Frank Zappa's studio development, especially the usage of sped up laughing. Bob Guy was the station manager of KCOP-TV 13 in Los Angeles, CA. He also portrayed the Jeepers Creepers character in his "Jeepers Creepers Theatre" program that aired on his station during 1962-1963. John Zacherle cracked the Top 10 with his "Dinner With Drac" in 1958, so Zappa asked Guy to use his Jeepers character on a similar record. This time, the premise involved readings of letters exchanged between Jeepers Creepers and Count Dracula after Dracula invited Jeepers and his wife Doris to his Transylvanian castle.

On "Dear Jeepers," Paul Buff produced an elaborate collage of horror sound effects which ran throughout the track, and he worked in snorks here and there. The music did not start until 30 seconds into the track, which involved a basic three-chord instrumental with stops in the middle following the priceless line "Doris, squeeze me a glass of mildew."

"Letter From Jeepers" was dictated by Jeepers to his wife Doris from Cucamonga rather than Los Angeles. The uplifting music bed that started 15 seconds into the sound effects track matched the excitement Jeepers expressed about the dinner he enjoyed with Count Dracula. In between laughing, Jeepers described Cucamonga's weather in full detail. One of his descriptions was that "…it's rainy and damp 400 days of the year." In fact, "400 Days Of The Year" was the initial title of the more commonly known "Nine Types Of Industrial Pollution" on early editions of the "Uncle Meat" album.

Jeepers' disappointment that Dracula was serving fish and chips quickly turned to thrills when the dish was revealed to be silverfish and buffalo chips. When describing the silverfish, Jeepers said, "The first one went down easy, but the second one was greasy!" Years later, the line was turned around in Zappa's song "Keep It Greasey" as "Keep it greasey so it'll go down easy." In terms of conceptual continuity, "Letter From Jeepers" has proven to be the more successful of the two single sides. Sped up vocals would be used greatly on Mothers singles and albums, especially "We're Only In It For The Money," "Cruising With Ruben & The Jets," and "Uncle Meat."

The Donna label once again licensed this single from Buff and Zappa. In retrospect, it would have been difficult to find a record company to release such crazed antics. Thankfully, Frank Zappa and Paul Buff would offer a more commercial single candidate by The Heartbreakers to go along with Bob Guy and Baby Ray And The Ferns. This single has been released numerous times, but once again, the Buff downloads and box set have the best sound on these tracks.

* * *

THE HEARTBREAKERS: Everytime I See You/ Cradle Rock (7" 45 rpm single)
Released April 22, 1963 as Donna 1381

A-side
Everytime I See You (2:15) (Frank Zappa – Raymond Eugene Collins) • Master #: DF-463-545 • MONO
Recorded: April 1963 at Pal Recording Studio, Cucamonga, CA
Personnel: Benny Rodriguez (co-lead vocal); Joe Rodriguez (co-lead vocal); Frank Zappa (lead guitar); Max Uballez (rhythm guitar); Richard Provincio (piano); Armando Mora (tenor saxophone); Chris Pasqual (bass); Manuel Mosqueda (drums)
Producer: Frank Zappa and Billy Cardenas
Engineer: Paul Buff

B-side
Cradle Rock (2:52) (Virgie Gallegos) • Master #: DF-463-544 • MONO
Recorded: April 1963 at Pal Recording Studio, Cucamonga, CA
Personnel: Benny Rodriguez (co-lead vocals); Joe Rodriguez (co-lead vocals); Max Uballez (rhythm guitar); Richard Provincio (piano); Chris Pasqual (bass); Manuel Mosqueda (drums, tambourine)
Producer: Frank Zappa and Billy Cardenas
Engineer: Paul Buff

Benny and Joe Rodriguez were 14 at the time they recorded this single at Pal. These two Mexican brothers from East Los Angeles had already released "Corrida Mash"/ "I'm Leaving It All Up To You" on the Brent label with instrumental backing by The Romancers. That recording was helmed by Robert "Bumps" Blackwell, who was Little Richard's producer. Romancers rhythm guitarist Max Uballez had already visited Pal for his single "Rock Little Darling" for Donna. Joining Zappa, Uballez and the rest of The Romancers would again back The Heartbreakers for this Donna-released session at Pal.

Frank Zappa and Heartbreakers manager Billy Cardenas produced this single and were not credited, which was typical for pre-Mothers singles. The A-side label should have shown 2:35 as the timing instead of 2:15, and using proper English, it should have been shown as "Every Time I See You." In a more romantic vein than we're used to hearing from Zappa, the A-side was written with Ray Collins. Its composition was similar to "Memories Of El Monte" except that it had numerous stops to accentuate the chorus. Zappa's guitar lead was in a commercial style and was unusual for him in that it followed the chord changes instead of staying put on one chord.

For the B-side that did not feature Frank, Benny and Joe's friend Virgie Gallegos wrote the East L.A.-styled slow ballad "Cradle Rock" by placing the children's tune "Rock-A-Bye Baby" in a different context. Compared to the A-side, the playing on "Cradle Rock" was a bit loose. Both sides were made available on the Buff releases. The Heartbreakers completed their recording career with the single "Please Answer"/ "She Is My Baby" for the Linda label. As for Zappa, Buff and Collins, an eventful release was next on the calendar.

* * *

BRIAN LORD AND THE MIDNIGHTERS: The Big Surfer/ THE MIDNIGHTERS: Not Another One! (7" 45 rpm single)
Released May 1963 as Vigah! V-001-A (A-side)/ V-001-B (B-side)
Released May 27, 1963 as Capitol 4981

A-side
The Big Surfer (2:25) (Frank Zappa) • Master #: none (Vigah!); 45-39841 (Capitol) • MONO
Recorded: May 1963 at Pal Recording Studio, Cucamonga, CA
Personnel: Brian Lord (lead vocal); Paul Buff (opening vocal, bass, saxophone, sound effects); Frank Zappa (lead guitar, rhythm guitar, drums, lead vocal, backing vocals); Ray Collins (lead vocal, backing vocals)
Producer: Paul Buff
Engineer: Paul Buff

"The Big Surfer" created the template for a Frank Zappa satirical work – putting people in ridiculous circumstances, with song quotes and humorous interludes spicing up the overall structure. The first voice heard is that of Paul Buff, followed by a quote of "Yankee Doodle." Adapted from its European roots, "Yankee Doodle" was written in 1755 by British Army surgeon Dr. Richard Shuckburgh. The drums stop and we first hear the title character, KMEN (San Bernardino, CA) radio personality Brian Lord, who's imitating US president John F. Kennedy. ("Yankee Doodle" was quoted on four occasions at the February 16, 1988 performance at Bushnell Memorial Hall in Hartford, CT.)

The Big Surfer's role here is to judge a dance contest on the beach in Santa Monica, CA. The music kicks in and the pseudo-JFK gives his opening speech and refers to his wife Jacqueline Kennedy and White House Press Secretary Pierre Salinger. The "girls" laughing in the background were sped up voices by Zappa. Other Kennedy references that Brian Lord made were of JFK's younger brother Teddy (whose baggies fell down), daughter Caroline, and brother Bobby. There is a reference to being under pressure that Brian Lord as JFK makes. Most of that pressure came from the communist state of Cuba – namely, the failed Bay Of Pigs Invasion to overthrow Fidel Castro and the Cuban Missile Crisis.

After the crowd cheers, pseudo-JFK picks out a couple in the corner. Why, it's Frank Zappa as a boy in awe of The Big Surfer, and a girl, voiced by Ray Collins. As winners of the dance contest, Brian Lord as JFK tells them that they have won an all-expense paid trip as the first members of the Peace Corps to be sent to

Alabama. John F. Kennedy had created The Peace Corps by executive order on March 1, 1961 to promote world peace and friendship. Unfortunately, peace and friendship were not present in the southern part of the United States. Birmingham, Alabama was ravaged by bombings and riots on May 11, 1963, which is what Zappa was referring to with the Peace Corps being sent to that state. In actuality, JFK called in Federal troops. "The Big Surfer" fades out with a quote of "Dixie" written in 1859 by Daniel Decatur Emmett. ("Dixie" was quoted in "Dupree's Paradise" at the September 11, 1974 late show performance at Kurhalle, Vienna, Austria, in "Jesus Thinks You're A Jerk" on the albums "Broadway The Hard Way" and "Understanding America," and in the version of "Jesus" on "Zappa '88: The Last U.S. Show").

The politics of this record meant that it had to be recorded and produced quickly. The reference to Alabama indicates that it was recorded immediately after the May 11, 1963 Birmingham incidents. Paul Buff and Frank Zappa created the Vigah! label and got the record pressed as fast as they could. "Vigah" would be how JFK (or Brian Lord, for that matter) would sound to most ears when pronouncing the word "vigor," so it was a good match for the record's contents. Zappa and Buff proved to Capitol Records that "The Big Surfer" was selling quickly, but that was because they bought all the available copies at local record stores! Capitol licensed the master and pressed up copies for a May 27, 1963 release.

After numerous threats on his life, 37-year-old Mississippi NAACP field secretary Medgar Evers was shot and killed in his driveway in Jackson, MS on June 12, 1963. Capitol honchos recalled "The Big Surfer" after they felt that having a record in release that referred to civil rights tensions was not a good idea. The Vigah! pressing was still available, but no one at the time knew that "The Big Surfer" was originally on that label.

In retrospect, Brian Lord's voicing of John F. Kennedy was quite effective. Ray Collins would use the same female voice as the character Nelda on the next single. The B-side featured guitarist Dave Aerni along with Paul Buff on all other instruments. "Not Another One!" was heavily influenced by The Tornadoes' "Bustin' Surfboards" and referred to the necessary evil of producing a quickly recorded B-side.

* * *

NED & NELDA: Hey Nelda/ Surf Along With Ned & Nelda (7" 45 rpm single)
Released June 1963 as Vigah! V-002-A (A-side)/ V-002-B (B-side)

A-side
Hey Nelda (2:05) (Frank Zappa – Raymond Eugene Collins) • Master #: none • MONO
Recorded: May 1963 at Pal Recording Studio, Cucamonga, CA
Personnel: Frank Zappa (guitar, drums, co-lead vocal); Ray Collins (co-lead vocal); Paul Buff (piano, organ, bass)
Producer: Paul Buff
Engineer: Paul Buff

B-side
Surf Along With Ned & Nelda (2:03) (Frank Zappa – Raymond Eugene Collins) • Master #: none • MONO
Recorded: May 1963 at Pal Recording Studio, Cucamonga, CA
Personnel: Frank Zappa (guitar, drums, co-lead vocal); Ray Collins (co-lead vocal); Paul Buff (piano, bass, saxophone)
Producer: Paul Buff
Engineer: Paul Buff

The Vigah! label would prove to be a necessary outlet because no label wanted this record! The early 1963 #1 record "Hey Paula" by Paul And Paula was a prime subject for satire, especially since it presented an overly sweet conversation of a couple in love. "Hey Paula" was originally issued in November 1962 on the Le Cam label as by Jill & Ray, and it was picked up for national distribution by Philips (with an artist credit of Paul And Paula) the next month. Ray Hildebrand (as Paul) wrote the song after enjoying Annette Funicello's hit "Tall Paul." His singing partner Jill Jackson took the role of Paula in the song.

Frank Zappa and Ray Collins used their most uncommercial voices to respectively play Ned and Nelda. While Ned had more of a positive persona, Nelda was nearly always miserable. The overall effect was to present the anti-Paul And Paula teenage couple. "Hey Nelda" used the same kind of organ-dominant backing as "Hey Paula," but the sweet vocal character of the hit was intentionally replaced by coarseness. Paul Buff was a master at creating that kind of backing track. Frank Zappa's patented early '60s drum rolls ran throughout the Ned & Nelda track, unlike the straight drumming on "Hey Paula."

"Surf Along With Ned & Nelda" continued the satire by mentioning Bruce Johnston's "Do The Surfer Stomp," a two-part Donna label single from January 1962. As expected, Ned and Nelda battled all the way through the song. Nelda liked Frank Zappa's guitar solo, but she started complaining that her fun in the studio with Ned was being interrupted by Paul Buff's subsequent sax break. The last verse got Ned and Nelda back on track until the ending stomp section irritated Nelda until the fade. Zappa, as Ned, maintained his composure until he lost it during the stomping. Collins and Zappa knew what they were creating was completely absurd.

Clearly off-center, the record closed the book on the Vigah! label. The Steve Allen-inspired comment "forget it" was used on both sides. The Buff box and downloads are again the most recent sources for these tracks.

* * *

THE HOLLYWOOD PERSUADERS: Tijuana/ **Grunion Run** (7" 45 rpm single)
THE PERSUADERS: Tijuana Surf/ **Grunion Run** (7" 45 rpm single)
Released July 15, 1963 as Original Sound OS-39 (both editions)

B-side
Grunion Run (2:20) (Frank Zappa) • Master #: or-083 • MONO
Recorded: June 1963 at Pal Recording Studio, Cucamonga, CA
Personnel: Frank Zappa (guitars, bass, drums); Paul Buff (saxophones)
Producer: Paul Buff
Engineer: Paul Buff

This single was the turning point for Frank Zappa and Paul Buff. It had a large impact on their individual and collective activities in the future. Similar to The Masters' single, Paul Buff needed a B-side to accompany a top-rate instrumental which had already been recorded. Buff spent a lot of time working on his saxophone playing. He experimented with overdubbing numerous saxophone parts over a Mexican-flavored backing track. He ended up playing all the instruments. That experiment became "Tijuana Surf," also copyrighted as simply "Tijuana." Art Laboe at Original Sound loved what he heard and asked to hear the potential flipside. There was none. There was also no artist name. Buff and Laboe made the executive decision to credit the song as "Tijuana" by The Hollywood Persuaders, and as "Tijuana Surf" by The Persuaders to respectively cover the pop and surf markets.

That was fine, but Buff still needed something to put on the other side. Paul asked FZ to come up with an instrumental. Frank quickly came back with "Grunion Run," a major step forward in his playing and reputation. Zappa's guitar tone was enhanced by a Buff-designed fuzz box that was created by accident. With Buff handling the saxophone parts and sitting in the control room while Frank did the rest, "Grunion Run" proved to be a very strong flipside. Zappa signed the publishing agreement with Art Laboe for "Grunion Run" on June 27, 1963.

Art Laboe licensed the single to record companies in Canada, Mexico, Argentina, and Brazil. The Mexican release on Gamma G 528 became a massive hit. It spent 17 weeks at #1 in Mexico and prevented The Beatles' "I Want To Hold Your Hand" from reaching the top spot. Gamma combined the two Original Sound credits, listing the A-side as "Tijuana" by Los Persuaders. The B-side was translated as "El Gruñon (Grunion Run)." The only problem was that the Mexican single profits could not be taken out of the country without the cash disappearing! Both sides of the single also appeared in Mexico on the self-titled Los Persuaders album (Diana LPD-18; released June 1964).

The success of "Tijuana" did a lot of things for Paul Buff. Art Laboe asked Paul to become Original Sound's recording engineer with a budget to create a new studio. The deal between Buff and Laboe also involved future records by The Hollywood Persuaders and any other artist names Paul wanted to use. The downside of the deal was that Paul Buff would have to remove himself from Pal Recording Studio. Buff eventually sold Pal to Zappa on August 1, 1964, when it officially became known as Studio Z. Three days before the studio sale, Buff created a stereo mix of "Grunion Run" that was a little shorter than the mono mix. The Buff downloads and box set covered the original mono mix, the stereo mix, and an alternate mono mix. An alternate stereo mix also exists but has not been released. The two most notable records that Buff made after leaving Pal were The Hollywood Persuaders' "Drums A-Go-Go" and The Buff Organization's "Studio 'A.'"

The record also helped Frank Zappa, but in a different way. After his arrest on March 26, 1965, Frank asked Art Laboe for a $1,500 advance against his publishing royalties for "Memories Of El Monte" and "Grunion Run" to cover attorney fees and to bail girlfriend Lorraine Belcher out of jail.

* * *

MR. CLEAN: Mr. Clean/ Jessie Lee (7" 45 rpm single)
Released July 15, 1963 as Original Sound OS-40

A-side
Mr. Clean (1:52) (Frank Zappa) • Master #: or-084 • MONO
Recorded: June 1963 at Pal Recording Studio, Cucamonga, CA
Personnel: Robert "Mr. Clean" Davis (lead vocal); Frank Zappa (lead guitar, rhythm guitar, drums, backing vocals); Paul Buff (electric piano, bass); Dorothy Berry & The Sweethearts (backing vocals)
Producer: Paul Buff
Engineer: Paul Buff

B-side
Jessie Lee (2:10) (Frank Zappa) • Master #: or-085 • MONO
Recorded: June 1963 at Pal Recording Studio, Cucamonga, CA
Personnel: Robert "Mr. Clean" Davis (lead vocal, backing vocals, harmonica); Paul Buff (fuzz bass); Frank Zappa (guitar, drums, percussion)

Producer: Paul Buff
Engineer: Paul Buff

From the picture sleeve of a record he made a year after this one, Robert Davis was probably the most unusual looking person that walked into Pal Recording Studio. He had all the physical characteristics of the Mr. Clean character that Procter & Gamble used for their like-named cleaning product – a dark-skinned, muscular bald man with an earring who posed with his arms folded. This Mr. Clean had a solid R&B voice, and Frank Zappa presented him with two quality songs to record.

The A-side had the added bonus of backing vocals by Dorothy Berry ("Louie, Louie" composer Richard Berry's wife) and her vocal group The Sweethearts. Cleanly recorded and perfectly executed, "Mr. Clean" was a very competitive plug side for a single. Frank Zappa did the male backing vocals on this side – especially "he's the greatest lover in the world" on the stops. The Zappa drum sound was also very much in evidence. The flipside "Jessie Lee" utilized Paul Buff's fuzz bass to great effect. It certainly sounded different than other current records.

This single, the previous Hollywood Persuaders 45, and a record that Paul Buff did with Dave Aerni as The Rotations were all submitted to, and accepted by, Original Sound. (The Rotations single is in the "Honorable Mentions" section.) Zappa signed a publishing agreement for both songs on the same day as "Grunion Run" – June 27, 1963. "Mr. Clean" and "Jessie Lee" have been released numerous times over the years. Both A-side mixes and the B-side were also part of the Buff downloads and box set. The label timings of both songs were interchanged by mistake.

An alternate mono mix of "Mr. Clean" was first released on the "Joe's Xmasage" album. It lacked the backing vocals from Dorothy Berry and The Sweethearts, and it was a few seconds shorter. As for Robert Davis, he based himself in Seattle, WA and put together the band The Cleansers in 1964. Mr. Clean And The Cleansers released two singles – the two-part "Karate" (Camelot CS-136) and "Think"/ "Poison Ivy" (Audio Recording AR-118). "Think" is the single with a classic picture sleeve.

* * *

RON ROMAN: Tell Me/ **Love Of My Life** (7" 45 rpm single)
Released July 29, 1963 as Daani D-101-1 (A-side)/ D-101-2 (B-side)

B-side
Love Of My Life (2:03) (Frank Zappa – David Lee Aerni) • Master #: none • MONO
Recorded: April 1963 (backing track) and June 1963 (vocal overdubs) at Pal Recording Studio, Cucamonga, CA
Personnel: Ron Roman (lead vocal); Ray Collins (backing vocals); Paul Buff (piano, drums, fuzz bass, saxophones); Frank Zappa (guitar)
Producer: Frank Zappa (backing track) and Dave Aerni (overdubs)
Engineer: Frank Zappa (backing track), Paul Buff (backing track and overdubs), Dave Aerni (backing track and overdubs)

This 45 has been the subject of a lot of debate about who did what and when they did it! Since Paul Buff was the one constant participant in the recording of the A-side and all three versions of the B-side, we'll go with his recollections. Zappa's "Love Of My Life" was a '50s-styled number that was first recorded in April 1963 with multiple overdubs by Ray Collins and Paul Buff. Collins redid some of his vocal parts for a version with the unknown Mary Gonzales. The same music track was used for that alternate version. Connecting together "Earth Angel" and "Memories Of El Monte," the backing vocals on Zappa's "Love Of My Life" quoted "Earth Angel." It was a song of great lasting value, as it was recorded later for the albums "Cruising With Ruben & The Jets," "Tinsel Town Rebellion," and "Zappa '88: The Last U.S. Show." The start of the backing track was also used at the tail end of the "Lonely Little Girl" single.

For some reason, only the Ron Roman version of "Love Of My Life" was used. (Also unused at this time were gems like "Any Way The Wind Blows," "Fountain Of Love," and the notorious "Masked Grandma.") Dave Aerni noticed that a tape of the original "Love Of My Life" was just sitting there and brought in vocalist Ron Roman during June 1963 to record a single of it. Before recording with Roman took place, Aerni took the liberty of changing some of the lyrics and giving himself half of the writer credit. Ron Roman sang this revised lyric set, and because Ray Collins' vocal parts could not be completely wiped off the five-track tape, Collins' falsetto remained in the final mix. Just as inexplicable as Zappa's lack of interest in releasing the song was that Dave Aerni considered Ron Roman's version to be a B-side. "Tell Me" (the A-side) was a nondescript song written by Kenny Williams (brother of Ronnie) and featured Roman's double-tracked vocals and Paul Buff playing piano, bass, and drums. If anything should have been a B-side, "Tell Me" was it. Suffering an even worse fate was the song "Please Tell Me They're Lying," whose master tape was lost altogether.

Dave Aerni went ahead and created the Daani imprint using Pal's address on the label. The record was so poorly distributed after its late July 1963 release that no one knew that it was available. Frank Zappa was not happy with what Aerni did, but they continued to work together when producing instrumental records as Curry & Irvin. Aerni would revive Daani for a single ("One Look"/ "Dirty Ways") by his group City Limits in 1966. Both sides were recorded at Original Sound with Paul Buff engineering. Ron Roman did not appear again on record for a few years after his debut in 1963. He recorded two LPs in 1967-1968 for GNP Crescendo's Carole label as lead vocalist with The Mystic Astrologic Crystal Band, and he recorded a single for Dot in 1969 ("I'll Be Your Baby Tonight"/ "Just To Let Rosemary Know") as Ron Roman & The Proposition.

The Mary Gonzales version of "Love Of My Life" debuted on "Greasy Love Songs," and all three versions were part of the Buff box and download series. The Buff releases had a longer introduction. Zappa's prolific recording output at this time was put together on a tape reel containing completed demos of "Why Don't You Do Me Right?," "Walkin' Out," "Cookin' Turnips" (later known as "Speed-Freak Boogie")," "Waltz," and "Can't Stand Up."

* * *

THE RHYTHM SURFERS: 502 (Like Getting Pinched On A 502)/ Big City Surfer (7" 45 rpm single)
Released September 1963 as Daytone D-6301

<u>A-side</u>
502 (Like Getting Pinched On A 502) (2:12) (The Rhythm Surfers) • Master #: D-6301-A • MONO
Recorded: June 1963 at Pal Recording Studio, Cucamonga, CA
Personnel: Dan Braymer (drums); other personnel unknown
Producer: Curry (Frank Zappa) & Irvin (Dave Aerni)
Engineer: Dave Aerni and Frank Zappa

B-side
Big City Surfer (2:01) (The Rhythm Surfers) • Master #: D-6301-B • MONO
Recorded: June 1963 at Pal Recording Studio, Cucamonga, CA
Personnel: Dan Braymer (drums); other personnel unknown
Producer: Curry (Frank Zappa) & Irvin (Dave Aerni)
Engineer: Dave Aerni and Frank Zappa

In addition to bringing The Tornadoes back to Pal in June 1963 for album recording, Dave Aerni invited The Pharos. Aerni worked with The Pharos on their "Pintor"/ "Rhythm Surfer" single for Bob Keane's Del-Fi label in April 1963. The Pharos had undergone some changes in the interim, and they recently hired drummer Dan Braymer to complete their lineup. While working for Dave Aerni's new Daytone label, The Pharos were in the process of renaming themselves The Rhythm Surfers after the B-side of their Del-Fi single. The lineup with Braymer was together for only about a month, and they had already broken up by the time this single was released.

Aerni noted that Buff had numerous record labels so that people would not know they were all by the same person when licensing them out. Aerni did the same thing with his Daytone, Ador and Daani labels, but he went one step further: he created the Jack Irvin persona for the records he worked on. When Frank Zappa participated in an Aerni release for Daytone, he became the mysterious Curry. Putting the two names together (Curry and Irvin), it had the similar look and sound of the defunct New York City printmaking company Currier And Ives.

The first song recorded by The Pharos/ Rhythm Surfers was a vocal blues number, "Steel Wheels." Dave Aerni wrote the song about his truck driving jobs. The next item they recorded was "502 (Like Getting Pinched On A 502)." A pinch was slang for an arrest. At that time in California, a "502" was the police code for misdemeanor drunk driving. The code is now 23152. Dan Braymer kicked off the freewheeling proceedings of "502" with various drunken laughs and yells livening up the track. "502" and "Steel Wheels" were paired on a Pal acetate credited to The Pharos. It was felt that another instrumental should be the B-side of the single rather than "Steel Wheels." That song fell by the wayside and was replaced by the last song recorded – "Big City Surfer." The guitar melody of "Big City Surfer" alternated low notes from the Duane Eddy songbook and higher-pitched surf picking. Incidentally, the timings of both Daytone sides are incorrect. They should respectively be 2:29 and 2:12.

"Steel Wheels" debuted on Volume 9 of the Buff download series (released June 18, 2010) and the Buff box. Both tracks on the Daytone 45 were released as downloads and the box set. The Pharos/ Rhythm Surfers were the first of a few groups that Dave Aerni brought to Pal for which very little is known.

* * *

THE TORNADOES: Phantom Surfer/ **Shootin' Beavers** (7" 45 rpm single)
Released December 20, 1963 as Aertaun 45-103

B-side
Shootin' Beavers (2:15) (Gerald Sanders) • Master #: 45-103-B • MONO
Recorded: June 1963 at Pal Recording Studio, Cucamonga, CA
Personnel: Gerald Sanders (shouted intro, second "Bag that pelt!" vocal, bass); James Norman "Roly" Sanders (lead guitar); Jesse Sanders (rhythm guitar); George White (saxophone, first "Bag that pelt!" vocal); Leonard

Delaney (drums)
Producer: Dave Aerni for Aertaun Productions
Engineer: Frank Zappa

This record was the subject of a great deal of consternation by everyone involved – the band, the producer, and even the audience. In fact, this is the first of three records released with the Aertaun catalog number 45-103. It is the only one of the three on which Zappa was involved. "Shootin' Beavers" was recorded at Pal during The Tornadoes' "Bustin' Surfboards" album sessions in June 1963. When "Shootin' Beavers" was released on the album, there were no complaints about its contents. However, when "Shootin' Beavers" was placed on the B-side of "Phantom Surfer," all hell broke loose. Parents were outraged that their children were listening to such a disgusting song. Considering that the song was mostly instrumental with the occasional side comments "shoot that beaver" and "bag that pelt," it must have been those comments that they were protesting. Today, we would equate "shooting beavers" to getting a female crotch shot, and "bagging a pelt" would be getting some pussy. As expected, those comments registered strongly with Zappa!

The A-side "Phantom Surfer" was a fresh vocal recording made at William Locy Sound Company in Riverside, CA during November 1963. It was written by Dorinda Morgan, wife of early Beach Boys producer Hite Morgan. Unlike their other recordings, The Tornadoes had John Huffman produce it instead of Dave Aerni. This occurred because the band was in the process of separating themselves from Aerni, who now based all his work at Pal. The Tornadoes also didn't appreciate that Aerni used an artist and repertoire (A&R) representative, Rue Barclay, who did nothing but put his name on the record labels.

The uproar about "Shootin' Beavers" occurred immediately upon release just before Christmas 1963 and continued into January 1964. A re-recording of "Shootin' Beavers" took place that January at Locy's studio and was released with "Phantom Surfer" on January 31, 1964. The protests continued. Gerald Sanders' yelled intro "Hey, shoot that beaver!" was excised and the track was renamed "Lightnin'" for its release on March 13, 1964. Confusingly, the catalog number never changed. For a while, anyone buying Aertaun 45-103 had no idea what they were getting – the original "Shootin' Beavers," the full re-recording, or the edited re-recording. The Tornadoes had enough and replaced manager Dave Aerni with John Huffman. This move effectively ended their deal with Aertaun. Even though they did some more recording, The Tornadoes never released another record in the '60s. The best source for "Shootin' Beavers" remains the "Now And Then" CD from 2005.

* * *

CONRAD AND THE HURRICANE STRINGS: Hurricane/ Sweet Love (7" 45 rpm single)
Released January 1964 as Daytone D-6401-A (A-side)/ D-6401-B (B-side)
CONRAD AND THE HURRICANES: Hurricane/ Sweet Love (7" 45 rpm single)
Released May 25, 1964 as Era 3130

A-side
Hurricane (2:12) (Ed Sigarlaki) • Master #: DA-6401-A (Daytone); 45-BSN-432 (Era) • MONO
Recorded: December 1963 at Pal Recording Studio, Cucamonga, CA
Personnel: Ed Sigarlaki (lead guitar); Coen "Conrad" Couwenberg (rhythm guitar); Don Sigarlaki (bass); Patrick Couwenberg (drums)
Producer: Curry (Frank Zappa) & Irvin (Dave Aerni)
Engineer: Frank Zappa

B-side
Sweet Love (2:01) (Ed Sigarlaki) • Master #: DA-6401-B (Daytone); 45-BSN-431 (Era) • MONO
Recorded: December 1963 at Pal Recording Studio, Cucamonga, CA
Personnel: Ed Sigarlaki (lead guitar); Coen "Conrad" Couwenberg (rhythm guitar); Don Sigarlaki (bass); Patrick Couwenberg (drums)
Producer: Curry (Frank Zappa) & Irvin (Dave Aerni)
Engineer: Frank Zappa

Talk about aggression! "Hurricane" was exactly that – an insistent, guitar melody over tumbling drums. The group, known originally as The Rocking Yings, consisted of Coen "Conrad" Couwenberg (rhythm guitar), Raul de Groen (drums), Ed Sigarlaki (lead guitar), and his brother Don Sigarlaki (bass). Conrad, his brother Patrick and the Sigarlaki brothers moved from the western part of Amsterdam, Holland to Ontario, CA in 1962, as Patrick Couwenberg took over the drums from Raul de Groen. Frank Zappa saw the band while he was hanging around the Ontario Music store and he invited them to record at Pal. Good old Curry & Irvin would produce the group, who now called themselves Conrad And The Hurricane Strings.

Ed Sigarlaki turned in a more romantic guitar-led tune for the B-side "Sweet Love." It was a nice contrast to the bombast of "Hurricane." Aerni released the record on Daytone in January 1964. The Era label licensed the master for nationwide distribution after they noticed the buzz surrounding the Daytone single. They also took the liberties of changing the group's name to Conrad And The Hurricanes and deleting the production credit. Era was much too late in cashing in on the action because it took them until late May to get their act together. Surf music was simply not competitive in the mid-1964 market. Unbelievably, these guys never made another record. "Hurricane" has proven to be a must-have surf instrumental for collectors and music fans alike.

In the conceptual continuity sweepstakes, Frank Zappa sampled the introduction of "Hurricane" for the "Bit Of Nostalgia" segment in the Verve edition of "Lumpy Gravy" in 1968.

* * *

THE CORDELLS: Happy Time/ I Love How You Love Me (7" 45 rpm single)
Released January 1964 as Ador D-6402-A (A-side)/ D-6402-B (B-side)

A-side
Happy Time (2:20) (T. Lessard) • Master #: DA-6402-A • MONO
Recorded: December 1963 at Pal Recording Studios, Cucamonga, CA
Personnel: T. Lessard (lead guitar); other personnel unknown
Producer: Irvin (Dave Aerni) & Curry (Frank Zappa)
Engineer: Frank Zappa

B-side
I Love How You Love Me (2:05) (Larry Kolber – Barry Mann) • Master #: DA-6402-B • MONO
Recorded: December 1963 at Pal Recording Studios, Cucamonga, CA
Personnel: T. Lessard (lead guitar); other personnel unknown
Producer: Irvin (Dave Aerni) & Curry (Frank Zappa)
Engineer: Frank Zappa

Dave Aerni was great for bringing in completely unknown groups to Pal. The Cordells came to the studio at the end of 1963 to record four songs – two on this single, and the other two ("Sand Flea" and "Down Under") were lost a long time ago. Dave Aerni signed them to his Ador label, which used the record number following the above Conrad And The Hurricane Strings single. "Happy Time" and "I Love How You Love Me" formed the only known Ador release in January 1964. The usual Curry & Irvin production credit was reversed for just this release.

"Happy Time" was another wild surfboard ride, pairing an uplifting guitar-led tune with drumming that was nearly always in the middle of a roll. One might have figured that The Paris Sisters' 1961 hit "I Love How You Love Me" would not translate well to a surf instrumental format, but you would be wrong. This relaxed guitar arrangement was a complete winner. It was too bad that the record was so badly distributed. Both sides were included as part of the Buff download series and the box set.

* * *

THE DECADES: Lonely Drummer/ The Phantom Strikes Back (7" 45 rpm single)
Released January 1964 as Daytone D-6403

A-side
Lonely Drummer (2:22) (J. Irvin [aka David Lee Aerni]) • Master #: DA-6403-A • MONO
Recorded: January 1964 at Pal Recording Studio, Cucamonga, CA
Personnel: unknown
Producer: Curry (Frank Zappa) & Irvin (Dave Aerni)
Engineer: Frank Zappa

B-side
The Phantom Strikes Back (2:18) (J. Irvin [aka David Lee Aerni]) • Master #: DA-6403-B • MONO
Recorded: January 1964 at Pal Recording Studio, Cucamonga, CA
Personnel: unknown
Producer: Curry (Frank Zappa) & Irvin (Dave Aerni)
Engineer: Frank Zappa

Absolutely nothing is known about The Decades, except that they were the only act to have more than one Daytone single. "Lonely Drummer" was a very sedate choice for an A-side, while "The Phantom Strikes Back" covered very familiar surf instrumental territory. They would be back in five months for their second single. Another unknown group, The Dynamic Five, recorded the single "Big Boy Pete"/ "Mo-So Boogie" in May 1964 as Daytone DA-6405. Both sides were produced by Bobby Sands. Dave Aerni's involvement as Irvin was in writing the B-side and engineering the tracks. With no mention of Zappa's alias Curry, Frank was not involved with The Dynamic Five's single.

* * *

THE WOODY WAGGERS: The Sahara Hop/ FRANK AND THE WOODY WAGGERS: Three Guns (7" 45 rpm single)
Released May 1964 as Daytone D-6407 (A-side)/ D-6408 (B-side)

A-side
The Sahara Hop (2:30) (F. & J. Irvin [aka David Lee Aerni]) • Master #: DA-6407-A • MONO
Recorded May 1964 at Pal Recording Studio, Cucamonga, CA
Personnel: unknown
Producer: Currie (Frank Zappa) & Irvin (Dave Aerni)
Engineer: Frank Zappa

B-side
Three Guns (3:10) (J. & J. Irvin [aka David Lee Aerni]) • Master #: DA-6408-A • MONO
Recorded May 1964 at Pal Recording Studio, Cucamonga, CA
Personnel: unknown
Producer: Currie (Frank Zappa) & Irvin (Dave Aerni)
Engineer: Frank Zappa

For a bunch of unknowns that never made another 45, this group created a first-class single at Pal for Daytone. The Woody Waggers were presented with Dave Aerni's energetic three-chord surf instrumental "The Sahara Hop" as their Daytone A-side. It was one of the last really fine surf tunes. The B-side "Three Guns," listed as by Frank And The Woody Waggers, was completely unexpected. It was a post-Civil War American frontier ballad which took place on the Chisholm Trail stretching from Texas to Kansas. The cattle owner in the song hired three armed men (three guns) to ensure the safe transfer of his cattle between those states, but two of the armed men were corrupt. The vocalist confirms that he killed the other two gunmen towards the end of the song. "Three Guns" would have been ideal as the theme for a mid-'60s Western program on TV. No one knows who Frank the vocalist was, but Frank Zappa certainly got the most out of him during the group's short studio existence. Note that Zappa's production credit was incorrectly spelled as Currie for this release. By this point, the distribution of Dave Aerni's record labels was so poor that very few copies were pressed and sold. This single and both Decades singles are extremely rare. Both sides of all three singles were released on the Buff box only, as their discovery came after the download series was completed.

* * *

THE DECADES: Dance Forever More/ Louie De Loop (7" 45 rpm single)
Released June 1964 as Daytone D-1306

A-side
Dance Forever More (2:01) (B. Davis) • Master #: D-6415 • MONO
Recorded: June 1964 at Pal Recording Studio, Cucamonga, CA
Personnel: unknown
Producer: Curry (Frank Zappa) & Irvin (Dave Aerni)
Engineer: Frank Zappa

B-side
Louie De Loop (1:56) (J. Irvin [aka David Lee Aerni]) • Master #: D-6416 • MONO
Recorded: June 1964 at Pal Recording Studio, Cucamonga, CA

Personnel: unknown
Producer: Curry (Frank Zappa) & Irvin (Dave Aerni)
Engineer: Frank Zappa

This appears to be the last record that Frank Zappa and Dave Aerni worked on together. It was also the last known Daytone release and the final time that Aerni worked at Pal. Clearly, that kind of music and recording studio were both on the way out. "Dance Forever More" was similar to a slower version of The Pharos' "Pintor" without the castanets. "Louie De Loop" was a standard three-chord "stop and go" instrumental with a very open drum sound.

FZ's purchase of Pal from Paul Buff came less than two months after this Decades 45. The studio became known as Studio Z. Very few outside clients came in to rehearse their material. At least one very muffled tape exists from this period. Zappa mostly used Studio Z to prepare for the proposed film "Captain Beefheart Vs. The Grunt People," the rock opera "I Was A Teen-age Malt Shop," and the recording of "The Uncle Frankie Show" for Pomona College radio station KSPC in Claremont, CA. Oh yes, there was the aforementioned bust on March 26, 1965, ten days in jail, and this group that Zappa joined the next month – The Soul Giants, which became The Mothers that May 9.

* * *

HONORABLE MENTIONS FROM THE EARLY YEARS (1961-1965)

THE VELVETEENS: Dog Patch Creeper/ Johnny's Jump (7" 45 rpm single)
Released September 1960 as Emmy E-1005-1 (A-side)/ E-1005-2 (B-side)

<u>A-side</u>
Dog Patch Creeper (2:55) (Mario John Valenzuela, Sr. – Mario John Valenzuela, Jr.) • Master #: none • MONO
Recorded: September 1960 at Pal Recording Studio, Cucamonga, CA
Personnel: Johnny Valenzuela (rhythm guitar, vocal asides); John Valenzuela, Sr. (piano); Danny Valenzuela (drums); Joe Valenzuela (bass); Danny Espinoza (saxophone); Polie Rodriguez (lead guitar)
Producer: Paul Buff
Engineer: Paul Buff

The Velveteens sounded rough. That was completely intentional, as was their infectious energy. Only Paul Buff and Frank Zappa recorded more tracks at Pal than The Velveteens, who laid down nearly twenty. This was their first recording venture, and they were listed as the backing band on many other singles for the next two years. The Pomona, CA-based Velveteens were led by Mario John Valenzuela, Jr., who was better known as Johnny. His father Mario (who also went by John) played piano, his other sons Danny and Joe respectively played drums and bass, and the lineup was completed by their friends Danny Espinoza (saxophone) and Polie Rodriguez (lead guitar). All the members were of Mexican-American descent. Rodriguez was promoted on both labels of the record.

"Dog Patch Creeper" started out with Polie Rodriguez' guitar riff, and what a riff it was. The Velveteens took that riff and beat it into the ground. Paul Buff referred to such a classic performance as "the power of amateurs." The Velveteens played "Dog Patch Creeper" at El Monte Legion Stadium in late 1960 when they shared the stage with Rosie And The Originals, Don & Dewey, and The Box Tops. When Frank Zappa went to Pal the first time, he made sure to grab a copy of the record which he kept for the rest of his life. Zappa incorporated the main riff of "Dog Patch Creeper" into his "Tryin' To Grow A Chin." This track was part of the Buff downloads and box set.

* * *

THE ROTATIONS: Heavies/ The Cruncher (7" 45 rpm single)
Released August 23, 1963 as Original Sound OS-41

<u>A-side</u>
Heavies (1:42) (David Lee Aerni – Paul Conrad Buff) • Master #: or-086 • MONO
Recorded: June 1963 at Pal Recording Studio, Cucamonga, CA
Personnel: Dave Aerni (lead guitar, rhythm guitar); Paul Buff (all other instruments)
Producer: Paul Buff
Engineer: Paul Buff

<u>B-side</u>
The Cruncher (2:12) (David Lee Aerni – Paul Conrad Buff) • Master #: or-087 • MONO
Recorded: June 1962 at Pal Recording Studio, Cucamonga, CA
Personnel: Dave Aerni (lead guitar, rhythm guitar); Mike Dineri (saxophone); Paul Buff (all other instruments and effects)
Producer: Paul Buff
Engineer: Paul Buff

As soon as Dave Aerni brought in The Tornadoes to Pal, Paul Buff put Aerni and his guitar playing to work to get in on the hot surf action. Buff had already recorded "Like Surf" and "Train To Infinity" with saxophone player Mike Dineri (who had played with FZ in Joe Perrino & The Mellotones) in June 1962. Both tracks lacked lead guitar, which was the instrument of choice for surf music. Paul Buff decided to add Dave Aerni guitar parts to "Train To Infinity," which was renamed "The Cruncher." Frank Zappa was so impressed by "The Cruncher" that he played it for The Tornadoes during their first Pal visit in December 1962.

The pressure to finish this project ratcheted up when the Hollywood Persuaders and Mr. Clean singles were completed for Art Laboe of Original Sound. It took a whole year for Buff and Aerni to come up with a strong A-side. Dave Aerni brought The Tornadoes back to Pal to finish their album for Josie, and it may have been their presence that inspired Buff and Aerni to create "Heavies." "Heavies" took the "Bustin' Surfboards" approach of starting with a tape of surf waves and a Buff drum pattern before Aerni kicked the song into gear. This brief song ended with surf waves and became a surf essential. This time, Buff played all the saxophone parts. Paul and Dave had to come up with a group name, so they called themselves The Rotations when the tapes were submitted to Art Laboe. Despite their fine efforts, "Heavies"/ "The Cruncher" was their only record.

Frank Zappa was not involved with this 45, but he ended up using the intro of "Heavies" as part of the audio collage "Nasal Retentive Calliope Music" on "We're Only In It For The Money." Both sides were part of the Buff downloads and box set.

* * *

FRANK ZAPPA, MOTHERS OF INVENTION & SESSIONS (1966-1993)

BOBBY JAMESON: Reconsider Baby/ Lowdown Funky Blues (7" 45 rpm single)
Released June 20, 1966 as Penthouse 501

<u>A-side</u>
Reconsider Baby (2:33) (Robert Parker Jameson) • Master #: P-66-7001-A • MONO
Recorded: May 1966 at H. & R. Studios, Hollywood, CA
Personnel: Bobby Jameson (lead vocal); other musicians unknown
Arranger: Ken Handler & Norm Ratner (credited); Frank Zappa (uncredited)
Producer: Norm Ratner (credited); Frank Zappa & Bobby Jameson (uncredited)
Engineer: John Haeny

The Mothers Of Invention recorded their first album "Freak Out!" in March 1966, but it took Verve a while to get their promotional machine together. The first Zappa-related single to be released after the formation of the MOI was for Bobby Jameson, a troubled artist who was overhyped, taken advantage of, ripped off, etc. by numerous record companies and managers. The cumulative effect of this mistreatment was that Jameson's well-being was negatively impacted for the rest of his life.

Jameson's first single, "Take This Lollipop"/ "Let's Surf," was a rare positive experience for him. Recorded for the Jolum label in Hollywood in 1963, the disc featured former Gamblers "Moon Dawg" member Elliot Ingber on guitar. Of course, Elliot was part of the MOI "Freak Out!" lineup. Bobby Jameson then recorded for Talamo, Current, London, Brit, Surrey and Mira before he ended up with Penthouse.

As the first signing for Penthouse Productions, Bobby Jameson was expecting a more positive outcome. After all, Penthouse was formed by Ken Handler and Pat Boone – yes, THAT Pat Boone! Pat was busy with his own recording and acting pursuits, so he left the day-to-day operations of the Penthouse label to Ken Handler and producer Norm Ratner. That proved to be a big mistake, as the label lasted for four releases before it was terminated. Penthouse's releases were distributed by Mira Productions, Inc., helmed by former Vee Jay label president Randy Wood. Randy handled Jameson's Surrey and Mira recordings. Mira released Jameson's single "Vietnam" (shown as "Viet Nam" on the label) b/w "Metropolitan Man." It was recorded with fellow Mira artist The Leaves, who included future Mothers bassist Jim Pons. Bobby performed the A-side in Robert Carl Cohen's film "Mondo Hollywood" with footage including his girlfriend Adelaide Gail Sloatman. Bobby met cocktail waitress Gail (as she was commonly known) at The Trip in West Hollywood. "Vietnam" was also featured on the "Mondo Hollywood" soundtrack LP.

Jameson ran into Frank Zappa on the numerous occasions that Frank played at Griffith Park in Los Angeles. After striking up a friendship, they agreed to work on a record. Bobby Jameson was inspired to write a song after he greatly appreciated Percy Sledge's #1 hit "When A Man Loves A Woman." His response was "Reconsider Baby," a similarly emotive number with soulful female backing vocals joined by full orchestration on the bridge and out-chorus. Frank Zappa was brought in as contractor and arranger for the session. No documentation of the session exists, but Jameson confirmed that Zappa, and not credited arrangers Ken Handler or Norm Ratner, arranged the session. Handler and Ratner booked the studio session and paid the bills. Jameson thought that The Dixie Cups were the backing vocalists, but he was not sure. After Zappa did this thing, Jameson recorded the 90-second flipside with just his vocals and guitar.

A month later, another session with Zappa was booked. Jameson demanded that Frank Zappa be given arranging credit on the record label before they recorded "Gotta' Find My Roogalator." That session follows chronologically after the first MOI single below. "Reconsider Baby" was also recorded as a Mira B-side by Rojay Gotee (aka Robert J. Youngs) in September 1967. It used a carbon copy of the Zappa arrangement with different musicians, but its overall execution was inferior. The A-side of Gotee's single was "She Don't Love Me Anymore (People Call Me Rover)," and it was released as Mira 244.

Penthouse is one of those labels whose content has fallen through the cracks. To address the injustices against his lack of compensation, Jameson made his Penthouse recordings available to YouTube and the Zappateers group as of August 28, 2011.

* * *

THE MOTHERS OF INVENTION: How Could I Be Such A Fool/ Help I'm A Rock 3rd Movement: It Can't Happen Here
(7" 45 rpm single)
Released June 29, 1966 as Verve VK 10418
Reissued November 25, 2016 as Barking Pumpkin BPR 1228 (Black Friday 7" 45 rpm numbered pink vinyl single)

A-side
How Could I Be Such A Fool (2:12 [both editions]) (Frank Zappa) • Master #: 100,237 (Verve); none (Barking Pumpkin) • MONO
Recorded: March 10-11, 1966 at T.T.G. Studios, Hollywood, CA
Personnel: Frank Zappa (lead guitar, leader, arranger, conductor, copyist, harmony vocal, backing vocals); Ray Collins (lead vocal); Johnny Rotella (piccolo); Elliot Ingber (rhythm guitar); Roy Estrada (bass); Jimmy Carl Black (drums); Kurt Reher (cello); Raymond Kelley (cello); Paul Bergstrom (cello); Emmet Sergeant (cello); Joseph Saxon (cello); Edwin V. Beach (cello); Arthur Maebe (brass); George F. Price (French horn); John T. Johnson (tuba); Carol Kaye (12-string guitar); Virgil Evans (trumpet); David Wells (trombone); Kenneth Watson (timpani); Gene P. Estes (vibraphone); Eugene DiNovi (piano); Plas Johnson (flute); Benjamin Barrett (contractor); Roy Caton (trumpet, copyist)
Producer: Tom Wilson
Engineer: Ami Hadani & Tom Hidley

B-side
Help I'm A Rock 3rd Movement: It Can't Happen Here (3:12 [both editions]) (Frank Zappa) • Master #: 100,526 (Verve); none (Barking Pumpkin) • MONO
Recorded: March 12, 1966 at T.T.G. Studios, Hollywood, CA
Personnel: Frank Zappa (leader, arranger, copyist, lead vocals, backing vocals); Ray Collins (backing vocals); Roy Estrada (backing vocals); Jimmy Carl Black (backing vocals); Jeannie Vassar (Suzy Creamcheese vocal); plus numerous unknown vocalists and woodwind players
Producer: Tom Wilson
Engineer: Ami Hadani & Tom Hidley

The first musical outpouring of The Mothers Of Invention with producer Tom Wilson at T.T.G. Studios in Hollywood covered a lot of ground. T.T.G. was located at 1441 North McCadden Place in Hollywood, close to where Sunset Boulevard and Highland Avenue intersected. The studio's Sunset-Highland proximity became part of its informal name. This single combined the unique T.T.G. studio sound with Wilson's ability to deliver challenging records. Future echoes of this producer/studio combination can be heard with The Velvet Underground, The Animals, and the subsequent Eric Burdon And The Animals lineup. Amnon "Ami" Hadani and Tom Hidley named their four-track studio T.T.G. at its founding on June 8, 1965. Hadani was a general in the Israeli Air Force and was familiar with the Jewish Brigade slang term "Tilhas Tizig Gesheften," which directly translates to "Lick My Ass Business," or loosely, "Up Your Ass." (It was not named for "Two Terrible Guys," even though it makes for a good story!) Both were veterans of A&R Studios in New York. Regardless of mono or stereo mixing, T.T.G. produced a spatial audio environment that sounded like no other recording location. The studio's processing of recorded vocals and drums brought more attention to those essential elements.

After varying degrees of success at various jazz labels, Tom Wilson became an East Coast staff producer for Columbia Records. While at Columbia, Wilson produced seminal folk-rock albums by Bob Dylan and Simon & Garfunkel. Tom Wilson added electric guitars, bass and drums to Simon & Garfunkel's "The Sounds Of Silence" to create a #1 hit. Before that record became successful, Wilson moved to California to work for MGM's Verve label. The Mothers were playing at the Whisky a Go Go on L.A.'s Sunset Strip in November 1965 when Tom Wilson heard them playing Zappa's recent song about the Watts riots, "Trouble Comin' Every Day." The renamed Mothers Of Invention were signed by Verve on March 1, 1966 and began recording at T.T.G. less than two weeks later.

The first MOI A-side was a very safe choice in commercial terms. Unlike contemporary singles, "How Could I Be Such A Fool" was in 3/4 time. The track was processed with a great deal of reverb. The final single mix was much stronger than the stereo album edition. This mono master was reissued on the double CD "The MOFO Project/Object (fazedooh)" before the single was reissued with a picture sleeve in 2016. The Australian release (Verve V-5122) might be the rarest of all foreign singles, with less than 30 copies known to exist.

Part of the basic track of "How Could I Be Such A Fool" (from 0:57 to 1:15) was combined with "What's The Ugliest Part Of Your Body?" vocals for the instrumental, mono, stereo and '80s re-recorded versions of "Lonely Little Girl" on "We're Only In It For The Money." All of these mixes were featured on "Lumpy Money." The acetate and single versions of "Lonely Little Girl" did not feature that "Fool" extract. "How Could I Be Such A Fool" was re-recorded for the "Cruising With Ruben & The Jets" album in 1968. The song was performed live in 1967, 1970, and 1974-1976, with regular, rearranged performances in the final two years.

The spirit of "It Can't Happen Here" (but not the content) can be traced to Mauricio Kagel's 1957-1958 work "Anagrama." The title "It Can't Happen Here" was a Sinclair Lewis novel in 1935 and an oil painting by first Mothers manager Mark Cheka in 1956. The mono single master lacked Zappa's piano solo, the "psychedelic" section, and FZ's comment "since you first took the shots." Frank's ending vocal was covered with repeated reverberations, which I have called a rippling reverb. The 1:15-1:19 segment of "It Can't Happen Here" quoted the 1880 Neapolitan classic "Funiculì Funiculà" by Luigi Denza and Giuseppe "Peppino" Turco.

Numerous mixes have been made of "It Can't Happen Here," but none of them have the exact edit sequence of the single master. The "Mothermania" edited stereo remix of "It Can't Happen Here" involved a loop of three "can't happen here" segments prior to the rippling. The complete original stereo mix of "Help I'm A Rock – It Can't Happen Here" was reissued on the 2013 single (discussed in the "Posthumous Releases" section) prior to the original debut single reissue three years later. "It Can't Happen Here" was quoted within the "Joe's Menage" track "What's The Ugliest Part Of Your Body?" and within "The Illinois Enema Bandit" on both "Zappa In New York" and "Läther."

Someone at Verve in England had a real sense of humor. The A-side of the British single was actually "It Can't Happen Here"! The record was released as Verve VS 545 on November 11, 1966.

* * *

BOBBY JAMESON: Gotta' Find My Roogalator/ Lowdown Funky Blues (7" 45 rpm single)
Released August 8, 1966 as Penthouse 503

<u>A-side</u>
Gotta' Find My Roogalator (2:30) (Robert Parker Jameson) • Master #: P-66-7005-A • MONO
Recorded: June 21, 1966 at H. & R. Studios, Hollywood, CA
Personnel: Bobby Jameson (lead vocal); Frank Zappa (lead guitar, leader, arranger); Benjamin Barrett (contractor); Louis Morell (guitar); Robert West (guitar, bass); Lawrence Knechtel (piano); Gene Estes (drums, tympani, tambourine); Carol Kaye (guitar); John Guerin (drums); Reginald Dale (R.D.) McMickle (trumpet); Billy Hughes (copyist); Robert Gibson (copyist); Russell Brown (copyist)
Producer: Norm Ratner (credited); Frank Zappa & Bobby Jameson (uncredited)
Engineer: John Haeny

The inspiration for Bobby Jameson's "Gotta' Find My Roogalator" came from Johnny Rivers. Johnny wrote an instrumental with vocal exhortations called "Roogalator" as the B-side of his late May 1966 single "(I Washed My Hands In) Muddy Water." Jameson liked the nebulous blues term "roogalator," which was a good luck charm similar to a "mojo." Bobby put together his song "Roogalator" and presented it to Frank Zappa. To separate Jameson's song from the Rivers flipside, the title was changed to "Gotta' Find My Roogalator" after its recording. (The union session sheet shows the original title. The apostrophe was unnecessarily used on the record label. Frank would use an apostrophe correctly later.)

Zappa brought life to "Gotta' Find My Roogalator" through his energetic arrangement and controlled use of guitar feedback. The FZ lead guitar sound was developing with the first-call session musicians that accompanied his instrument and Jameson's vocal. Once again, Norm Ratner put his name as producer on the label without actually doing that work. Carol Kaye did not play on "Roogalator" because of her dissatisfaction with the song, but she was paid anyway.

The second track recorded at the session was Girl From The East." Written about the Philadelphia, PA-born Gail Sloatman, "Girl From The East" was originally written and recorded to satisfy a contract for the Mira budget label Surrey in 1965. The label asked folk performers Chris Ducey and The Trio Of Time to record an album called "Songs Of Protest And Anti-Protest." Surrey discovered that Ducey was signed to another label and the album was shelved after the front and back covers were prepared. For some reason, Brian Jones of The Rolling Stones was shown playing harmonica on the front cover instead of Ducey. In order to avoid a complete loss, Surrey hired Bobby Jameson to record brand new songs using Ducey's original front cover titles. Jameson was billed as Chris Lucey, with Surrey changing the "D" to an "L" in a manual front cover touch-up. Surrey released the album in this way, but the early '70s British release on the Joy label (called "Too Many Mornings") was credited to Bobby Jameson. Having survived this experience, Jameson proceeded to record the aforementioned "Vietnam" for Mira and "Reconsider Baby" for Penthouse. "Girl From The East" was recorded by The Leaves for their Mira album "Hey Joe" and as the B-side for three different singles.

Bobby Jameson wanted to re-record "Girl From The East" using Zappa's band arrangement. Jameson's re-recording with Zappa only featured his lead vocal, unlike The Leaves' version with a fully developed vocal arrangement. Even though Bobby Jameson could never figure out why he decided not to use this re-recording as the B-side of "Gotta' Find My Roogalator," it is most likely due to The Leaves' superior vocal treatment. The previous B-side was used instead. Trumpeter R.D. McMickle is clearly not on "Girl From The East," but it does sound like Carol Kaye's playing on the track.

Stock copies are extremely difficult to locate. Jameson made all three of his Penthouse tracks available through Zappateers and YouTube, but the recording of "Girl From The East" from the original acetate cuts off at the end. There is no other way to obtain this recording, so we will have to live with whatever Jameson shared with fans.

Bobby Jameson frequently brought Gail Sloatman to Frank's place on 8404 Kirkwood Drive in the Laurel Canyon section of Los Angeles. What Bobby didn't know was that a relationship was forming between Gail and Frank. Zappa and Gail were crazy about each other, and Frank asked Bobby if he was serious about her. Bobby said it was OK if they got together, and their relationship officially began.

In his way of thanking Bobby for being open about his feelings concerning Gail, Zappa helped Jameson obtain his next recording arrangement with the Verve label. Frank asked MOI producer Tom Wilson to make sure Bobby's project was handled well. Noted producer Curt Boettcher, fresh off his success with The Association, worked with Bobby Jameson on the album "Color Him In." The songs were written by Jameson while at Frank's house, and the 1967 album "Color Him In" was simply credited to his last name.

Van Dyke Parks was occasionally playing electric harpsichord with The Mothers at this time. He suggested to Frank Zappa that he contact Delton Kacher (known as Del Casher) to do some studio work for actress Florence Marly. Florence was an alien vampire queen in the March 1966 film "Queen Of Blood" (aka "Planet Of Blood") directed by Curtis Harrington. Marly wrote the song "Space Boy" which she wanted to use in "Queen Of Blood," but it was not recorded for the film. In August 1966, FZ went to Del Kacher's garage studio in Los Angeles to record Marly's song. Del engineered the track and played guitar and bass, while Frank contributed drums and orchestration. That orchestration involved sound effects by Forrest Ackerman and Cole (aka Ronald Stein). Not known as a vocalist or a composer, Florence Marly provided vocals which perfectly matched the backing track. She had a small role in Curtis Harrington's next film "Games" (released September 1967). The recording of "Space Boy" has not been officially released, but a transfer from an existing Audiodisc acetate has been widely circulated. The acetate mistakenly lists the song's inclusion in the film. Florence Marly never gave up on her song. She re-recorded "Space Boy" with electronic music pioneers Bebe and Louis Barron in 1971, and it was completed in 1973 for the "Blood" sequel "Space Boy! Night, Neal And Ness." It was a low budget short subject which was shot on 16mm film.

* * *

THE MOTHERS OF INVENTION: Trouble Comin' Every Day/ Who Are The Brain Police? (7" 45 rpm single)
Released November 14, 1966 as Verve VK 10458

<u>A-side</u>
Trouble Comin' Every Day (2:28) (Frank Zappa) • Master #: 101,372 • MONO
Recorded: March 9, 1966 at T.T.G. Studios, Hollywood, CA
Personnel: Frank Zappa (lead vocals, lead guitar, leader, arranger, conductor, copyist); Elliot Ingber (rhythm guitar); Roy Estrada (bass); Jimmy Carl Black (drums); Ray Collins (harmonica)
Producer: Tom Wilson

Engineer: Ami Hadani & Tom Hidley

B-side
Who Are The Brain Police? (3:22) (Frank Zappa) • Master #: 100,234 • MONO
Recorded: March 9, 1966 at T.T.G. Studios, Hollywood, CA
Personnel: Frank Zappa (co-lead vocal, leader, arranger, conductor, copyist); Ray Collins (co-lead vocal, kazoo); Elliot Ingber (rhythm guitar); Roy Estrada (bass, backing vocals); Jimmy Carl Black (drums); Eugene DiNovi (piano); Gene Estes (timpani, gong); Neil Levang (fuzztone guitar); Benjamin Barrett (contractor)
Producer: Tom Wilson
Engineer: Ami Hadani & Tom Hidley

The second MOI single for Verve was a brilliant combination of the serious and the absurd. "Trouble Comin' Every Day" (which FZ later called "Trouble Every Day" or "More Trouble Every Day" in its retooled arrangement) captured the ugly spectacle of the Watts riots. The whole mess started when police pulled over an African-American robbery parolee, Marquette Frye, for reckless driving in the Watts section of Los Angeles on August 11, 1965. An argument between Frye and the police became a fight. People in the area spread the word that police injured a pregnant woman in the melee. Six days of rioting lasted until the 16th. The Army National Guard was called in to quell the situation, but not before 34 people died and $40 million of property damage occurred. A similar situation occurred with Rodney King in 1991, which led to further rioting the next year.

Through "Trouble Comin' Every Day," Frank Zappa incisively dealt with the Watts event and the shameful television coverage of it. The same problems with events and television coverage exist today. As for the recording itself, three electric guitars, bass, drums and a Zappa vocal were laid down first. Added to this foundation were Zappa's second vocal, a fourth electric guitar track, and Ray Collins' harmonica.

The mono album mix and single master of "Trouble Comin' Every Day" contained the ending number "4" of the countoff and snare hit leading into the song. The single master edited out the 0:01-0:09 segment from the album mix, kept the next 1:25, and then used the next 1:06 from the 4:18 point of the album edition before fading out early. The truncated British edition of "Freak Out!" used the single master for the mono edition, and most importantly, used an otherwise unavailable stereo mix of the single master with the countoff for the stereo edition. The most recent release of the mono single master is the 4-CD edition of "The MOFO Project/Object."

"Trouble Comin' Every Day" was performed throughout the life of the original MOI, and on the album "The Mothers 1970." It did not appear again until its new "More Trouble Every Day" arrangement during the 1974 tour. The song laid dormant again until it was included in the 1984 and 1988 tours. The "blow your harmonica, son" and other harmonica variant lyrics were used in "The Downtown Talent Scout," "Prelude To The Afternoon Of A Sexually Aroused Gas Mask," "Harmonica Fun," "Diptheria Blues," and "In France." The heat (as in police) were also mentioned in "Wowie Zowie," "Son Of Suzy Creamcheese," and "The Downtown Talent Scout." The Great Society lyric reference in "Trouble" also turned up in "Hungry Freaks, Daddy."

"Who Are The Brain Police?" was a devastating look inside all of us. It started ominously with bass and two opening chords before Neil Levang's fuzztone on a Stratocaster. The Ray Collins-led vocals evolved into rippling echo at the end of each line. The chorus was equally ominous. After the "I think I'm going to die" freak-out section (known as Section B), Zappa is most audible on the following chorus, verse, and next chorus. A kazoo lead over the pounding chords took the song to its fadeout. The single master of

"Who Are The Brain Police?" was reissued on "The MOFO Project/Object (fazedooh)" (the 2-CD version). The basic tracks and single master were also used as the B-side for the 2013 single of "Help I'm A Rock – It Can't Happen Here."

The Section B freak-out piece was used in "Help I'm A Rock." "Who Are The Brain Police?" was performed live in 1970 and 1971. Three excerpts of "Brain Police?" were used in "Porn Wars Deluxe" on the "Understanding America" collection. Chrome allusions were also made in numerous songs: "The Chrome Plated Megaphone Of Destiny," "Uncle Meat," "Magic Fingers," "Sofa" and its backwards use in "Ya Hozňa," "Muffin Man," "A Token Of My Extreme," "Stick It Out," and "Sy Borg."

The Canadian single (Verve V-10458X) was the same as the US release. The Japanese single (Verve DV 5010) came with a picture sleeve, but was belatedly released in November 1967. In Holland, the sides were reversed for their January 27, 1967 single (Verve 58 509). Unbelievably, "Freak Out!" was not released in Japan until 1969, so a further single was produced for that market: "Motherly Love"/ "I Ain't Got No Heart." The record had a picture sleeve, and was released as Verve DV 5012 in mid-September 1968.

* * *

BURT WARD: Boy Wonder I Love You/ Orange Colored Sky (7" 45 rpm single)
Released November 14, 1966 as MGM K 13632

A-side
Boy Wonder I Love You (2:25) (Frank Zappa) • Master #: L77 • MONO
Recorded: June 9, 1966 at T.T.G. Studios, Hollywood, CA
Personnel: Frank Zappa (leader, arranger, conductor, copyist); Esther Roth (contractor); Jimmy Carl Black (drums); Eugene DiNovi (piano); Roy Estrada (bass); Elliot Ingber (guitar); Dennis Budimir (guitar); Plas Johnson (saxophone); Justin Gordon (bass clarinet, clarinet); James Zito (French horn, trumpet); George Callender (tuba); Benjamin Barrett (cello); plus unknown backing vocalists
Producer: Tom Wilson
Engineer: Ami Hadani & Tom Hidley

B-side
Orange Colored Sky (1:46) (Milton DeLugg – William Stein) • Master #: L80 • MONO
Recorded: June 10, 1966 at T.T.G. Studios, Hollywood, CA
Personnel: Frank Zappa (leader, arranger, conductor); Billy Hughes (contractor); John Guerin (drums); Gene DiNovi (piano); Elliot Ingber (guitar); William Pitman (guitar); Lou Morell (guitar); Dennis Budimir (guitar); Kenneth Watson (tympani, traps, mallets); Plas Johnson (saxophone); Jack Nimitz (bass clarinet, clarinet); Frederick Dutton (contrabassoon, bassoon); Anthony Terran (trumpet); John T. Johnson (tuba); Benjamin Barrett (cello); Vincent Bartold (copyist); Robert Gibson (copyist); Russell Brown (copyist); plus unknown backing vocalists and strings
Producer: Tom Wilson
Engineer: Ami Hadani & Tom Hidley

Offering a record deal to a celebrity has always been a bad idea. The success of the ABC television series "Batman" respectively starring Adam West and Burt Ward as Batman and Robin, The Boy Wonder, was the source of merchandising madness. Veteran actor Adam West had a distinctive speaking voice and he could sing well. Burt Ward (born Bert John Gervis, Jr.) was an unproven actor still in his teens. What did

ABC do? They signed Burt Ward to a contract with their ABC-Paramount record label. ABC was so excited that they reported Ward's signing to Billboard magazine. The label couldn't get anything off the ground with Burt, so they quietly dropped him. Billboard didn't report that development. In early June 1966, the MGM label stepped in and reported their signing of Burt Ward to a record deal. MGM was hoping to get two Burt Ward singles.

Coming off his work on Bobby Jameson's first Penthouse single, Frank Zappa was looking for another project. The camp humor of "Batman" was undeniable. Tom Wilson was assigned to work with Burt Ward, and Wilson in turn brought in Zappa to realize the project as arranger and conductor. It was immediately obvious that Burt Ward could not sing. He could speak over a musical backing, but that was about it. Frank Zappa invited Jimmy Carl Black, Roy Estrada and Elliot Ingber from The Mothers Of Invention to join a sizable collection of studio musicians for the sessions at T.T.G.

Zappa came up with the idea of Burt Ward reading Boy Wonder fan mail over a backing track. The session sheet listed the work as "Boy Wonder (Why I Love You)," but it ended up being called "Boy Wonder I Love You." A backing track for the song "Gotta Fall In Love" (titled "I Love" on the tape box) was not used. The other track worked on during the first session date was the Nat King Cole hit "Orange Colored Sky." The song was written by Milton DeLugg and Willie Stein in 1930, and Cole's version was recorded with Stan Kenton and his orchestra. Burt Ward's attempt to cover "Orange Colored Sky" was disastrous and required another session the next day (June 10, 1966).

"Boy Wonder I Love You" began with female vocals singing the title before Burt Ward started speaking about catching up with his fan mail. A gushing fan wrote that she wanted a personalized response from the Boy Wonder instead of something from his agent. Burt continued to read the letter that requested his presence the following Saturday for a visit that could last all summer. That visit would involve the fan doing everything for him. The letter ended comically with the line "I hope you know this is a girl writing." "Boy Wonder I Love You" concluded with fan response and backing vocals. In the mayhem, Frank Zappa can be heard repeating "Boy Wonder." There was no question that "Boy Wonder I Love You" would be the A-side of the single.

The second session started with the unused instrumental "Variant I," listed as "The Comedian" on the tape box. This was followed by a complete take of vocalist Robert John and record executive Russ Regan's "Teenage Bill Of Rights," on which Burt Ward went through demands for American teens in political terms. It was now time for "Orange Colored Sky." Ward's singing on the number was deliciously atrocious, and the spoken parts involved exclamatory words like those used in "Batman" fight scenes ("Flash!," "Bam!," "Alakazam!"). It was Zappa's idea for Burt to say "Hotcha!" during the song. "Orange Colored Sky" had a very Zappa-like "bump" ending. Elliot Ingber was the only Mothers member invited for this day's session. A final unused music track with backing vocals, "Tears Come From Loving You," was the last piece recorded before time ran out. There would not be two singles drawn from these sessions! The mono mixdown session tape includes various scraps of countoffs and outtakes.

It took MGM five months to release this single. Promo copies of this single outnumber stock copies by a ratio of at least 10 to 1. The B-side was misspelled "Oranged Colored Sky" on promos, but was correctly depicted on super-rare stock copies. This single has never been reissued, but the session tapes have been widely circulated.

Burt Ward did not learn his lesson from this experience! In 1970, he recorded the A-side "I've Got Love For

My Baby" with The Bobby Sanders Singers for the Soultown label. The B-side "Robin's Theme" was thankfully an instrumental. As for Adam West, he sang "Orange Colored Sky" quite well in his Batman costume for the October 8, 1966 episode of the TV show "The Hollywood Palace." There was some comedy going on around Adam West while he did his thing, but his performance of "Orange Colored Sky" was miles ahead of his Batman co-star.

* * *

BARRY GOLDBERG: Carry On/ Ronnie Siegel From Avenue L (7" 45 rpm single)
Released March 6, 1967 as Verve/Folkways KF 5045

A-side
Carry On (2:45) (Barry Joseph Goldberg) • Master #: 101,791 • MONO
Recorded: between December 10-14, 1966 at an unknown studio, New York, NY
Personnel: Barry Goldberg (vocals, organ, rhythm guitar, piano); Mike Bloomfield (lead guitar); Frank Zappa (rhythm guitar); other personnel unknown
Producer: Tom Wilson
Engineer: unknown

By this time, FZ had built up a reputation as an unusual performer and guitarist who got things done. Blues veteran Barry Goldberg had recorded with his group The Tempters before playing on "Devil With The Blue Dress On"/ "Good Golly Miss Molly" by Mitch Ryder & The Detroit Wheels. Barry recorded two singles with vocalist/guitarist Steve Miller (yes, THAT Steve Miller) before he did this solo single for Verve/Folkways. With Tom Wilson as producer, Zappa was brought in for an unusual role – that is, as rhythm guitarist on Goldberg's song "Carry On." Paul Butterfield Blues Band guitarist Mike Bloomfield took the lead. The first verse of "Carry On" strangely fades into the section prior to the first chorus. While very interesting, "Carry On" did not have commercial potential.

Looking at MGM/Verve master numbers, the recording date for "Carry On" is between December 10-14, 1966. Butterfield and Zappa were both free and in New York during that time period. The B-side was recorded on February 15, 1967 and was an organ-led instrumental. Both sides of this record have never been reissued. The only copies that seem to turn up are promotional, but it is quite possible that stock copies exist.

* * *

THE MOTHERS OF INVENTION: Why Don't You Do Me Right/ Big Leg Emma (7" 45 rpm single)
Released April 10, 1967 as Verve VK 10513
Reissued November 23, 2012 as Barking Pumpkin BPR 1221 (7" 45 rpm Black Friday numbered single with reversed sides)

A-side
Why Don't You Do Me Right (2:38) (Frank Zappa) • Master #: L 260 (Verve); BPR 1221 B (Barking Pumpkin; B-side) • MONO
Recorded: March 6, 1967 at T.T.G. Studios, Hollywood, CA
Personnel: Frank Zappa (lead vocal, lead guitar); Ray Collins (backing vocals); Roy Estrada (bass); Don Preston (electric harpsichord); Jimmy Carl Black (drums); Billy Mundi (drums)
Producer: Tom Wilson

Engineer: Ami Hadani & Tom Hidley

B-side
Big Leg Emma (2:32) (Frank Zappa) • Master #: L 258 (Verve); BPR 1221 A (Barking Pumpkin; A-side) • MONO
Recorded: March 6, 1967 at T.T.G. Studios, Hollywood, CA
Personnel: Frank Zappa (co-lead vocals, guitar); Ray Collins (vocals, tambourine); Roy Estrada (vocals, bass); Don Preston (keyboards); Bunk Gardner (soprano saxophone); Jimmy Carl Black (co-lead vocals, drums); Billy Mundi (drums)
Producer: Tom Wilson
Engineer: Ami Hadani & Tom Hidley

The second MOI album "Absolutely Free" was recorded in the middle of November 1966, but packaging battles with Verve led to delays until the end of May 1967. A standalone single would have to keep things going until "Absolutely Free" was ready. "Why Don't You Do Me Right" (later called "Why Don'tcha Do Me Right?") was a song that Zappa wrote in 1962 during his troubled first marriage. Frank recorded two demos of the song at Pal. The first was a solo demo in January 1963, and the second was done in the middle of that year with his friend Floyd. The Floyd version was part of the "Joe's Xmasage" collection, and the Buff box had both versions.

The first band arrangement of "Why Don't You Do Me Right" and "Big Leg Emma" were done at a separate session at T.T.G. By this point, Billy Mundi had come into the band as the second drummer. Keyboardist Don Preston and woodwind master Bunk Gardner were the other new band additions. Frank took a considerably heavier approach for the revised "Why Don't You Do Me Right," using a guitar riff derived from Howlin' Wolf's "Smokestack Lightnin'." The breakdown prior to the out-chorus referred to The Troggs' "Wild Thing." "Why Don't You Do Me Right" was actually the A-side of the single, with Billboard reviewing that side in their May 13, 1967 issue.

"Big Leg Emma" sounded more old-fashioned, thanks to Bunk Gardner's soprano saxophone. The light humor of the song's lyrics dealt with the title character, who suffered from skin and weight problems in addition to the size of her legs! Frank's passing comment "Sock it to me!" referred to the Mitch Ryder & The Detroit Wheels hit "Sock It To Me – Baby!". MGM listed "Big Leg Emma" as "Dilemma" on their tape logs, but FZ's title was the correct one.

This conscious effort to create a hit single was met with complete radio indifference, despite the inoffensive nature of both sides. The only time that Zappa performed "Why Don't You Do Me Right" live was at a Boston soundcheck on February 19, 1988. "Big Leg Emma" was rarely performed from 1967-1970, but it was frequently played between December 1976 and December 1977. One such case (December 29, 1976) is on the 40th anniversary edition of "Zappa In New York."

The multi-track tapes for this single disappeared early on, so we only have mono mixes of both sides. The first time that both sides of this single appeared on an album took place on the 1975 British LP that people commonly refer to as "Transparency." The sonics on that album were reduced because of long playing times. The original LP box set "The Old Masters Volume One" featured both single tracks on the "Mystery Disc," but with reverb added. CDs of "Absolutely Free" added both sides as bonuses with the same reverb issue. The 2012 CD edition has the unadulterated mono single masters, as does the 2-LP edition in 2017.

On the analog front, the original mono single masters were reissued in 2012 with a picture sleeve as a 7"

Black Friday vinyl release with the sides reversed. The reissue picture sleeve duplicated the one used for the Norwegian release (Verve VK 58 303) from September 22, 1967. The British single issued the same day (Verve VS 557) had "Big Leg Emma" as the top side, but the Swedish single (Verve VK 58 303) was like the American release. France had the most unconventional release, pairing "Son Of Suzy Creamcheese" with "Big Leg Emma" (Verve 58 516).

* * *

THE KNACK: Softly, Softly/ The Spell (7" 45 rpm single)
Released April 10, 1967 as Capitol 5889

A-side
Softly, Softly (2:24) (Michael Chain – Michael "Dink" Kaplan) • Master #: 45-57212 • MONO
Recorded: February 28, 1967 at Capitol Studios, Hollywood, CA
Personnel: Michael Chain (lead vocal, rhythm guitar); Michael "Dink" Kaplan (lead guitar); Larry Gould (bass); Howard "Pug" Baker (drums); Frank Zappa (piano); Jimmy Carl Black (percussion); Ray Collins (backing vocals)
Producer: Nick Venet
Engineer: John Krauss

The first Los Angeles band called The Knack was signed to Capitol and produced four challenging pop singles between 1966 and 1968. Their first release, "Time Waits for No One" b/w "I'm Aware," did not chart but created a solid following. The Knack started working on their second 45 on December 12, 1966. The excellent B-side "The Spell" was laid down at Capitol Studios on that date. It took main songwriters Michael Chain and Dink Kaplan a couple of months to come up with a strong A-side candidate in "Softly, Softly." When recording it on February 28, 1967, they concluded that it needed a piano to complete the arrangement.

It was The Knack's good fortune that Frank Zappa was preparing "Lumpy Gravy" material for the next Capitol sessions that would take place in mid-March 1967 with Nick Venet producing. Jimmy Carl Black and Ray Collins also happened to be on hand. Nick Venet was handling The Knack's sessions, so he asked Zappa and the guys to come in and help the group with "Softly, Softly." The subtle touches that these Mothers added to the song produced a very professional final single master. The single met the same fate as its predecessor, but it was released in Japan, Germany, and New Zealand. The mono single masters of "Softly, Softly" and "The Spell" were included on the British compilation CD "Time Waits For No One: The Complete Recordings" (Now Sounds CRNOW 38; released August 7, 2012). As for the other Knack, you know, the "My Sharona" guys, Frank Zappa would make fun of them much later!

* * *

FRANK ZAPPA: Sink Trap/ Gypsy Airs (8" 45 rpm Capitol acetate single)
Acetate Pressing Date: June 15, 1967
NOT COMMERCIALLY RELEASED

A-side
Sink Trap (3:04) (Frank Zappa) • Master #: 57290 • STEREO
Recorded: March 14, 1967 at Capitol Studios, Hollywood, CA
Personnel: Frank Zappa (arranger, conductor); The Abnuceals Emuukha Electric Symphony Orchestra – Sidney Sharp (contractor, violin); Ted Nash (flute, bass flute, alto saxophone, clarinet, bass clarinet, contrabass clarinet);

Jules Jacob (oboe, English horn, flute, piccolo, tenor saxophone); Johnny Rotella (flute, baritone saxophone, E flat contrabass clarinet, clarinet, bass clarinet); John L. "Bunk" Gardner (flute, clarinet, bassoon, bass saxophone, soprano saxophone, tenor saxophone); Emil Radocchia (aka Emil Richards) (mallets, percussion, timpani, Latin); Gene P. Estes (mallets, percussion, timpani, Latin); James C. Zito (trumpet, flugelhorn, piccolo trumpet); Thomas J. Tedesco (guitar, bells, bongos); Kenneth Shroyer (tenor trombone, bass trombone); Frank Capp (drums, Latin); Don Christlieb (bassoon, contrabassoon); Michael A. Lang (piano); John Balkin (bass); Alfred Viola (guitar); Robert West (bass guitar); Dennis Budimir (guitar); Arthur E. Briegleb (French horn); George F. Price (French horn); Lyle Ritz (bass); Joan Steele (copyist); Robert M. Calderwood (copyist); Russell N. Brown (copyist); Vincent Bartold (copyist); Jack DuLong (copyist)
Producer: Nick Venet
Engineer: Joe, Rex, Pete, Jim, Bob and Gary

B-side
Gypsy Airs (1:40) (Frank Zappa) • Master #: 57320 • STEREO
Recorded: March 15, 1967 at Capitol Studios, Hollywood, CA
Personnel: Frank Zappa (arranger, conductor); The Abnuceals Emuukha Electric Symphony Orchestra – Sidney Sharp (contractor, violin); John L. "Bunk" Gardner (piccolo, flute, bassoon, baritone clarinet); Johnny Rotella (piccolo, flute, E flat clarinet, clarinet, E flat contrabass clarinet); Gene P. Estes (mallets, percussion, timpani, Latin); Victor Feldman (timpani, Latin, percussion, mallets); Ted Nash (flute, bass flute, alto saxophone, clarinet); Gene Cipriano (oboe, flute, bass flute, E flat clarinet); Kenneth Shroyer (tenor trombone, bass trombone, bass trumpet); James C. Zito (trumpet, flugelhorn, piccolo trumpet); Thomas J. Tedesco (guitars, bells, bongos); Don Christlieb (bassoon, contrabassoon); Robert West (bass guitar); John Balkin (bass); Charles Berghofer (bass); Lincoln Mayorga (keyboards); George F. Price (French horn); David A. Duke (French horn); Alfred Viola (guitar); Trefoni (Tony) Rizzi (guitar); Shelly Manne (drums); Leonard Malarsky (violin); William Kurasch (violin); Arnold Belnick (violin); Ralph Schaeffer (violin); Jerome A. Kessler (cello); Raymond J. Kelley (cello); Leonard Selic (viola); Joseph DiFiore (viola); Harry Hyams (viola); Philip Goldberg (viola); Joseph Saxon (cello); Jesse Erlich (cello), Tibor Zelig (violin); Harold Ayres (violin), Jerome J. Reisler (violin), Robert Ross (copyist); R.D. McMickle (copyist); John Donahue (copyist); Robert Calderwood (copyist); C.D. Goodwin (copyist); Russell N. Brown (copyist); Joan Steele (copyist)
Producer: Nick Venet
Engineer: Joe, Rex, Pete, Jim, Bob and Gary

These Capitol "Lumpy Gravy" extracts correspond directly with the titles on the stereo album acetate rather than the mono masters used for the "Lumpy Gravy Primordial" 12-inch from 2018. According to Capitol's tape files, no release number was assigned for this track coupling. There are no known test pressings. Other than a handful of "Lumpy Gravy" 4-track cartridges in the Muntz Stereo-Pak series (Capitol 4CL-2719; released August 7, 1967), these mixes have not been made available commercially. Despite its extreme rarity, the stereo acetate has been widely circulated. The original 4-track tape does in fact exist, contrary to what the Zappa Family Trust has claimed.

The "Sink Trap" (aka "Envelops The Bath Tub") segment, called "Lumpy Gravy (Excerpt)/ Improvisation," was recorded live at UCLA's Royce Hall on September 18, 1975. It was released on the 40th anniversary edition of "Orchestral Favorites." Extracts of that recording were previously used in "QuAUDIOPHILIAc" (indexed as "Lumpy Gravy"), "Tinsel Town Rebellion" (as part of "Easy Meat"), and "One Shot Deal" (included in the track "Hermitage").

* * *

ERIC BURDON & THE ANIMALS: It's All Meat/ **The Other Side Of This Life** (7" 45 rpm single)
Released August 21, 1967 as MGM K 13795 (Record 5 of an "MGM Celebrity Scene" 5-single box set: MGM Box CS-11-5)

B-side
The Other Side Of This Life (3:43) (Fred Neil) • Master #: L 111 • MONO
Recorded: July 4, 1966 at T.T.G. Studios, Hollywood, CA
Personnel: Eric Burdon (lead vocal); Frank Zappa (guitar, bass, arranger, leader); Benjamin Barrett (contractor); John Guerin (drums); William Roberts (guitar); Lawrence Knechtel (organ); Carol Kaye (guitar)
Producer: Tom Wilson
Engineer: Ami Hadani

As we know, MGM and its subsidiary labels usually had no idea what they were doing. One of the things that MGM's labels did was to create box sets of special promotional singles that coin operators would use for jukeboxes. Unrelated bits and pieces of an artist's output were spread out over multiple singles. A handful of stock copies of these box sets were created for so-called regular fans. It was a strange way to promote the MGM/Verve catalog.

The "MGM Celebrity Scene" set dealing with The Animals covered the second edition of the band (with Eric Burdon, guitarist Hilton Valentine, keyboardist Dave Rowberry, bassist Chas Chandler, and drummer Barry Jenkins) as well as the more psychedelic-leaning Eric Burdon And The Animals lineup (guitarist Vic Briggs, guitarist/violinist John Weider, bassist Danny McCulloch, and Barry Jenkins). By the time this record was released, the more recent lineup had issued the album "Winds Of Change." To smooth over the transition of the band, MGM misleadingly credited all five records in the set to Eric Burdon And The Animals.

The final disc of the MGM singles set used "It's All Meat" (a "Winds Of Change" album track and single B-side) as the top side, with the earlier group's cover of Fred Neil's "The Other Side Of Life" on its reverse. Funny enough, "It's All Meat" expressed Frank Zappa's "project/object" in Eric Burdon's own terms, that is, music of all kinds is all meat from the same bone. Burdon also namechecked Zappa in the title track of the 1967 album "Winds Of Change" by stating that "Frank Zappa zapped."

Eric Burdon loved Frank Zappa, Tom Wilson, and the T.T.G. sound. Wilson had previously worked with the second lineup of The Animals, who were about to break up. Afternoon and evening sessions from 2:30-5:30 and 5:30-9:00 were hastily arranged at T.T.G. for July 4, 1966. Tom Wilson asked Frank Zappa to arrange some tracks for The Animals.

Zappa and Wilson were at T.T.G., but none of The Animals were. Eric Burdon and company had spent the previous night partying. This was the Independence Day holiday, and studio musicians worked at triple scale. Without a band to work with, Frank called up American Federation of Musicians Local 47 to obtain some unionized session musicians to cover the date.

The Animals were completely unprepared when they eventually arrived at T.T.G. Eric Burdon and Barry Jenkins came in first. The session players sat around while Burdon decided what he was going to sing. His band was not there, so Eric decided to record "The Other Side Of Life" and Frank Zappa's song "All Night Long" with the session cats. (Fred Neil's own version of "The Other Side Of Life" featured producer Nick Venet and drummer Billy Mundi.) This was the first time that Burdon would record with session musicians. (He would do the same thing two months later with the "Eric Is Here" album after this Animals lineup quit.)

Larry Knechtel (organ), William Roberts (composer of "Hey Joe"; harmonica, guitar), Carol Kaye (guitar) and John Guerin (drums) formed the backing band. Zappa played lead guitar and bass. "All Night Long" was an early version of a song that Zappa would call "No Matter What You Do," and it was called "Song X" on the session sheet. It drew upon "Smokestack Lightnin'" and other blues influences that Eric Burdon could relate to. "No Matter What You Do" appeared on the bootleg "Tis The Season To Be Jelly." William Roberts played the harmonica on "All Night Long." Both tracks were laid down very quickly and professionally.

The missing members of The Animals, namely Hilton Valentine, Dave Rowberry and Chas Chandler, arrived at T.T.G. towards the end of the recording process. Hilton Valentine told me that they were furious when they found that Eric had recorded without them and that the band name would be attributed to the tracks. With the exception of organist Don Randi substituting for Larry Knechtel, the same set of musicians had been booked for the next session.

With the full band now in attendance, they weren't going to allow other musicians to play on their tracks again. The Animals had their own T.T.G. session from 11:00 PM to 2:30 AM. Tom Wilson would continue producing, and Zappa and the session people were dismissed and paid without working. Eric Burdon and the rest of The Animals laid down "Hit The Road Jack," "Lucille," "Smokestack Lightnin'" and "Louisiana Blues" on their own. The two tracks with Zappa and all four of these "real" Animals tracks were included on the US-only album "Animalism" (MGM E/SE-4414; released November 21, 1966). The album has been officially reissued on CD in 2006 and on LP in 2010, and it should be noted that the mono and stereo mixes have different lengths.

* * *

VARIOUS ARTISTS: MGM, Verve, Verve/Forecast Radio Commercials (12" 33 1/3 rpm sampler)
Released September 11, 1967 as MGM ADVS 1A (A-side)/ ADV 1B (B-side)

B-side – Track 3
Freak Out (1:01) • Master #: none • MONO
Recorded: March 6, 1967 at T.T.G. Studios, Hollywood, CA
Personnel: unknown (voice)
Producer: unknown
Engineer: Ami Hadani

B-side – Track 4
Freak Out & Absolutely Free (1:01) • Master #: none • MONO
Recorded: November 15, 1966 ("Son Of Suzy Creamcheese" fragments) and March 6, 1967 (voice-over) at T.T.G. Studios, Hollywood, CA
Personnel: Frank Zappa (voice-over; lead guitar, backing vocals); Roy Estrada (bass, backing vocals); Ray Collins (lead vocal); Jimmy Carl Black (backing vocals); Don Preston (piano); Bunk Gardner (tenor saxophone); Billy Mundi (drums); Jim Fielder (12-string guitar)
Producer: Frank Zappa
Engineer: Ami Hadani

B-side – Track 5
Absolutely Free (1:01) • Master #: none • MONO
Recorded: November 18, 1966 ("Brown Shoes Don't Make It" fragments) and March 6, 1967 (voice-over) at

T.T.G. Studios, Hollywood, CA
Personnel: Frank Zappa (lead guitar, co-lead vocal, voice-over); Roy Estrada (bass, co-lead vocal); Ray Collins (co-lead vocal, mallets); Jimmy Carl Black (co-lead vocal); Don Preston (electric piano, piano, clavinet); Bunk Gardner (tenor saxophone, flute, bassoon, clarinet); Billy Mundi (drums); Jim Fielder (12-string guitar); Lisa Cohen (voice); Benjamin Barrett (contractor); James Getzoff (violin); Marshall Sosson (violin); Alvin Dinkin (viola); Armand Kaproff (cello); Donald Ellis (trumpet); Johnny Rotella (contrabass clarinet); Bob Hartley (copyist); Bill Hughes (copyist)
Producer: Frank Zappa
Engineer: Ami Hadani

This unassuming record came in a plain sleeve without a cover. It was not labelled as a promotional item, but it was meant to be used for non-commercial purposes only. Most of the commercials consisted of an album track with a voice-over. The first side of the record was stereo and featured commercials for the original cast album of "You're A Good Man, Charlie Brown," Nico's "Chelsea Girl," Jameson's "Color Him In," The Alan Lorber Orchestra's "The Lotus Palace" (two ads), The James Cotton Blues Band's self-titled debut, Tim Hardin's "Tim Hardin 2," and Sam The Sham And The Pharaohs' "The Sam The Sham Revue," which would be later retitled "Nefertiti." The second side was mono and included commercials for Johnny Tillotson's "Here I Am," Tim Hardin's "Tim Hardin 1," Laura Nyro's "More Than A New Discovery" (later titled "The First Songs…"), and the three Mothers Of Invention spots listed above. The record was pressed on September 7, 1967 and was ready for distribution on the following Monday (September 11).

The first spot for "Freak Out!" was a generic spot with a voice-over. However, the other two spots are of great interest to fans. Both ads were first issued commercially as bonus tracks on the second LP (Tracks 1 and 4, respectively) of the 180g release "Absolutely Free" to celebrate its 50th anniversary on October 6, 2017 (Zappa ZR 3835-1). Side two of the second LP had a laser etching of Zappa.

Fans who happened to be listening to the radio at the right time could hear taped interviews and commercials with Frank Zappa. However, this record was the first official document of Zappa's alternative methods of promotion and his viewpoints on radio corruption. It was all done in an "in your face" style. The commercial covering "Absolutely Free" and "Freak Out!" started out with a four-second clip of "Son Of Suzy Creamcheese" before FZ and Roy Estrada sang "deedle-deedle-dee-deedle-deedle-dee-deet." This idea would be fleshed out later in 1967 for the recording of "Lonely Little Girl." Frank's commentary started with a soft-sell of both albums, including his "Freak Out!" comment that "we sock it to you for $3.98." Another clip of "Suzy" flowed into this shocking conclusion: "Pigs! Radio is an ugly medium. Listen to The Mothers Of Invention in the privacy of your own home on Verve Records." Thus, the purpose of FZ's commercial was to use radio to get potential fans to listen to The Mothers instead of their radio! MGM's originally filed the tape of "Suzy" under the title "Suzy Creamcheese (What's Got Into You)."

The radio spot that concentrated solely on "Absolutely Free" began with Frank's introduction of a segment from "Brown Shoes Don't Make It." Zappa again tried to sock it to listeners by referring to pigs and the fact that Mothers records were not played on the radio. Another clip of "Brown Shoes" went into Zappa's promotion of their record label and The Mothers Of Invention's stint at Café Au Go Go in New York City (May 2-21, 1967). By the time this record was made available, the band was nowhere near New York! It was very bad planning by MGM, but then again, it was not surprising to FZ or to us.

* * *

TOMMY FLANDERS: Friday Night City/ Reputation (7" 45 rpm single)
Released September 18, 1967 as Verve Forecast KF 5064

A-side
Friday Night City (2:25) (Tommy Flanders) • Master #: L 449 • MONO
Recorded: April 1, 1966 at T.T.G. Studios, Hollywood, CA
Personnel: Frank Zappa (leader, arranger, guitar, bass); Henry Roth (contractor); Armand Kaproff (cello); Harold Schneier (cello); Gerald Wiggins (piano); James Gordon (drums); Lou Morell (guitar); David Wells (trumpet, trombone); Johnny Rotella (contrabass flute, saxophone); Robert Hartley (copyist)
Producer: Tom Wilson
Engineer: Ami Hadani & Tom Hidley

B-side
Reputation (4:35) (Tim Hardin) • Master #: L 450 • MONO
Recorded: April 1, 1966 at T.T.G. Studios, Hollywood, CA
Personnel: Frank Zappa (leader, arranger, guitar, bass); Henry Roth (contractor); Armand Kaproff (cello); Harold Schneier (cello); Gerald Wiggins (piano); James Gordon (drums); Lou Morell (guitar); David Wells (trumpet, trombone); Johnny Rotella (contrabass flute, saxophone); Robert Hartley (copyist)
Producer: Tom Wilson
Engineer: Ami Hadani & Tom Hidley

This session with former Blues Project vocalist Tommy Flanders was actually the first one that Zappa did since the creation of The Mothers, and it even predated the first Bobby Jameson single. Note that this single was released more than 17 months after it was recorded. The delay was not related to the quality of the record. In fact, the single is an excellent representation of what Flanders and Zappa did best. Flanders mysteriously disappeared for a long time after laying down these tracks.

Tommy Flanders was not an unknown commodity to Frank Zappa. As vocalist for the Verve/Folkways act The Blues Project, Flanders was a Mick Jagger-like front man for the New York blues band which began in the summer of 1965. His girlfriend Maxine had convinced him that he was too good for The Blues Project, and Tommy left in early January 1966. Tommy and Maxine were present at Zappa's late night "Freak Out!" session that took place the month before the T.T.G. recording of Flanders' own single for Verve/Forecast.

"Friday Night City" (original title "Motown [Friday Night City]") described street scenes in New York, and specifically, Greenwich Village. Zappa's arrangement and guitar playing effectively accompanied Flanders' vocal. While not overly commercial as an A-side, its subject matter and performance was well worth repeated listenings. Based on the original song title, the subject matter must have been Detroit before Flanders relocated his composition to the more familiar New York City.

"Reputation" was written by Tim Hardin. No bassist was listed on the Flanders session sheet, but evidence of the bassist on both sides (namely, Zappa) can be found on the bass line running throughout "Reputation." That bass line would be later used for the "King Kong" segment of "Lumpy Gravy." Only Frank Zappa would have known that part since it was his composition. (The bass line can be heard during the first 42 seconds of the "Foamy Soaky" segment of the Capitol edition, the 7:39-8:21 Part Two segment of the Verve edition, and from 0:05-0:47 with overdubs on the "Lumpy Money" track "Section 8, Take 22.") This take of "Reputation" has all of the lead guitar, rhythm and brass touches of a prototypical Zappa arrangement. Flanders proves himself worthy with another top-notch performance.

When Flanders was finally located after a period in the wilderness, this single was released. Flanders went on to record an MGM single and the Verve/Forecast album "The Moonstone" that was accompanied by a single. He later rejoined The Blues Project for another brief stint, but that was it for his career.

The mono single master of "Friday Night City" was reissued in 1997 on the double CD "Anthology" by The Blues Project. "Reputation" has not been made available since its original single issuance.

* * *

THE MOTHERS OF INVENTION: Lonely Little Girl/ Mother People (7" 45 rpm single)
Released November 20, 1967 as Verve VK 10570

A-side
Lonely Little Girl (2:44) (Frank Zappa) • Master #: 103,858 • MONO
Recorded: July 27-September 1967 at Mayfair Studios, New York, NY, and October 1967 at Apostolic Studios, New York, NY
Personnel: Frank Zappa (acoustic guitar, electric guitar [including electric guitar on the "Love Of My Life" intro at the end of this track], piano, celeste, lead vocals, backing vocals, arranger, conductor); Ian Underwood (piano, woodwinds); Bunk Gardner (woodwinds); Roy Estrada (bass, backing vocals); Jimmy Carl Black (tambourine); Billy Mundi (drums); Dick Barber (cough); Paul Buff (piano, drums, fuzz bass and saxophones on "Love Of My Life" intro at the end of this track)
Producer: Frank Zappa
Executive Producer: Tom Wilson
Engineer: Gary Kellgren (Mayfair); Dick Kunc (Apostolic)

B-side
Mother People (2:30) (Frank Zappa) • Master #: 103,861 • MONO
Recorded March 14-16, 1967 at Capitol Studios, Hollywood, CA (the "I Don't Know If I Can Go Through This Again" segment), July 26-September 1967 at Mayfair Studios, New York, NY, and October 1967 at Apostolic Studios, New York, NY
Personnel: Frank Zappa (electric guitar, acoustic guitar, lead vocals, backing vocals, arranger, conductor); Ian Underwood (piano, woodwinds); Bunk Gardner (woodwinds – see below); Roy Estrada (bass, backing vocals); Billy Mundi (drums); The Abnuceals Emuukha Electric Symphony Orchestra musicians on the "I Don't Know If I Can Go Through This Again" segment – Sidney Sharp (contractor, violin); Robert H. Ross (copyist); Esther Roth (orchestra manager); Robert West (bass guitar); James Bond (bass); Ted Nash (flute, bass flute, alto saxophone, clarinet, bass clarinet, contrabass clarinet); Jules Jacob (oboe, English horn, flute, piccolo, tenor sax); Johnny Rotella (flute, alto saxophone, bass saxophone, baritone saxophone, clarinet, E flat clarinet, E flat contrabass clarinet, bass clarinet, piccolo); John L. "Bunk" Gardner (flute, clarinet, baritone clarinet, bass clarinet, bassoon, bass saxophone, soprano saxophone, tenor saxophone, piccolo); Emil Radocchia (aka Emil Richards) (mallets, percussion, timpani, Latin); Gene P. Estes (mallets, percussion, timpani, Latin); James C. Zito (trumpet, flugelhorn, piccolo trumpet); Thomas J. Tedesco (guitar, bells, bongos); Kenneth Shroyer (tenor trombone, bass trombone, bass trumpet); Frank Capp (drums, Latin); Don Christlieb (bassoon, contrabassoon); Michael A. Lang (piano); John Balkin (bass); Alfred Viola (guitar); Dennis Budimir (guitar); Arthur E. Briegleb (French horn); George F. Price (French horn); Lyle Ritz (bass); Joan Steele (copyist); Robert M. Calderwood (copyist); Russell N. Brown (copyist); Vincent Bartold (copyist); Jack DuLong (copyist); Victor Feldman (timpani, Latin, percussion, mallets); Gene Cipriano (oboe, flute, bass flute, E flat clarinet); Charles Berghofer (bass); Lincoln Mayorga (piano); David A. Duke (French horn); Trefoni (Tony) Rizzi (guitar); Shelly

Manne (drums); Leonard Malarsky (violin); William Kurasch (violin); Arnold Belnick (violin); Ralph Schaeffer (violin); Jerome A. Kessler (cello); Raymond J. Kelley (cello); Leonard Selic (viola); Joseph DiFiore (viola); Harry Hyams (viola); Philip Goldberg (viola); Joseph Saxon (cello); Jesse Erlich (cello); Tibor Zelig (violin); Harold Ayres (violin); Jerome J. Reisler (violin); R.D. McMickle (copyist); John Donahue (copyist); Robert Calderwood (copyist); C.D. Goodwin (copyist); Russell N. Brown (copyist); Joan Steele (copyist); Alan Estes (timpani, mallets, percussion, Latin); Pete Jolly (piano); Lew McCreary (trombone); Vincent DeRosa (French horn); Richard Parisi (French horn); Arthur Maebe (French horn); Harold G. Bemko (cello); Alexander Koltun (violin); Bernard Kundell (violin); James Getzoff (violin)

Producer: Nick Venet ("I Don't Know If I Can Go Through This Again" segment only); Frank Zappa ("Mother People" original recording)

Executive Producer: Tom Wilson ("Mother People" original recording)

Engineer: Joe, Rex, Pete, Jim, Bob and Gary (Capitol); Gary Kellgren (Mayfair); Dick Kunc (Apostolic)

The next attempt to create a Mothers hit single would lead to an unusual result. Vocals and instrumental backing for the tracks that ended up on the album "We're Only In It For The Money" were recorded and/or played back at different speeds. Of all the tracks laid down during the sessions, "Lonely Little Girl" was selected to be the A-side of a potential single. The "Lonely Little Girl" track itself was only 1:10, so Zappa decided to create an exclusive construct drawn from different sources to create a 2:44 single master.

The single master of "Lonely Little Girl" began with the first 0:39 from the mono-mixed album version. After the word "unreal," the next seven seconds (0:39-0:46) came from the "Money" acetate mix (using the 3:10-3:17 segment of "Lonely Little Girl" and the first two seconds of the track "Theme From Burnt Weeny Sandwich."). That portion did not end up as part of the finished album. The 0:46-0:48 segment of the single master came from the mono "Lumpy Gravy Part One" celeste and cough (played in real time) at the 11:27-11:28 mark. That piece was an outtake from the Luden's Cough Drops television commercial animated by Ed Seeman that won Zappa a Clio Award. From 0:48-2:20, the single used the first 92 seconds of "Take Your Clothes Off When You Dance" in its mono "Money" album mix. (The last "deedle-deedle-dee" is missing from the mono mix when compared to the stereo.) The next second (2:20-2:21) used the Apostolic Blurch Injector sound effect heard during "Nasal Retentive Calliope Music" on the mono "Money" LP (heard at 0:02-0:03). From 2:21-2:44, the "Lonely Little Girl" single surprisingly ended with a sped up Pal Recording Studio backing track of "Love Of My Life." The Apostolic Blurch Injector was also used on the "Money" track "The Chrome Plated Megaphone Of Destiny," the "Bit Of Nostalgia," "Bored Out 90 Over" and "I Don't Know If I Can Go Through This Again" segments of the Verve "Lumpy Gravy" album, and "Dwarf Nebula Processional March & Dwarf Nebula" on "Weasels Ripped My Flesh."

Apparently, Zappa thought that this single was commercial! It certainly sounded different than the competition, but radio stations completely ignored it. The single made its album debut on "The Lumpy Money Project/Object." It is impossible to create a stereo mix of the single master, as some of the source materials are not available in multi-track form. The three Cucamonga-era versions of "Love Of My Life" were discussed in the Ron Roman single listing.

To get an idea of what the end of the "Lonely Little Girl" single sounds like in real time, you will need to slow it down about one octave. There are two ways to accomplish this:

1) Slow down the 2:21-2:44 segment of the single master by 50% using Audacity or other software, or

2) After the initial drum roll of any of the three original versions of "Love Of My Life," speed up the track by

100% using similar software.

By using either method, you will mainly hear Paul Buff's multiple saxophone parts and drums. The other instruments are submerged in the mix. If you are wondering why Frank Zappa would have brought the 1963 backing track of "Love Of My Life" to Mayfair and Apostolic, the backing tape was used for reference in order for the MOI to re-record the song during the upcoming "Cruising With Ruben & The Jets" sessions.

"Lonely Little Girl" was performed live as part of a "Money" medley between September 1975 and March 1976. A fragment of the "Lonely Little Girl" album version was used in a reversed form within "Ya Hozña." A few different iterations of "Lonely Little Girl" also appeared in "Lumpy Money." As previously mentioned, the 0:45-0:58 part of the song's album version used the original "How Could I Be Such A Fool" backing track with "What's The Ugliest Part Of Your Body?" vocals on top of it. The 0:59-1:01 segment of the LP version also quoted "Plastic People."

The single predated the album "We're Only In It For The Money" by about 3½ months. The official release date of the album was March 4, 1968, but there is evidence that copies were floating around before that date. Billboard magazine listed "Money" in their "New Action LPs" section for the February 17, 1968 issue, and there was an ad for the album and "Lonely Little Girl" in the next issue (February 24). "Money" was belatedly reviewed by Billboard in the March 16, 1968 issue.

"Mother People" was a catchy but challenging MOI B-side. It shared a similar theme with "Motherly Love." Unfortunately, the full impact of "Mother People" was neutered by the powers that be at MGM. All versions of the original "Money" album were edited. The first 59 seconds matched up exactly with the subsequent mono album mix. Instead of a second "C" section which involved the words "fuckin'" and "shitty," a copy of the first "C" section (from 0:41-0:47) was used in its place. A clear edit can be heard going into the second chorus starting at 1:06. Three seconds of record scratches (timed from 1:39-1:42) led into the 1:42-2:19 section derived from the "I Don't Know If I Can Go Through This Again" segment of "Lumpy Gravy Part One" (indexed at 13:07-13:44). Incidentally, Bunk Gardner was the only common performer for both the basic track and the orchestral fragment. The last verse of "Mother People" carried the song from 2:19 to its 2:31 conclusion.

The unfortunate record that was scratched was Monkees vocalist Davy Jones' self-titled Colpix LP "David Jones." It is not known if a mono or stereo LP was involved! The so-called offending section of "Mother People" was reversed and called "Hot Poop" on some Verve "Money" LPs. The word "fuckin'" was slightly edited, but "shitty" was left intact.

The "Mothermania" album featured a different mono mix of "Mother People" with the offending verse intact but it ended before the scratches, orchestral segment, and final verse. Like the entirety of the "Money" album, "Mother People" was also released with revised bass and drum tracks recorded in August 1983. The mono single equates to the mono album master on "Lumpy Money" and the "Money" picture disc edition. "Mother People" was performed between June and December 1970 as the back end of a medley with "Dog Breath." The VPRO "Piknik" broadcast featured a performance later included on "The Mothers 1970."

The Luden's commercial led to Zappa being approached by Remington, the electric shavers brand of the Sperry Rand Corporation. Remington offered Zappa $1,000 to create a different kind of radio commercial. Conveniently, Zappa's manager Herb Cohen also had Stone Poneys lead vocalist Linda Ronstadt as a client. FZ and Ian Underwood recorded the backing track for "Remington Electric Razor" and added Linda

Ronstadt's vocals. Remington bigwigs were not thrilled with Zappa's tape and shelved it. Thankfully, the commercial has been widely distributed ever since. Other short-term Zappa commercials and public service announcements were distributed on reel-to-reel tape. The most notable spots that Zappa did during this period were for Hagstrom guitars and public service announcements dealing with voting in the 1968 election and against the use of speed.

* * *

THE MOTHERS OF INVENTION: Mother People – Flower Punk/ Nasal Retentive Calliope Music – Absolutely Free (cassette single; third track misspelled "Nasal Retentive Caliope Music")
Released July 22, 1968 as Verve VV 795

Side 1 – Track 1
Mother People (2:30) (Frank Zappa) • Master #: Z7 • STEREO
same information as the previous single

Side 1 – Track 2
Flower Punk (3:04) (Frank Zappa) • Master #: Z7 • STEREO
Recorded July 26-September 1967 at Mayfair Studios, New York, NY, and October 1967 at Apostolic Studios, New York, NY
Personnel: Frank Zappa (electric guitar, lead vocals, clavinet, arranger, conductor); Ian Underwood (piano, woodwinds, voice); Bunk Gardner (woodwinds); Roy Estrada (bass, voice); Billy Mundi (drums); Jimmy Carl Black (voice, tambourine)
Producer: Frank Zappa
Executive Producer: Tom Wilson
Engineer: Gary Kellgren (Mayfair); Dick Kunc (Apostolic)

Side 2 – Track 1
Nasal Retentive Calliope Music (2:03) (Frank Zappa) • Master #: Z7 • STEREO
Recorded October 1967 at Apostolic Studios, New York, NY
Personnel: Eric Clapton (voice); Frank Zappa (musique concrète assembly); Paul Buff (alto saxophone, bass and drums on "Rotations" segment); Dave Aerni (guitar on "Rotations" segment)
Producer: Frank Zappa
Executive Producer: Tom Wilson
Engineer: Dick Kunc

Side 2 – Track 2
Absolutely Free (3:24) (Frank Zappa) • Master #: Z7 • STEREO
Recorded: July 31-September 1967 at Mayfair Studios, New York, NY, and October 1967 at Apostolic Studios, New York, NY
Personnel: Frank Zappa (lead vocal, acoustic guitar, electric guitar, tambourine, marimba); Don Preston (piano); Ian Underwood (harpsichord); Roy Estrada (bass); Billy Mundi (drums); Pamela Zarubica (Suzy Creamcheese vocal)
Producer: Frank Zappa
Executive Producer: Tom Wilson
Engineer: Gary Kellgren (Mayfair); Dick Kunc (Apostolic)

The first pre-recorded cassettes were released in the US by the Mercury Record Corp. in July 1967. At the beginning of the cassette market, Mercury was manufacturing tapes of their own releases. Mercury was also paid by other labels to make cassettes until those companies obtained the equipment to make their own cassette tapes. MGM wanted no part of Mercury, as they wanted to manufacture jazz and pop cassettes for their entire family of labels. (The label also entered the world of PlayTapes, which were more like edited versions of albums due to their 24-minute maximum playing time.) Cassette singles were already in production in England, so MGM wanted to debut this format in the US. A small selection of MGM and Verve cassette singles was released in July 1968.

MGM took what they thought was a representative sample of tracks from the MOI album "We're Only In It For The Money." All four masters were taken from the censored stereo edition of the album. Side one featured the aforementioned "Mother People" along with "Flower Punk."

The "musique concrète" of "Nasal Retentive Calliope Music" used the Apostolic Blurch Injector (0:02-0:03), the voice of Eric Clapton (0:23-0:26), The Rotations' "Heavies" in rechanneled stereo (1:38-1:57) and record scratches (1:57-2:02) from Davy Jones' "What Are We Going To Do?," the first track on side one of Jones' self-titled Colpix LP. As reported earlier, the Blurch Injector was used on the "Lonely Little Girl" single from 2:20 to 2:21. Paul Buff and Dave Aerni were not told about the use of their track and did not receive any payments.

"Flower Punk" was a complete parody of both the "flower power" movement and William Roberts' "Hey Joe." Roberts had played on the aforementioned Animals session. Zappa did both sped up vocals and he played clavinet with a wah-wah pedal. The hippie riff was used to great effect throughout. A quote of The Troggs' "Wild Thing" was made from 1:42-1:49. The words "balling" and "flower power sucks" were edited out. The '80s remix version used Arthur Barrow's bass quote of The Knack's "My Sharona" from 1:55 to 2:28. This time, we're talking about the later Knack group!

This was not the first time that The Mothers Of Invention recorded the anti-"flower power" anthem "Absolutely Free." They recorded an unused version at T.T.G. with the rough title "Electric Banana" on March 6, 1967 during the "Why Don't You Do Me Right"/ "Big Leg Emma" session. Its original title was "Arabesque." "Absolutely Free" made references to Santa's reindeer, S&H Green Stamps, and Donovan's "Mellow Yellow." On the live front, "Absolutely Free" was performed instrumentally from 1966 to 1968.

* * *

WILD MAN FISCHER: The Circle/ Merry-Go-Round (7" 45 rpm single)
Released October 9, 1968 as Bizarre/Reprise 0781

A-side
The Circle (2:54) (Larry Fischer) • Master #: (L6825) (mono promos and stock copies) • MONO; (L6825)S (stereo promos) • STEREO
Recorded: September 1968 at Sunset Sound Studios, Los Angeles, CA
Personnel: Larry Fischer (vocals); Frank Zappa (all instruments, conductor)
Producer: Frank Zappa
Engineer: Jerry Hansen

B-side
Merry-Go-Round (1:47) (Larry Fischer) • Master #: (L6826) (mono promos and stock copies) • MONO; (L6826)S (stereo promos) • STEREO
Recorded: September 1968 at Sunset Sound Studios, Los Angeles, CA
Personnel: Larry Fischer (vocals); The Bizarre Percussion Ensemble – Art Tripp (percussion); Frank Zappa (percussion, conductor)
Producer: Frank Zappa
Engineer: Jerry Hansen

Anyone walking the streets of Los Angeles from 1967 onward saw Larry Fischer offering songs for sale. In-between his two institution stints, Fischer was dubbed "Wild Man" by R&B vocalist Solomon Burke. Larry was a paranoid schizophrenic and manic depressive that sought to vent his frustrations via homemade songs. A member of The Leaves introduced Frank Zappa to Larry Fischer at Canter's Deli in Los Angeles. A session with producer Tom Wilson was arranged and was a complete disaster. The idea to record Wild Man was shelved for the time being. Three of Larry's songs were released on a 7" 33 1/3 rpm custom pressing called "Laminas 1" in May 1968. For that record, a group of UCLA art students put together a single of their works. Initial versions of Wild Man Fischer's "Merry-Go-Round," "Autumn Leaves" and "Linda And Laurie" were included on that record.

Frank Zappa and manager Herb Cohen's success in creating the Bizarre and Straight custom labels distributed by Reprise was the catalyst in getting a Wild Man Fischer project off the ground. Fischer's completely undisciplined material and presentation would find a home at the Bizarre label, even though Larry would be a street denizen.

Live field recordings and studio tracks at Sunset Sound were captured within a three-month period. These tracks captured Fischer's essence and demons – sometimes within the same recording. Making a cohesive album from all of these tapes was going to take some time. The game plan was to release a single prior to the eventual release of the double album "An Evening With Wild Man Fischer." The top side would be "The Circle," and Larry's most popular song, "Merry-Go-Round," would form the B-side. For the single, FZ would produce, coax the best performances out of Fischer, and create backing tracks on his own and with new Mothers drummer Art Tripp.

Larry Fischer would re-record "Merry-Go-Round" and "Autumn Leaves," the latter under the new title "The Leaves Are Falling." There is enough unreleased material from the Zappa sessions to create another album, so it is quite possible that Wild Man Fischer re-recorded "Linda And Laurie." Much later, Larry recorded "Linda" again as "Oh Linda, No Laurie" for his "Pronounced Normal" album.

Reprise, the Warner Bros. – Seven Arts Records label linked with Zappa's Bizarre and Straight custom imprints, was just starting to offer stereo-mixed promotional copies in addition to the standard mono promo discs. Stock copies would be the same as the mono promos.

"The Circle" contained an increasingly intense vocal performance from the Wild Man. It is probably the only song which involves the geometric terms "diangle" and "biangle." It goes to show what used to be taught in math classes many years ago! Zappa created the entire backing track on his own, and it turned out to be the perfect accompaniment for Larry's ravings. "Merry-Go-Round" lacked Fischer's spoken intro on the album, but it captured him in full flight. Billed as The Bizarre Percussion Ensemble, FZ and Tripp added percussion flourishes throughout. Quotes of "Merry-Go-Round" were made in "Lumpy Gravy Part

Two" (from 1:20-1:26) and the track "This Is Phaze III" on "Civilization Phaze III" (from 0:34-0:38). "The Circle" ended with an obvious edit and a cymbal crash.

Obtaining any copy of the single – especially stock copies – is a difficult task. The mono mixes of both sides are noticeably different than their stereo counterparts, as Fischer's vocals are much louder in mono. Neither of the mono mixes have ever been reissued. The stereo promotional mixes are exactly the same as the subsequent stereo album that appeared 6½ months later.

"An Evening With Wild Man Fischer" was briefly reissued on CD by Gonzo Multimedia, but it was obviously mastered from a non-mint record that was processed with amateur audio restoration. It is not recommended. In all likelihood, an official reissue of the Wild Man Fischer project will be accompanied by the material that was not included on the original double album.

* * *

RUBEN AND THE JETS: Anyway The Wind Blows/ Jelly Roll Gum Drop (7" 45 rpm promo single)
Released December 9, 1968 as Verve VK 10632

A-side
Anyway The Wind Blows (2:58) (Frank Zappa) • Master #: 105,605-BW • STEREO
Recorded: July-September 1967 at Mayfair Studios, New York, NY, and October 1967–February 1968 at Apostolic Studios, New York, NY
Personnel: Ray Collins (lead vocal, backing vocals); Frank Zappa (acoustic guitar, backing vocals); Roy Estrada (bass, backing vocals); Don Preston (piano); Ian Underwood (organ, tenor saxophone, alto saxophone); Motorhead Sherwood (baritone saxophone, tambourine); Bunk Gardner (tenor saxophone, alto saxophone); Jimmy Carl Black (drums); Arthur Dyer Tripp III (drums)
Producer: Frank Zappa
Engineer: Dick Kunc

B-side
Jelly Roll Gum Drop (2:17) (Frank Zappa) • Master #: 105,599-BW • MONO
Recorded: July-September 1967 at Mayfair Studios, New York, NY, and October 1967–February 1968 at Apostolic Studios, New York, NY
Personnel: Ray Collins (lead vocal, backing vocals); Frank Zappa (acoustic guitar, backing vocals); Roy Estrada (bass, backing vocals); Don Preston (piano); Ian Underwood (organ, alto saxophone); Motorhead Sherwood (baritone saxophone, tambourine); Bunk Gardner (tenor saxophone); Jimmy Carl Black (drums); Arthur Dyer Tripp III (timpani)
Producer: Frank Zappa
Engineer: Dick Kunc

The recording for "We're Only In It For The Money," "Cruising With Ruben & The Jets" and "Uncle Meat" all ran together, as Zappa and the Mothers rehearsed and recorded all different kinds of material. An album of the MOI playing doo-wop inspired tunes was quicker to knock out, and Zappa decided that a compilation album (later called "Mothermania") would complete their contractual requirements with Verve. "Uncle Meat" was turning out to be a much bigger project which would be held in reserve for another label. The Wild Man Fischer single was the first output from Zappa's new deal with Reprise, and that label would be the home for "Uncle Meat". The above single was credited to Ruben And The Jets to disguise the MOI's identity with the hope that airplay would result.

"Any Way The Wind Blows" was spelled incorrectly on numerous releases, including this one. The song's original arrangement was first recorded at Pal during March 1963. It debuted on "The Lost Episodes" before a mix with a longer ending turned up as a Buff download and box set inclusion. The 1965 Mothers lineup's version was part of "Joe's Corsage." The first official release of "Any Way The Wind Blows" came from the March 1966 "Freak Out!" sessions at T.T.G. Numerous iterations/mixes of the "Any Way" master and segments were featured on "The Worst Of The Mothers" and both editions of "The MOFO Project/Object."

Both recordings were more than a year old by the time they were selected for this single. This arrangement of "Any Way The Wind Blows" lacked some of the lyrics and instrumental sections present in the "Freak Out!" version. The original Mothers are not known to have performed the song live. Art Tripp replaced Billy Mundi's drums in late February 1968 to complete the master of the track that was later released on "Cruising With Ruben & The Jets." The album was subjected to July 1983 UMRK overdubs for CD releases between 1985 and 1995. These remixed editions lacked Motorhead Sherwood's baritone saxophone, but featured Arthur Barrow on bass and Chad Wackerman on drums. Fans were excited to hear the original stereo album master again on "Greasy Love Songs." Non-US mono releases of the "Cruising" album were simply mono fold-downs of the stereo mixes.

The Flo & Eddie lineup of The Mothers Of Invention performed "Any Way The Wind Blows" live during 1971, and two live versions can be heard on "Beat The Boots II: Swiss Cheese/ Fire!" and "Carnegie Hall." The September 1975 band performed "Any Way The Wind Blows" only at the first date of their tour.

After initial recording was done for "Jelly Roll Gum Drop," it was briefly played live during the September-October 1967 European MOI tour. The song's title was a combination of Richard Berry And The Dreamers' "Jelly Roll" (released on a Flair 45 and 78 in 1955) and Otis Williams And His Charms' "Gum Drop" (a track on their "Otis Williams And His Charms" EP for DeLuxe in 1956).

Unlike the stereo A-side, the B-side "Jelly Roll Gum Drop" was mixed in mono. In fact, it is the only official mono Ruben And The Jets mix. The timing on the label reflects the album length and not the additional 4 seconds on the single mix. The single master used a single Ray Collins lead vocal. The stereo album mix and the '80s remix relied on twin Collins leads. In addition, the mono single accentuated the backing vocals, guitar, and Tripp's timpani. The '80s remix dropped the saxophones, timpani, and organ. All mixes included real time and sped up backing vocals by Collins. The "Greasy Love Songs" album included the mono single master and an alternate mono mix.

"Jelly Roll Gum Drop" also referred to Chuck Higgins And His Mellotones' "Pachuko Hop" (a Combo single from 1952) and The Olympics' "The Slop" (the May 1960 Arvee B-side of "Big Boy Pete"). Incidentally, the flip of Higgins' single was "Motor Head Baby," which is presumed to be the source of Jim "Motorhead" Sherwood's nickname. Another Zappa track that mentioned "Pachuko Hop" was "Debra Kadabra" on "Bongo Fury."

Stock copies of this single are not known to exist. They were pressed by Bestway Products Inc. in New Jersey. The A-side is the same mix as the subsequent stereo album master. Perhaps for commercial reasons, the A-side "Any Way The Wind Blows" was replaced by "Deseri" on the release below.

* * *

REUBEN AND THE JETS: Deseri/ Jelly Roll Gum Drop (7" 45 rpm single with misspelled artist name)
RUBEN AND THE JETS: Deseri/ Jelly Roll Gum Drop (7" 45 rpm single)
Released December 30, 1968 as Verve VK 10632 (both editions)

A-side
Deseri (2:04) (Raymond Eugene Collins – Paul Conrad Buff) • Master #: 105,597 • STEREO
Recorded: July-September 1967 at Mayfair Studios, New York, NY, and October 1967–February 1968 at Apostolic Studios, New York, NY
Personnel: Ray Collins (lead vocal, backing vocals); Frank Zappa (acoustic guitar); Roy Estrada (bass); Don Preston (piano); Ian Underwood (organ, alto saxophone); Motorhead Sherwood (baritone saxophone, tambourine); Bunk Gardner (tenor saxophone); Jimmy Carl Black (drums); Arthur Dyer Tripp III (drums)
Producer: Frank Zappa
Engineer: Dick Kunc

B-side
Jelly Roll Gum Drop (2:17) (Frank Zappa) • Master #: 105,599 • MONO
same information as previous single

Three weeks went by before Verve unleashed the revised version of the Ruben And The Jets single with the same release number and B-side. Bestway handled the promotional copies, but two different pressing plants manufactured the stock copies. One pressing misspelled the group's pseudonym as Reuben And The Jets. That edition is much rarer than the correctly spelled pressing.

In the preparation of the Buff box set, Paul Buff told me that the correct spelling of the song should be "Deserie," like The Charts' June 1957 A-side for the Everlast label. Paul Buff and Ray Collins wrote the song that was originally recorded in March 1963 at Pal Recording Studio. Buff played all the instruments. This recording was first released on "Looking Up Granny's Dress," a Grandmothers compilation album by Rhino in 1982. It was reissued with its correct title on the Buff box and as a download. Those were the first releases on which Buff was paid, as he was not consulted or paid for the Ruben version of the song.

The single mix of "Deseri" is in stereo and is the same as on the "Cruising With Ruben & The Jets" album, but its stereo image is reversed. Ray Collins started his backing vocals and spoken piece too early on this version. The remixed/overdubbed version of "Deseri" digitally shifted these parts into the correct positions within the track, and the originally unused organ track by Ian Underwood became audible. The lyrics of "Deseri" used the line "hear my plea," which can also be heard on the "Cruising" track "Cheap Thrills" and on two "Uncle Meat" tracks: "Dog Breath, In The Year Of The Plague" and "Electric Aunt Jemima." "Greasy Love Songs" used the original stereo mix of the recording. "Deseri" was not performed live by any Zappa-related lineups. The Australian issue of this single had reversed sides. Issued as Verve VS-11, the A-side was misspelled as "Jelly Roll Gum Drops."

* * *

THE MOTHERS OF INVENTION: Radio Spots For Bizarre/Reprise Album – The Mothers Of Invention – Uncle Meat
(7" 45 rpm promo single)
Released April 21, 1969 as Reprise PRO 332

A-side – Track 1
Band One (0:30) (Frank Zappa) • Master #: 10,948 • MONO
Recorded: October 1967 – February 1968 at Apostolic Studios, New York, NY ("Cruising For Burgers" fragment), and March 1969 at an unknown studio (voice-over)
Personnel: Frank Zappa (electric guitar, acoustic guitar); Ray Collins (lead vocals); Bunk Gardner (clarinet); Ian Underwood (organ); Roy Estrada (bass); Jimmy Carl Black (drums); Art Tripp (drums); unknown (voice-over)
Producer: Frank Zappa
Engineer: Dick Kunc

A-side – Track 2
Band Two (0:30) (Frank Zappa [all fragments except "Ella Guru"]; Don Vliet ["Ella Guru" fragment]) • Master #: 10,948 • MONO
Recorded: October 1967 – February 1968 at Apostolic Studios, New York, NY (basic tracks for Mothers fragments), September 1968 at Sunset Sound Studios, Los Angeles, CA (percussion overdubs for Mothers fragments), August 1968 – March 1969 at Whitney Studios, Glendale, CA (Captain Beefheart "Ella Guru" fragment), and March 1969 at unknown studio (voice-over)
Personnel: Mothers fragments – Frank Zappa (guitar, vocals); Ray Collins (lead vocals); Jimmy Carl Black (drums, voice); Roy Estrada (bass, lead vocals, backing vocals); Bunk Gardner (woodwinds); Art Tripp (drums, percussion); Jim Sherwood (saxophone); Ruth Komanoff (marimba, vibes); Pamela Zarubica (Suzy Creamcheese voice); Captain Beefheart fragment – Captain Beefheart (aka Don Vliet) (lead vocal); Rockette Morton (aka Mark Boston) (bass); Drumbo (aka John French) (drums); Zoot Horn Rollo (aka Bill Harkleroad) (guitar); The Mascara Snake (aka Victor Hayden) (clarinet); Antennae Jimmy Semens (aka Jeff Cotton) (steel-appendage guitar, flesh horn); unknown (voice-over)
Producer: Frank Zappa
Engineer: Dick Kunc (Apostolic and Whitney); Jerry Hansen (Sunset Sound)

A-side – Track 3
Band Three (1:00) (Frank Zappa [all fragments except "Ella Guru"]; Don Vliet ["Ella Guru" fragment]) • Master #: 10,948 • MONO
Recorded: October 1967 – February 1968 at Apostolic Studios, New York, NY (basic tracks for Mothers fragments), September 1968 at Sunset Sound Studios, Los Angeles, CA (percussion overdubs for Mothers fragments), August 1968 – March 1969 at Whitney Studios, Glendale, CA (Captain Beefheart "Ella Guru" fragment), and March 1969 at unknown studio (voice-over)
Personnel: Mothers fragments – Frank Zappa (guitar, vocals); Ray Collins (lead vocals); Jimmy Carl Black (drums, voice); Roy Estrada (bass, lead vocals, backing vocals); Bunk Gardner (woodwinds); Art Tripp (drums, percussion); Jim Sherwood (saxophone); Ruth Komanoff (marimba, vibes); Pamela Zarubica (Suzy Creamcheese voice); Dick Kunc (voice); Captain Beefheart fragment – Captain Beefheart (aka Don Vliet) (lead vocal); Rockette Morton (aka Mark Boston) (bass); Drumbo (aka John French) (drums); Zoot Horn Rollo (aka Bill Harkleroad) (guitar); The Mascara Snake (aka Victor Hayden) (clarinet); Antennae Jimmy Semens (aka Jeff Cotton) (steel-appendage guitar, flesh horn); unknown (voice-over)
Producer: Frank Zappa
Engineer: Dick Kunc (Apostolic and Whitney); Jerry Hansen (Sunset Sound)

A-side – Track 4
Band Four (1:00) (Frank Zappa) • Master #: 10,948 • MONO
Recorded: October 1967 – February 1968 at Apostolic Studios, New York, NY (basic tracks for "The Air" fragment), September 1968 at Sunset Sound Studios, Los Angeles, CA (percussion overdubs for "The Air"

fragment), and March 1969 at Whitney Studios, Glendale, CA (Dick Kunc voice-over)
Personnel: Frank Zappa (guitar, vocals); Ray Collins (lead vocals); Jimmy Carl Black (drums, voice); Roy Estrada (bass, lead vocals, backing vocals); Bunk Gardner (woodwinds); Art Tripp (drums, percussion); Jim Sherwood (saxophone); Ruth Komanoff (marimba, vibes); Pamela Zarubica (Suzy Creamcheese voice); Dick Kunc (voice-over)
Producer: Frank Zappa
Engineer: Dick Kunc (Apostolic); Jerry Hansen (Sunset Sound)

B-side
same as A-side

Frank Zappa's Bizarre and Straight labels were positioned as the two outlets for his various projects. Greater budgets were allocated for recording and promotion. This was the first promotional single created for Zappa-related releases. Along with the usual fragments of songs from "Uncle Meat," these promotional spots featured some material not related to the project being promoted. With album-oriented programming proliferating on stereo FM radio stations, it is not known why these commercials were created in mono.

The first half-minute spot ("Band One") was a basic commercial using an unknown voice-over artist speaking over the "Uncle Meat" track "Cruising For Burgers." "Band Two" was another half-minute spot, but it was anything but ordinary. Record scratches and sound effects were interspersed with occasional voice-over commentary, an "Uncle Meat" fragment of "Mr. Green Genes," pieces of "Ella Guru" by Captain Beefheart & His Magic Band, and "Uncle Meat" tracks "The Air," "If We'd All Been Living In California…," and "Our Bizarre Relationship." The spot concluded with two clips not on the album: an Art Tripp percussion flourish (similar to his playing on "We Can Shoot You" from "Uncle Meat" or "Enigmas 1 Thru 5" on the "Finer Moments" set), and Suzy Creamcheese saying "Ah."

"Band Three" was similar in content to the second commercial, but it was one minute long with different ad copy. The musical sequence was the same, but additional material was added after Suzy Creamcheese's brief comment. That additional content was a further Suzy comment ("I must confess – it's just humanly impossible to do that"), followed by engineer Richard "Dynamite Dick" Kunc laughing and saying "Dynamite!" before the concluding clip of "Sleeping In A Jar." The fourth ad, "Band Four," used "The Air" as its music bed. Kunc did the voice-over for that spot.

Strangely enough, the most recent track used in these spots was not by the MOI – it was actually Captain Beefheart's "Ella Guru." All the others were well over a year old at the time of their release on "Uncle Meat." These spots have still not been released commercially. The "Meat Light" album would have been an excellent place to feature them, but more important released and unreleased material was presented instead.

* * *

THE MOTHERS OF INVENTION: My Guitar/ Dog Breath (7" 45 rpm single)
Released September 1, 1969 as Bizarre/Reprise 0840
Reissued April 16, 2016 as Barking Pumpkin BPR 1227 (7" 45 rpm Record Store Day numbered green splatter vinyl single)

A-side
My Guitar (3:07) (Frank Zappa) • Master #: (M7401) (Bizarre/Reprise); none (Barking Pumpkin) • MONO

Recorded: June 1969 at A&R Studios, New York, NY
Personnel: Frank Zappa (lead vocal, lead guitar, arranger); Roy Estrada (bass); Don Preston (keyboards, electronics); Ian Underwood (alto saxophone); Bunk Gardner (tenor saxophone); Motorhead Sherwood (baritone saxophone); Jimmy Carl Black (drums); Arthur Dyer Tripp III (drums)
Producer: Frank Zappa
Engineer: Dick Kunc

B-side
Dog Breath (2:56) (Frank Zappa) • Master #: (M7442) (Bizarre/Reprise); none (Barking Pumpkin) • MONO
Recorded: October 1967 – February 1968 at Apostolic Studios, New York, NY
Personnel: Frank Zappa (lead guitar, backing vocals, arranger); Ray Collins (backing vocals); Jimmy Carl Black (drums); Roy Estrada (bass, backing vocals); Don Preston (electric piano); Bunk Gardner (piccolo, flute, clarinet, bass clarinet, soprano saxophone, alto saxophone, tenor saxophone, bassoon); Ian Underwood (electric organ, piano, harpsichord, celeste, flute, clarinet, alto saxophone, baritone saxophone); Arthur Dyer Tripp III (drums, timpani, vibes, marimba, xylophone, wood blocks, bells, small chimes); Euclid James Motorhead Sherwood (tenor saxophone, tambourine)
Producer: Frank Zappa
Engineer: Dick Kunc

Zappa was constantly playing catch-up with MOI releases. The extensive backlog of material tended to reflect previous lineups, and "Uncle Meat" did not have an obvious single. By the time this single was released, The Mothers Of Invention ceased to exist. Their last appearance was at CJOH-TV in Ottawa, Ontario, Canada on August 19, 1969. The month before, FZ started recording the solo album "Hot Rats."

Another standalone single would hold things over until Frank Zappa's next project came to life. The genesis of "My Guitar" (also known as "My Guitar Wants To Kill Your Mama") was recorded at Apostolic during the "Uncle Meat" sessions. It was first released as "My Guitar (Proto I – Excerpt)" on the "Meat Light" collection in 2016. The fully formed song was revisited in February 1969 at Criteria Studios in Miami, FL. Subsequent overdubs were recorded at T.T.G. and Whitney shortly afterward, and that version first appeared on "Weasels Ripped My Flesh" in 1970. Zappa recorded solos on acoustic guitar and electric guitar. Its unique instrumental portion before FZ's acoustic solo involved sped up clarinets and tenor saxophone, and it did not use organ in its arrangement.

A more relaxed rearrangement of "My Guitar" was cut at Phil Ramone's A&R Studios in New York during June 1969 for potential single release. The entire backing track had a different feel. Zappa's guitar soloing approach and Roy Estrada's bass part were different, and Ian Underwood played organ. Everything was recorded and played back in real time. The third verse was a repeat of the second verse, and the single master faded on Zappa's guitar solo. The lyrical content of attacking a girl's parents because they did not approve of Frank being with their daughter was not exactly ideal for a commercial single, but the song itself had great appeal. A shorter edit of the single version was included on "You Can't Do That On Stage Anymore Vol. 5" in 1992. "My Guitar" would be used again as the B-side of "WPLJ" (listed below), and the mono single masters of "My Guitar" and "Dog Breath" were reissued in 2016 with a picture sleeve.

"My Guitar" would be performed by The Mothers Of Invention between November 1968 and August 1969. A live version from Boston, MA (July 8, 1969) was released on "Beat The Boots I: The Ark." The song would also be performed between October 1976 and February 1977. The guitar intro of "My Guitar" recorded live in London (January 17, 1977) was released as the first part of "Duck Duck Goose" on the album "Läther," and that album also included a longer version of that track under the title "Leather Goods." The fall 1977 band rehearsed the tune but did not play it live. A slower arrangement of "My Guitar" was used as the backing track of "The Central Scrutinizer" on "Joe's Garage Act I." A shorter "Central Scrutinizer" can be found on "Understanding America." The fall 1984 lineup performed "My Guitar" during a North American tour. The December 23, 1984 performance was part of "Stage, Vol. 4." "My Guitar" was played between February and June 1988. A Syracuse, NY recording of "My Guitar" on March 21, 1988 was a download track on "The Frank Zappa AAAFNRAAAA Birthday Bundle" in 2010.

Numerous iterations of "Dog Breath" were recorded during the sessions for "Uncle Meat." One of them was the mono single master. The single used the first 1:02 of the "Uncle Meat" album track called "Dog Breath, In The Year Of The Plague." The next 1:02 (from 1:02-2:04) involved the track that was later released as "Dog Breath (Instrumental)" on "Meat Light – The Uncle Meat Project/Object Audio Documentary." The remaining 52 seconds were unique to the single. "Meat Light" also included a stereo remix of the single version. In actuality, the majority of the stereo mix is in mono with just Roy Estrada's vocals panned left and right, and a Zappa guitar track panned right. "Uncle Meat" also included "The Dog Breath Variations," and an alternate mix of that version was on "Meat Light." Sped up basic tracks from "Dog Breath" were used as a music bed for a hidden track within "Roxy – The Movie."

"Dog Breath" would become a Zappa standard that was adaptable to rock band or orchestral arrangements on its own or in conjunction with "Uncle Meat" (known as "Dog/Meat"). In 1968, "Dog Breath" was performed without vocals or played on top of "Little House I Used To Live In." Examples of both 1968 treatments can be heard on "Beat The Boots II: Electric Aunt Jemima." "Dog Breath" is on its own from Amsterdam (October 20) and with "Little House" from Denver, CO (May 3). On "Uncle Meat," "The Dog Breath Variations" and "Dwarf Nebula Processional March & Dwarf Nebula" quote each other! The early show on April 28, 1968 at the Grande Ballroom in Detroit, MI featured a performance of "The Orange County Lumber Truck Medley" with a quote of "Dog Breath."

The 1970 Mothers band represented "Dog Breath" on "Beat The Boots II: Disconnected Synapses," "Road Tapes, Venue #3," and "The Mothers 1970." "Dog Breath" recordings from the next year's lineup were issued on "Just Another Band From L.A.," "Carnegie Hall," and "Beat The Boots II: Swiss Cheese/ Fire!" (the latter with "Magdalena"). The Los Angeles performance was repeated on both "Zappa Picks" CDs. No "Dog/Meat" performances from the Grand Wazoo lineup from September 1972 have been issued. Numerous "Dog/Meat" versions from the 1973 band were released: "Road Tapes, Venue #2," "The Roxy Performances" (four versions), and "Halloween 73" (two versions). The "Roxy By Proxy" CD uses the version from the December 9, 1973 early show, as does "Roxy – The Movie" and "Roxy – The Soundtrack." The next night's late show version was first issued in inferior quality on "Beat The Boots III: Disc Five" before its deluxe release on "The Roxy Performances."

The super-tight 1974 band also got a lot of mileage out of "Dog/Meat." "The Dub Room Special!" CD and video along with the CD and video of "A Token Of His Extreme" all feature the August 27, 1974 take. "The Dog Breath Variations" from a Helsinki performance in September 1974 can be heard on "Stage, Vol. 2." The Abnuceals Emuukha Electric Symphony Orchestra from September 1975 performed "Dog Breath" twice, with one version making it to the 40th anniversary edition of "Orchestral Favorites." Later on, the fall 1984 band quoted "Dog Breath" during a performance of "Sharleena" on December 17 at the Paramount Theater in Seattle, WA. "Dog Breath" was rehearsed in 1987 but was not performed. Ensemble Modern played "The Dog Breath Variations" in Germany and Austria during September 1992, with the track from the September 19 show at Alte Oper in Frankfurt, Germany ending up on "The Yellow Shark."

"My Guitar"/ "Dog Breath" was a very popular coupling for foreign 45s. The German issue (Reprise RA 0840) came with a brilliant picture sleeve. Mexico issued this single (Reprise G-913) and a promo featuring "My Guitar" and Nancy Sinatra's "Drummer Man" (Gamma NO.236). Argentina (Reprise G-913), France (Reprise RV.20221), New Zealand (Reprise RO.840) and South Africa (Reprise R21.108) also duplicated the American release. The South African issue was the only Frank Zappa/ Mothers single that the country received. Even though no commercial singles from "Uncle Meat" were issued, Mexican fans received the "My Guitar" EP that included "My Guitar" and "Dog Breath" on side one, with "Mr. Green Genes" and "The Mothers Play 'Louie Louie' At The Royal Albert Hall" on side two. It was released as Gamma/Reprise GX 07-622. Of course, the song titles for the Mexican and Argentinian releases were translated into Spanish.

Released on September 29, 1969 was the only single by The GTO's. Frank Zappa produced all but two tracks on their album "Permanent Damage," but the two he was not involved with ended up on a single. Lowell George produced "Circular Circulation"/ "Mercy's Tune" (Straight ST 104).

* * *

FRANK ZAPPA: Radio Spots For Bizarre Reprise Album "Hot Rats" (7" 45 rpm promo single)
Released October 15, 1969 as Reprise PRO 347

A-side – Track 1
Band One (1:00) (Luther McDaniels – Ray Dobard) • Master #: 30,969 • STEREO
Recorded: July 24, 1969 at T.T.G. Studios, Hollywood, CA ("WPLJ" extract), and September 1969 at unknown studio (voice-over)
Personnel: Frank Zappa (co-lead vocal, backing vocals, acoustic guitar, electric guitar); Lowell George (guitar, co-lead vocal); Roy Estrada (backing vocals); Janet Ferguson (backing vocals); Buzz Gardner (trumpet); Ian Underwood (electric piano); Bunk Gardner (tenor saxophone); John Balkin (electric bass); Arthur Dyer Tripp III (drums); David Ossman (voice-over)
Producer: Frank Zappa
Engineer: Jack Hunt & Cliff Goldstein

A-side – Track 2
Band Two (0:50) (Frank Zappa) • Master #: 30,969 • STEREO
Recorded live on March 2, 1969 at Philadelphia Arena, Philadelphia, PA ("Passacaglia" extract), and September 1969 at unknown studio (voice-over)
Personnel: Frank Zappa (guitar, voice); Lowell George (guitar); Roy Estrada (bass); Jimmy Carl Black (drums); Art Tripp (drums); Ian Underwood (woodwinds); Don Preston (keyboards); Bunk Gardner (woodwinds); Motorhead Sherwood (saxophone); Buzz Gardner (trumpet); David Ossman (voice-over)
Producer: Frank Zappa
Engineer: Dick Kunc

B-side
same as A-side

The first of two promo 45s for Zappa's solo LP "Hot Rats" did not feature any music from it! The ad copy involved David Ossman and Phil Austin of Columbia Records comedy group The Firesign Theatre. Ossman and Austin were hired as writers/narrators for radio spots dealing with labels under the Warner Bros. – Seven Arts, Inc. umbrella.

The first spot ("Band One") used "WPLJ," which The Mothers Of Invention recorded in the last month of their existence. "WPLJ" would not be officially released until the February 1970 album "Burnt Weeny Sandwich" and its subsequent use as an A-side. It was the first time that Lowell George and Buzz Gardner appeared on a Mothers record. Electric bassist John Balkin had already contributed to the albums "Absolutely Free" and "Lumpy Gravy." For the one-minute spot, David Ossman affected an accent which was nothing like his regular speaking voice.

Ossman sounded more like himself when he narrated the "hip" 50-second "Band Two." A live Mothers fragment of "Passacaglia" recorded at the Philadelphia Arena on March 2, 1969 was the musical background. "Passacaglia" was part of an Artisan Sound Recorders acetate intended for release on the cancelled box set "The History & Collected Improvisations Of The Mothers Of Invention." The acetate has made the rounds in numerous forms. Musically, "Passacaglia" involved "Igor's Boogie, Phase One" played against the vamp of "King Kong." No tapes of the March 2 show have circulated among fans, and the acetate is the only source for "Kung Fu" and "Igor's Boogie" from that date. Like the "Uncle Meat" promo single, the same ads were on both sides. "The Hot Rats Sessions" did not include "Band One," but "Band Two" (mastered from vinyl) was titled "Hot Rats Vintage Promotion Ad #3."

* * *

FRANK ZAPPA: Radio Spots For Reprise Album 6356 - Frank Zappa - Hot Rats (7" 45 rpm promo single)
Released December 8, 1969 as Reprise PRO 366

A-side – Track 1
Band One (0:50) (Frank Zappa) • Master #: 31,031 • STEREO
Recorded: July 28-29, 1969 (basic tracks for "Peaches En Regalia" extract) and August 1969 (numerous undocumented "Peaches" overdub sessions) at T.T.G. Studios, Hollywood, CA, August 26, 1969 at Sunset Sound Recorders, Hollywood, CA (final "Peaches" overdubs), and September 1969 at unknown studio (voice-over)
Personnel: Frank Zappa (guitar, octave bass, percussion); Ian Underwood (pipe organ, piano, Hammond organ, flute, clarinet, soprano saxophone, alto saxophone, tenor saxophone); Ron Selico (drums); Shuggie Otis (bass); Phil Austin (voice-over)
Producer: Frank Zappa
Engineer: Jack Hunt & Cliff Goldstein (T.T.G.); Brian Ingoldsby (Sunset Sound)

A-side – Track 2
Band Two (1:00) (Frank Zappa) • Master #: 31,031 • STEREO
Recorded: July 28-29, 1969 (basic tracks for "Peaches En Regalia" extract) and August 1969 (numerous undocumented "Peaches" overdub sessions) at T.T.G. Studios, Hollywood, CA, August 26, 1969 at Sunset Sound Recorders, Hollywood, CA (final "Peaches" overdubs), and September 1969 at unknown studio (voice-over)
Personnel: Frank Zappa (guitar, octave bass, percussion); Ian Underwood (pipe organ, piano, Hammond organ, flute, clarinet, soprano saxophone, alto saxophone, tenor saxophone); Ron Selico (drums); Shuggie Otis (bass); Phil Austin (voice-over)
Producer: Frank Zappa
Engineer: Jack Hunt & Cliff Goldstein (T.T.G.); Brian Ingoldsby (Sunset Sound)

A-side – Track 3
Band Three (1:00) (Frank Zappa) • Master #: 31,031 • STEREO
Recorded: July 29, 1969 at T.T.G. Studios, Hollywood, CA (basic tracks for "Little Umbrellas" extract), August

25, 1969 at Sunset Sound Studios, Hollywood, CA ("Little Umbrellas" overdubs), August 29, 1969 at Whitney Recording Studio, Glendale, CA ("Little Umbrellas" overdubs), and September 1969 at unknown studio (voice-over)
Personnel: Frank Zappa (vibraphone); Ian Underwood (Hammond organ, piano, electric piano, alto recorder, clarinet, bass clarinet, soprano saxophone, alto saxophone, tenor saxophone, baritone saxophone); John Guerin (drums); Max Bennett (string bass); Phil Austin (voice-over)
Producer: Frank Zappa
Engineer: Jack Hunt & Cliff Goldstein (T.T.G.); Brian Ingoldsby (Sunset Sound); Dick Kunc (Whitney)

A-side – Track 4
Band Four (0:50) (Frank Zappa) • Master #: 31,031 • STEREO
Recorded: July 18, 1969 at T.T.G. Studios, Hollywood, CA ("The Gumbo Variations" extract), and September 1969 at unknown studio (voice-over)
Personnel: Frank Zappa (guitar); Don "Sugarcane" Harris (violin); Max Bennett (bass); Paul Humphrey (drums); Phil Austin (voice-over)
Producer: Frank Zappa
Engineer: Jack Hunt & Cliff Goldstein (T.T.G.)

B-side
same as A-side

The second "Hot Rats" promo disc represented the album well. All four radio spots came from the LP, and both sides had the same content. This time, Firesign's own Phil Austin did the voice-over honors. The 50-second "Band One" spotlighted "Peaches En Regalia" with Austin's main sales pitch: "Hi there, kids. The name of this song is called 'Peaches En Regalia.' It tells the story of a bowl of peaches that lives in the Royal Garden Hotel, across the street from the Kensington Market in London." "Band Two" was ten seconds longer, which allowed for a longer background sample of "Peaches" with the same ad copy. "Band Two," "Band Three" and "Band Four" were released on "The Hot Rats Sessions," but they were sourced from vinyl. The box set notes confusingly titled them as the first, second and fourth "Hot Rats Vintage Promotional Ad" spots.

The one-minute "Band Three" used "Little Umbrellas" with a similar narration: "The name of this song is called 'Little Umbrellas.' Well, it tells the story of a bowl of umbrellas that lives in the Royal Garden Hotel, across the street from the Kensington Market in London." In other words, it was typical Firesign humor. The 50-second "Band Four" was the most interesting of the bunch, using an extract of "The Gumbo Variations" in the background.

* * *

FRANK ZAPPA: Peaches En Regalia/ Little Umbrellas (7" 45 rpm single)
Planned for release on January 26, 1970 as Bizarre/Reprise 0889, but cancelled

A-side
Peaches En Regalia (3:30) (Frank Zappa) • Master #: unknown • MONO
Recorded: July 28-29, 1969 (basic tracks) and August 1969 (numerous undocumented overdub sessions) at T.T.G. Studios, Hollywood, CA, and August 26, 1969 at Sunset Sound Recorders, Hollywood, CA (final overdubs)
Personnel: Frank Zappa (guitar, octave bass, percussion); Ian Underwood (pipe organ, piano, Hammond organ, flute, clarinet, soprano saxophone, alto saxophone, tenor saxophone); Ron Selico (drums); Shuggie

Otis (bass)
Producer: Frank Zappa
Engineer: Jack Hunt & Cliff Goldstein (T.T.G.); Brian Ingoldsby (Sunset Sound)

B-side
Little Umbrellas (3:04) (Frank Zappa) • Master #: unknown • MONO
Recorded: July 29, 1969 at T.T.G. Studios, Hollywood, CA (basic tracks), August 25, 1969 at Sunset Sound Studios, Hollywood, CA (overdubs), and August 29, 1969 at Whitney Recording Studio, Glendale, CA (final overdubs)
Personnel: Frank Zappa (vibraphone); Ian Underwood (Hammond organ, piano, electric piano, alto recorder, clarinet, bass clarinet, soprano saxophone, alto saxophone, tenor saxophone, baritone saxophone); John Guerin (drums); Max Bennett (string bass)
Producer: Frank Zappa
Engineer: Jack Hunt & Cliff Goldstein (T.T.G.); Brian Ingoldsby (Sunset Sound); Dick Kunc (Whitney)

The nonissuance of Frank Zappa's signature instrumental work was very curious. The only mention of this single was made by the weekly record industry subscription service One Spot Reporter, which listed current single and album releases. Normally, One Spot Reporter would receive a physical copy of each release mentioned in its publication. In this case, no such copy was submitted to that publication, as not one acetate, test pressing, promotional copy or stock copy has surfaced to date. The only explanation for the listing in One Spot Reporter would be that a Reprise staffer jumped the gun and mistakenly reported that the above mono single would be released with Bizarre/Reprise catalog number 0889. Both sides were unique mono mixes, with "Peaches" faded nine seconds earlier than the stereo "Hot Rats" album master.

Tom Hidley of T.T.G. created the first 16-track recorder which used 2-inch wide tape. Zappa's "Hot Rats" would be the first album recorded with that equipment. Hidley's approach for his proprietary studio was similar what Paul Buff was thinking for his 10-track Original Sound recorder, in that a T.T.G. 16-track project had to be started and completed there. However, knowledgeable people could get around the intent of those studio creators: The Monkees started "As We Go Along" at Wally Heider's and finished it at Original Sound, while Frank Zappa started "Hot Rats" at T.T.G. and completed the LP at Sunset Sound.

The lure of all those tracks contributed to how each piece on "Hot Rats" would be created at T.T.G. The song arrangements were ongoing as overdubs were laid down on tape instead of being written out. The rhythm tracks by the four musicians playing on "Peaches En Regalia" required 10 hours of recording time, but Frank Zappa and Ian Underwood spent ten times as many hours overdubbing various parts. Many of those Zappa/Underwood sessions were not reported to Local 47, but the final overdub session at Sunset Sound was. Seven FZ overdubs were of octave bass, in which Zappa sped up a bass track one octave for much longer sustain. Some of Ian Underwood's saxophone parts were also sped up. In a sense, the massive overdubbing of "Peaches" was a return to the Pal days.

Shuggie Otis (born Johnny Alexander Veliotes, Jr.), oldest son of Zappa's musical idol Johnny Otis, played bass on "Peaches En Regalia" as a 15-year-old. Veteran drummer Ron Selico was playing with Shuggie at the time. As a teenager, Selico played drums on Sam Cooke's "Wonderful World." Ron Selico played bongos on the James Brown albums "James Brown Sings Raw Soul" and "Live At The Apollo Volume II," and he also played drums on the latter. The July 29, 1969 session for "Peaches" listed Jimmy Carl Black and Don Preston, but they did not figure in the final version. Exactly a week before, Roy Estrada and Ian Underwood helped Lowell George's pre-Little Feat group Rocky Karma record "Juliet" at T.T.G.

The final result of "Peaches En Regalia" was a classic instrumental that even non-Frank Zappa fans greatly appreciate. "Peaches En Regalia" was regularly performed live in 1971, 1976-1979, and 1988. The song was rehearsed by the 1980 band, and it was quoted during the 1982 and 1984 tours. After its initial release on "Hot Rats," live versions of "Peaches En Regalia" were included on "Fillmore East – June 1971," "Tinsel Town Rebellion," "Does Humor Belong In Music?," "Beat The Boots I: Any Way The Wind Blows," "Beat The Boots II: Swiss Cheese/ Fire!," "Beat The Boots III: Disc Six," "Hammersmith Odeon," "The Frank Zappa AAAFNRAAAAAM Birthday Bundle," "Carnegie Hall," "Halloween 77" (six versions), "Zappa In New York 40th Anniversary Deluxe Edition," and "Zappa '88: The Last U.S. Show." The studio version was featured on the "Strictly Commercial" and "ZAPPAtite – Frank Zappa's Tastiest Tracks" compilations. A video of "Peaches En Regalia" was included on the VHS version of "Baby Snakes" in 1987. The DVD does not include this video. A Synclavier realization of "Peaches En Regalia" was excerpted in the "Duckman" episode "It's The Thing Of The Principal" (Season 1, Episode 9).

In 2006, Dweezil Zappa used the multi-tracks of "Peaches" to create a new mix with fresh guitar overdubs on the 2006 album "Go With What You Know." The studio chatter was included, and the song had a longer fade than the "Hot Rats" album master. A double album release was originally planned for "Hot Rats." The material that did not make the single album cut remains unreleased.

"Little Umbrellas" (original title: "Natasha") was a studio creation that is not known to have been performed live. Its recording was almost as extensive as "Peaches En Regalia" but with a rhythm section of bassist Max Bennett and drummer John Guerin. Frank Zappa only played vibraphone and directed/produced all of Ian Underwood's studio overdubs. In fact, Underwood created a veritable woodwind orchestra for "Little Umbrellas." Unusually, work was done at three studios to complete the final master: T.T.G, Sunset Sound, and Whitney.

After its release on "Hot Rats," "Little Umbrellas" was included on the compilations "Strictly Genteel" and "Zappa Picks By Larry LaLonde Of Primus." The track was sampled by the Belgian band dEUS in 1994 as part of the "Worst Case Scenario" track "W.C.S. (First Draft)." Both singles tracks were remixed for CD releases prior to 2012, with "Little Umbrellas" sounding quite different than the "Hot Rats" album master. The original LP mixes were reinstated for the 2012 CD edition.

* * *

THE MOTHERS OF INVENTION: WPLJ/ My Guitar (7" 45 rpm single)
Released February 23, 1970 as Bizarre/Reprise 0892

A-side
WPLJ (3:02) (Luther McDaniels – Ray Dobard) • Master #: (M17611) (mono promos and stock copies); (M17611)S (stereo promos)
Recorded: July 24, 1969 at T.T.G. Studios, Hollywood, CA
Personnel: Frank Zappa (co-lead vocal, backing vocals, acoustic guitar, electric guitar); Lowell George (guitar, co-lead vocal); Roy Estrada (backing vocals); Janet Ferguson (backing vocals); Buzz Gardner (trumpet); Ian Underwood (electric piano); Bunk Gardner (tenor saxophone); John Balkin (electric bass); Arthur Dyer Tripp III (drums)
Producer: Frank Zappa
Engineer: Jack Hunt & Cliff Goldstein

B-side
My Guitar (3:07) (Frank Zappa) • Master #: (M7401) (mono promos and stock copies); (M7401)S (stereo promos) see "My Guitar"/ "Dog Breath" listing

The 4 Deuces' "W-P-L-J" and its B-side "Here Lies My Love" by Mr. Undertaker (real name: Roy Hawkins) made up both sides of a Frank Zappa teenage single favorite. The single was released by Berkeley, CA label Music City in 1955 (catalog number 790). "WPLJ" (as Zappa stylized it) extolled the virtues of drinking white port wine and lemon juice. The song was included on the "Burnt Weeny Sandwich" album before its single release three weeks later. The title of the song was noticed by Allen Shaw, the president of ABC's FM stations. Shaw decided to change New York progressive rock radio station WABC-FM to the album-oriented rock WPLJ-FM on February 14, 1971. The AOR format lasted until the end of June 1983. WPLJ ended their operations on May 31, 2019.

The Mothers Of Invention played "Here Lies My Love" at the McMillin Theater at Columbia University in New York City on February 14, 1969. The venue has been known as the Miller Theatre since 1988. "Here Lies My Love" was released on "Stage, Vol. 5" in 1992. The set of the early show on February 23, 1969 at the Rockpile in Toronto, Ontario, Canada included "WPLJ."

The studio version of "WPLJ" was laid down on T.T.G.'s new 16-track deck just a few days before recording for "Hot Rats" got underway. The MOI treatment of "WPLJ" kept the intent of The 4 Deuces' original but in a vastly superior recording environment. The lead vocal was shared by FZ and Lowell George. As he tended to do with doo-wop vocals throughout his career, Frank added a bass vocal for support. Janet Ferguson sang the "dit-dit-doo-wop" backing vocals. Roy Estrada's contributions were falsettos throughout and Chicano narration (sometimes X-rated) at the end. However, the single mix faded out way before any variations of the Spanish verb "chingar" ("to fuck" in English) could be heard. The timing of the single is completely wrong – it was actually about 2:06 rather than the 3:02 album length shown on the label. Zappa revived "WPLJ" during the 1984 tour. Two live versions from that tour appear on "Beat The Boots III: Disc Six" and "Does Humor Belong In Music?".

The single version of "My Guitar" was covered earlier, but something strange happened with how the song was presented this time. Mono promotional copies and stock copies of the record had the same mono master as the earlier single "My Guitar"/ "Dog Breath." Stereo promos actually had a 4:09 mix, leading to another timing error on the record label. As stated earlier, the mono single master faded on a guitar solo by Zappa. The stereo single mix featured the entire verse-long solo, another chorus, and faded on yet another Zappa solo. Most fans are still not aware of this major difference. Warner Bros. and Reprise were notorious for springing otherwise unavailable stereo mixes on their specially-marked promo singles. Most notably, the stereo promo of Jethro Tull's "Living In The Past"/ "Driving Song" also had unique mixes. While these Tull mixes were finally released on the "Benefit" deluxe edition, this stereo mix of Zappa's "My Guitar" has had no such reissue. Until the stereo mix of "My Guitar" is either reissued on vinyl or CD, it can be heard on "His-Story #1" (2-CD; Snowball Entertainment FZ1A/B) or in lesser quality on "Lumpy Gravy & Elsewhere" (Zipperman ZAP 012). The Italian release had "WPLJ" as the A-side, and the B-side was listed as "My Guitar" (Reprise R 02.140). The B-side actually played "Dog Breath."

One of Frank Zappa's most notable productions from this period was Captain Beefheart & His Magic Band's album "Trout Mask Replica." No US single was issued, but France received a picture sleeve 45: "Pachuco Cadaver"/ "Wild Life." The record was released during March 1970 as Straight/Pathè 2c 006-91.200. The single and its sleeve were reissued on white vinyl in June 2018 as Third Man TRM-559.

The Do It Now Foundation asked Frank Zappa to create six radio spots to steer people away from drugs. Frank created six mono spots (roughly 30 seconds each) that were issued on a 33 1/3 rpm promotional single called "Public Service Anti-Drug Abuse Spots – Series #1." This promo was accompanied by a letter dated April 16, 1970 which outlined the foundation's aims with this record.

* * *

FRANK ZAPPA: Sharleena/ Bognor Regis (10" 45 rpm Artisan Sound Recorders acetate)
Acetate Pressing Date: June 1970
NOT COMMERCIALLY RELEASED

A-side
Sharleena (2:54) (Frank Zappa) • Master #: none • STEREO
Recorded: Late June 1970, Trident Studios, London, England
Personnel: Frank Zappa (guitar, backing vocals); Eddie (aka Howard Kaylan) (lead vocal); The Phlorescent Leech (aka Mark Volman) (backing vocals); Ian Underwood (grand piano, tenor saxophone); George Duke (organ); Jeff Simmons (bass, backing vocals); Aynsley Dunbar (drums)
Producer: Frank Zappa; Dick Barber (special help)
Engineer: Roy Thomas Baker

B-side
Bognor Regis (4:45) (Frank Zappa) • Master #: none • STEREO
Recorded: July 29, 1969 at T.T.G. Studios, Hollywood, CA
Personnel: Frank Zappa (lead guitar); Max Bennett (bass); John Guerin (drums); Donald "Sugarcane" Harris (violin); Ian Underwood (tack piano)
Producer: Frank Zappa; Dick Barber (special help)
Engineer: Jack Hunt & Cliff Goldstein

Warner Bros., the parent company of Reprise, reported in September 1970 that this single would be released very soon. It never materialized. Frank Zappa brought an Artisan Sound Recorders acetate of these tracks with him while visiting London in mid-June 1970. The acetate was played at the Roundhouse in London before the regular crowd came in. The A-side was an edit of the "Chunga's Revenge" track. As a big fan of The Zombies and the breathy vocal asides of Colin Blunstone on the big hit "Time Of The Season," Howard Kaylan did his best Blunstone impression as he sighed during "Sharleena."

Regardless of the lineup, "Sharleena" proved to be a live number that almost always guaranteed an exciting guitar solo from Frank. The Hot Rats lineup debuted the song in March 1970. The subsequent Mothers band with Flo & Eddie performed "Sharleena" between June 1970 and December 1971. The song disappeared from live sets until the 1981, 1982, 1984 and 1988 tours. The earliest studio version of "Sharleena" was done at The Record Plant in Los Angeles in March 1970 and was later released on "The Lost Episodes" in 1996.

Live "Sharleena" performances from the Flo & Eddie lineup can be heard on "Road Tapes, Venue #3" (two versions), "Beat The Boots II: Tengo Na Minchia Tanta," "Carnegie Hall," as the centerpiece of a medley with "Wonderful Wino" and "Cruisin' For Burgers" on "Beat The Boots II: Swiss Cheese/Fire!," and on its own within "Playground Psychotics." Studio and live versions of "Sharleena" were included on "The Mothers 1970." The 1982 band represented the song on "Beat The Boots I: As An Am" and "Them Or Us." The December 4, 1984 guitar solo from "Sharleena" was released as "Winos Do Not March" on the Guitar" album. Dweezil Zappa joined his father on stage during the December 23, 1984 take of "Sharleena" that was excerpted on the Guitar Player flexidisc before the full track appeared on the "Stage Sampler" and "Stage, Vol. 3." The 1988 band version of "Sharleena" was released on "Zappa '88: The Last U.S. Show."

"Bognor Regis" was named after the British seaside village in West Sussex. The song title was mentioned during the "Stage, Vol. 1" track "Once Upon A Time" and the "Road Tapes, Venue #3" version of "It Can't Happen Here." Despite being nearly one year older than the A-side, "Bognor Regis" was a distinctive and fresh instrumental with extensive solo excursions. "The Hot Rats Sessions" box set (a December 2019 release) included the 10:59 "Unedited Master" and 8:10 "1970 Record Plant Mix" of "Bognor Regis." The June 1970 acetate of "Bognor Regis" was dubbed from a Record Plant mix with engineer Stan Agol on March 4, 1970. The acetate was a 4:45 edit that used seven segments from the "Unedited Master." One segment, lasting only one second long, was not part of the "1970 Record Plant Mix." Therefore, the acetate edit can be recreated despite the non-existence of the mixdown tape used to create the one-off disc. As revealed in the liner notes for the "Hot Rats" box set, the basic tracks of "Bognor Regis" were used for an early take of "Conehead." In the development of that more recent composition, the original "Bognor Regis" basics were erased in the process.

* * *

THE MOTHERS OF INVENTION: Radio Spot For Mothers Of Invention – Weasels Ripped My Flesh – Reprise Album MS 2028 (7" 45 rpm promo single)
Released August 10, 1970 as Reprise PRO 420

A-side – Track 1
Band One (1:00) (Frank Zappa) • Master #: 11,115 • MONO
Recorded: October 1967 – February 1968 at Apostolic Studios, New York, NY ("Our Bizarre Relationship" and "JCB Spits It" extracts), and July 1970 at unknown studio (voice-over and audio collage)
Personnel: Frank Zappa (voice); Pamela Zarubica (Suzy Creamcheese voice); Jimmy Carl Black (coffee slurping); unknown (voice-overs and interviewees)
Producer: Frank Zappa
Engineer: Dick Kunc

A-side – Track 2
Band Two (1:00) (Frank Zappa) • Master #: 11,115 • MONO
Recorded: October 1967 – February 1968 at Apostolic Studios, New York, NY ("Our Bizarre Relationship" and "JCB Spits It" extracts), and July 1970 at unknown studio (voice-over and audio collage)
Personnel: Frank Zappa (voice); Pamela Zarubica (Suzy Creamcheese voice); Jimmy Carl Black (coffee slurping); unknown (voice-overs and interviewees)
Producer: Frank Zappa
Engineer: Dick Kunc

A-side – Track 3
Band Three (1:00) (Frank Zappa) • Master #: 11,115 • MONO
Recorded: October 1967 – February 1968 at Apostolic Studios, New York, NY ("Our Bizarre Relationship" and "JCB Spits It" extracts), and July 1970 at unknown studio (voice-over and audio collage)
Personnel: Frank Zappa (voice); Pamela Zarubica (Suzy Creamcheese voice); Jimmy Carl Black (coffee slurping);

unknown (voice-overs and interviewees)
Producer: Frank Zappa
Engineer: Dick Kunc

A-side – Track 4
Band Four (1:00) (Frank Zappa) • Master #: 11,115 • MONO
Recorded: October 1967 – February 1968 at Apostolic Studios, New York, NY ("Our Bizarre Relationship" and "JCB Spits It" extracts), and July 1970 at unknown studio (voice-over and audio collage)
Personnel: Frank Zappa (voice); Pamela Zarubica (Suzy Creamcheese voice); Jimmy Carl Black (coffee slurping); unknown (voice-overs and interviewees)
Producer: Frank Zappa
Engineer: Dick Kunc

B-side
same as A-side

"Weasels Ripped My Flesh" was an archival album covering different lineups of The Mothers Of Invention. Once again, no material from the album was included on these radio spots. All four one-minute mono spots followed the same sequence: Jimmy Carl Black slurping warm coffee (from the "Meat Light" segment "JCB Spits It"), Zappa and then Suzy Creamcheese saying "Bizarre!" (from the "Uncle Meat" track "Our Bizarre Relationship"), the first voice-over, an "in the street" interview with people's thoughts about the album cover, the second voice-over, another JCB slurp, and finally, FZ saying "Bizarre!" and then fading on Suzy's first "Bizarre!" syllable (namely, "Biz") repeated six times using a similar sound effect as the conclusion of "It Can't Happen Here."

All four spots used a different street interview, and each person was presented with Neon Park's "Weasels" album cover without the title and artist name. As trivial as it may be, the JCB contribution was part of the original running order of "Uncle Meat" but did not make the final cut. The voice-overs were recorded by two different voice-over artists. Both sides had the same spots.

The execution of these radio spots was most likely the worst of all the promo singles that were created for Zappa or MOI albums. The only saving grace was the first voice-over, which used a Brooklyn, NY-accented voice to say, "If de Mothers put out an album with a cover like dis, will dey ever sell rekkids again?"

"Weasels Ripped My Flesh" was not represented by any US singles. In Venezuela, the album version of "My Guitar Wants To Kill Your Mama" was paired on a promo single with "The Orange County Lumber Truck" (Reprise REP 3468). Argentina released "My Guitar Wants To Kill Your Mama" with "Directly From My Heart To You" (Music Hall/ Reprise 31.654). As expected, the song titles were translated into Spanish.

* * *

FRANK ZAPPA: Radio Spots For Frank Zappa "Chunga's Revenge" Reprise Album MS 2030 (7" 45 rpm promo single)
Released October 23, 1970 as Reprise PRO 432

A-side – Track 1
Band One (1:00) (Frank Zappa) • Master #: 11,148 • MONO
Recorded: August 28, 1970 at Whitney Studios, Glendale, CA, and August 29, 1970 at The Record Plant, Hollywood, CA ("Would You Go All The Way?" extract), and September 1970 at unknown studio (voice-over)
Personnel: Frank Zappa (guitar, backing vocals); Ian Underwood (electric piano); George Duke (trombone); Jeff Simmons (bass); Aynsley Dunbar (drums); The Phlorescent Leech (aka Howard Kaylan) (co-lead vocal); Eddie (aka Mark Volman) (co-lead vocal); unknown (voice-over)
Producer: Frank Zappa
Engineer: Dick Kunc (Whitney); Stan Agol (The Record Plant)

A-side – Track 2
Band Two (1:10) • Master #: 11,148 • MONO
Recorded: September 1970 at unknown studio (voice-over)
Personnel: unknown (voice-over)
Producer: unknown
Engineer: unknown

B-side
same as A-side

Even though this record solely credited Frank Zappa, more than half of the tracks on "Chunga's Revenge" were by a revised Mothers group that toured from June to December 1970. Both mono radio spots used more than one person for voice-over purposes, and used the ad copy "'Chunga's Revenge' will stimulate precious bodily fluids."

The one-minute spot "Band One" used "Would You Go All The Way?" as its music bed. "Band Two" was a 70-second spot that used a baseball theme and crowd as its background while someone pretending to be a baseball player read the same ad copy as the first ad. Both ads spent more time discussing "Hot Rats" than "Chunga's Revenge." In addition, the spots made the erroneous claim that "Hot Rats" entered the US charts at #90 and then disappeared, when the album actually peaked at #173 in Billboard.

"Would You Go All The Way?" was released as a single two weeks after the October 23, 1970 issuance of "Chunga's Revenge." This would be the final Zappa-related Reprise radio commercial issued on a 7" vinyl single. Like the other album promo singles, both sides contained the same commercials. Clearly, these single releases were not effective uses of promotional budgets. Five 60-second radio spots were created for the 1972 Zappa/Mothers album "The Grand Wazoo," but they were circulated via 5-inch, 7½ IPS reel-to-reel tape.

* * *

FRANK ZAPPA: Tell Me You Love Me/ Will You Go All The Way For The U.S.A.? (7" 45 rpm single)
Released November 9, 1970 as Bizarre/Reprise 0967 (some stock copies released as Reprise 0967)

A-side
Tell Me You Love Me (2:43) (Frank Zappa) • Master #: (N19012)S • STEREO
Recorded: August 28, 1970 at Whitney Studios, Glendale, CA, and August 29, 1970 at The Record Plant, Hollywood, CA
Personnel: Frank Zappa (guitar, Condor); Ian Underwood (rhythm guitar, pipe organ); George Duke (electric piano); Jeff Simmons (bass); Aynsley Dunbar (drums); The Phlorescent Leech (aka Howard Kaylan) (lead vocal, backing vocals); Eddie (aka Mark Volman) (backing vocals)
Producer: Frank Zappa
Engineer: Dick Kunc (Whitney); Stan Agol (The Record Plant)

B-side
Will You Go All The Way For The U.S.A.? (2:30) (Frank Zappa) • Master #: (N19011)S • STEREO
Recorded: August 28, 1970 at Whitney Studios, Glendale, CA, and August 29, 1970 at The Record Plant, Hollywood, CA
Personnel: Frank Zappa (guitar, backing vocals); Ian Underwood (electric piano); George Duke (trombone); Jeff Simmons (bass); Aynsley Dunbar (drums); The Phlorescent Leech (aka Howard Kaylan) (co-lead vocal); Eddie (aka Mark Volman) (co-lead vocal)
Producer: Frank Zappa
Engineer: Dick Kunc (Whitney); Stan Agol (The Record Plant)

Considering how long previous singles were released after their recording, these tracks were turned into a single very quickly. This disc was credited to Frank Zappa even though both sides featured the MOI lineup with Flo & Eddie. Stereo-only promos and blue label stock copies were released on Bizarre/Reprise, and a handful of extremely elusive stock copies were issued on Reprise. As a rarity for FZ, both sides of the record were exactly the same as their album masters.

"Tell Me You Love Me" and "Would You Go All The Way?" were originally meant for the upcoming film "Frank Zappa's 200 Motels." Frank's prepared script for the film shoot dropped some of the vocal numbers, with five of the songs ending up on "Chunga's Revenge." "Tell Me You Love Me" and "Would You Go All The Way?" were two of the five "200 Motels" castoffs which joined various "Chunga's" live and studio tracks with different lineups. Other unused songs initially meant for "200 Motels" would be recorded live for the "Fillmore East – June 1971" LP. The guitar riff used on "Tell Me You Love Me" was intimately related to the riffs played on the subsequent "200 Motels" LP and film track "Daddy, Daddy, Daddy" and two other film castoffs that would be performed at the Fillmore: "Bwana Dik" and "Do You Like My New Car?".

Sonically, "Tell Me You Love Me" featured Zappa's guitar with and without an early guitar synthesizer – the Condor GSM by the Hammond Organ Company's Innovex imprint. This particular recording was compiled on the albums "Strictly Commercial" and "ZAPPAtite." Quotes of "Tell Me You Love Me" can be found in "The Groupie Routine" on "Stage, Vol. 1" (from L.A. on August 7, 1971) and in "Daddy, Daddy, Daddy" and "What Kind Of Girl Do You Think We Are?" on the "Philly '76" album (from Philadelphia on October 29, 1976). "The Mothers 1970" featured "Daddy, Daddy, Daddy" with a "Tell Me You Love Me" quote. The song itself was revived during the August-October 1978 and October-December 1980 tours, with the Berkeley, CA performance from December 5, 1980 represented on "Tinsel Town Rebellion" and the second volume of Steve Vai's "Secret Jewel Box" series. The May-July 1982 tour captured "Tell Me You Love Me" on "Stage, Vol. 1" (Pistoia, Italy – July 8, 1982).

When "Tell Me You Love Me" was played by the summer 1984 band in North America, the song underwent some lyric changes and became "Why Don't You Like Me?" and "Don't Be A Lawyer" depending on the show. Further lyric modifications relating to the somewhat odd behavior of singer Michael Jackson created a revised arrangement of "Why Don't You Like Me?" for the February-March 1988 band. A live version of the Jackson-themed song was released on the CD edition of "Broadway The Hard Way" in 1989. This new arrangement included a listing of people not related to Michael Jackson.

For single release, the title of "Would You Go All The Way?" was presumably modified to "Will You Go All The Way For The U.S.A.?" to avoid any controversy about its content. George Duke's trombone frequently quoted the opening six notes of "The Star-Spangled Banner" from 1:40 to 2:09. The lyrics referred to monster movies, which the later FZ song "Cheepnis" would deal with in great detail. "Would You Go All The Way?" was played at the August 21, 1970 Civic Auditorium gig in Santa Monica, CA, at Florida State University (the October 9, 1970 show captured on "The Mothers 1970"), and during the fall 1976 North American tour. "Philly '76" has a live version from that tour. The last known performance of "Would You Go All The Way?" was in the middle of a medley with "Road Ladies" and "Daddy, Daddy, Daddy" on September 29, 1977 at Maple Leaf Gardens, Toronto, Ontario, Canada. Flo & Eddie provided guest vocals for all three songs at that show.

* * *

JUNIER MINTZ: Tears Began To Fall/ JUNIER MINTZ FEATURING BILLY DEXTER ON GUITAR: Junier Mintz Boogie
(7" 45 rpm single)
Released July 21, 1971 as Straight/Reprise 1027

A-side
Tears Began To Fall (2:50) (Billy Dexter [aka Frank Zappa]) • Master #: (RCA 0472)S • STEREO
Recorded live on June 5-6, 1971 at Fillmore East, New York, NY, and June 1971 at Whitney Studios, Glendale, CA (vocal overdubs)
Personnel: Billy Dexter (aka Frank Zappa) (guitar, vocal introduction); Mark Volman (co-lead vocal, backing vocals); Howard Kaylan (co-lead vocal, backing vocals); Ian Underwood (woodwinds, keyboards); Aynsley Dunbar (drums); Jim Pons (bass, backing vocals); Bob Harris (keyboards)
Producer: Billy Dexter (aka Frank Zappa)
Engineer: Barry Keene (Fillmore East); Toby Foster (Whitney)

B-side
Junier Mintz Boogie (2:53) (Billy Dexter [aka Frank Zappa]) • Master #: (RCA 0473)S • STEREO
Recorded live on May 25, 1971 at Olympia Stadium, Detroit, MI
Personnel: Billy Dexter (aka Frank Zappa) (guitar, vocals); Mark Volman (vocals); Howard Kaylan (vocals); Ian Underwood (keyboards, woodwinds); Bob Harris (keyboards, vocals); Jim Pons (bass, vocals); Aynsley Dunbar (drums)
Producer: Billy Dexter (aka Frank Zappa)
Engineer: unknown

"Tears Began To Fall" was one of FZ's most commercial and direct A-sides and he turned it into a single master quickly. Unfortunately, Warner Bros.' promotional brilliance undermined Zappa and the MOI's efforts. Warners decided the record would definitely receive radio airplay if it did not mention Zappa or the MOI on the label. The deception was carried out by crediting the artist as Junier Mintz (adapted from the name of Nabisco's chocolate covered mint product Junior Mints) and attributing Zappa's guitar presence, production and songwriting to Billy Dexter. Warner Bros. mistakenly thought that people would not notice that they were listening to Frank Zappa And The Mothers Of Invention. A further clue was that the single was released on Zappa's Straight custom label for Reprise. Frank was not happy with this promotional innovation.

The mid-concert sequence of the band's Fillmore East set on June 5-6, 1971 featured "Peaches En Regalia," "Tears Began To Fall," and the "200 Motels" work "She Painted Up Her Face." "Peaches En Regalia" was completed by an Aynsley Dunbar drum roll, over which Zappa said, "The name of this song is 'Tears Began To Fall.'" This six-second transition is how the single master began. The subsequent album version did not have this intro. Despite the credit on the label, anyone listening could tell who the real group was. Flo & Eddie added Whitney Studios vocal overdubs to "Tears Began To Fall" and "Happy Together." Those vocals were mixed louder on the single than on the "Fillmore East" album. "Tears Began To Fall" quoted Max Steiner's well-known film theme "Gone With The Wind." Prior to the final chorus of "Tears Began To Fall," Zappa trimmed Aynsley Dunbar's drum break, and the recording faded on the intro of the next song in the set, "She Painted Up Her Face." Other live recordings of "Tears Began To Fall" can be heard on "Swiss Cheese/Fire!" and "Carnegie Hall." The song was only performed live in 1971 while Flo & Eddie were on board.

"Junier Mintz Boogie" was sourced from a stereo cassette recorded on May 25, 1971 at the Olympia Stadium in Detroit, MI. It was a Zappa guitar solo from the transition between "Latex Solar Beef" and "Willie The Pimp." The single credited Zappa's guitar playing to Billy Dexter as well as the other Dexter billings. Other than the studio overdubs on the A-side, this was FZ's first live single.

For a release that the record company thought had hit potential, all these machinations led to a poor-selling single that received minimal airplay. Stock copies of the Junier Mintz disc are super rare, especially since both sides are unique and have not been reissued in any form. Promotional copies included stereo and mono presentations of the A-side only, reflecting a change in how record companies serviced radio stations. Warner Bros. would have another opportunity three months later to correct the complete injustice of this single product.

* * *

MOTHERS OF INVENTION: Tears Began To Fall/ Junier Mintz Boogie (7" 45 rpm single)
Released August 20, 1971 as Reprise K 14100 (England) (promos were dated August 13, 1971, but stock copies were not released until a week later)

A-side
Tears Began To Fall (2:50) (Billy Dexter [aka Frank Zappa]) • Master #: K 14100 A • STEREO
same as previous single

B-side
Junier Mintz Boogie (2:53) (Billy Dexter [aka Frank Zappa]) • Master #: K 14100 B • STEREO
same as previous single

Meanwhile in England, Reprise wanted to release their own edition of the Junier Mintz single. The UK single ended up as a hybrid, in that the artist was listed as Mothers Of Invention, but all mentions of Frank Zappa were still credited to Billy Dexter. Promotional and stock copies were released with a pushout center, and other stock copies were pressed with a solid center. Unlike the US issue, the British promo copies came with the B-side. A slight delay in manufacturing stock copies led to their unavailability on the August 13,

1971 date listed on promotional copies.

The A-side was exactly the same as the Junier Mintz 45, but the B-side master was a raw presentation of the track with insufficient bass and a slightly longer ending. Clearly, the Brits did not use the properly equalized US master for "Junier Mintz Boogie" for their release. With its longer ending, the correct timing for the B-side should have been listed as 2:54. The revised American single credited to Frank Zappa And The Mothers Of Invention would be released exactly two months after this one.

* * *

FRANK ZAPPA: Special Radio Spot Commercial – Frank Zappa's "200 Motels" (7" 45 rpm promo single)
Released October 18, 1971 as United Artists SP-65-A (A-side)/ SP-65-B (B-side)

A-side
Special Radio Spot Commercial (1:00) • Master #: K-543 • MONO

B-side
Special Radio Spot Commercial (0:30) • Master #: K-544 • MONO

United Artists secured the film rights for Zappa's "200 Motels" project which was filmed in late January and early February 1971. The soundtrack and film masters were completed, so it was time for United Artists to promote them via two promotional singles and a film trailer. This mono single was prepared before any of the materials were ready, so these spots were typically silly in-house events with voice-overs and sound effects. The one-minute commercial discussed Frank Zappa and the soundtrack album, while the half-minute commercial talked about the soundtrack and the film that had not been released when this single was initially distributed.

* * *

(NO ARTIST LISTED): "200 Motels" (7" 33 1/3 rpm one-sided promo single which just listed the name of the film)
Released October 18, 1971 as United Artists UAC 115

A-side – Track 1
Cut 1 (1:00) (Frank Zappa) • Master #: none • STEREO
Recorded live on January 28 – February 5, 1971 at Pinewood Studios, London, England, and April 1971 at Whitney Studios, Glendale, CA (vocal and instrumental overdubs for "Strictly Genteel" and "I'm Stealing The Towels" extracts and voice-overs)
Personnel: Frank Zappa (guitar, ending voice-over); Howard Kaylan (co-lead vocal, voice-overs); Mark Volman (co-lead vocal, voice-overs, tambourine, maracas); Ian Underwood (keyboards, woodwinds); Aynsley Dunbar (drums); Ruth Underwood (orchestral drum set); George Duke (trombone); Martin Lickert (bass); The Royal Philharmonic Orchestra – Elgar Howarth, conductor; The Top Score Singers – David Van Asch, conductor
Producer: Frank Zappa
Engineer: Bob Auger (Pinewood); Barry Keene (Whitney)

A-side – Track 2
Cut 2 (1:00) (Frank Zappa) • Master #: none • STEREO
Recorded live on January 28 – February 5, 1971 at Pinewood Studios, London, England, and April 1971 at Whitney Studios, Glendale, CA (vocal and instrumental overdubs for "I'm Stealing The Towels," "Strictly Genteel," and "Does This Kind Of Life Look Interesting To You?" extracts and voice-overs), and September 1971 at unknown studio (main voice-over)
Personnel: Frank Zappa (guitar, ending voice-over); Howard Kaylan (co-lead vocal, voice-overs); Mark Volman (co-lead vocal, voice-overs, tambourine, maracas); Ian Underwood (keyboards, woodwinds); Aynsley Dunbar (drums); Ruth Underwood (orchestral drum set); George Duke (trombone); Martin Lickert (bass); The Royal Philharmonic Orchestra – Elgar Howarth, conductor; The Top Score Singers – David Van Asch, conductor; unknown (voice-over)
Producer: Frank Zappa
Engineer: Bob Auger (Pinewood); Barry Keene (Whitney)

A-side – Track 3
Cut 3 (0:30) (Frank Zappa) • Master #: none • STEREO
Recorded: April 1971 at Whitney Studios, Glendale, CA
Personnel: Howard Kaylan (voice-over); Mark Volman (voice-over); Frank Zappa (voice-over)
Producer: Frank Zappa
Engineer: Barry Keene

A-side – Track 4
Cut 4 (0:15) (Frank Zappa) • Master #: none • STEREO
Recorded live on January 28 – February 5, 1971 at Pinewood Studios, London, England, and April 1971 at Whitney Studios, Glendale, CA (vocal and instrumental overdubs for "I'm Stealing The Towels" extract and voice-overs)
Personnel: Frank Zappa (guitar, ending voice-over); Howard Kaylan (co-lead vocal, voice-over); Mark Volman (co-lead vocal); Ian Underwood (keyboards, woodwinds); Aynsley Dunbar (drums); Ruth Underwood (orchestral drum set); George Duke (trombone); Martin Lickert (bass); The Royal Philharmonic Orchestra – Elgar Howarth, conductor; The Top Score Singers – David Van Asch, conductor
Producer: Frank Zappa
Engineer: Bob Auger (Pinewood); Barry Keene (Whitney)

B-side
(blank)

United Artists' UAC series issued one-sided 33 1/3 rpm discs which promoted film soundtracks. The label copy for the singles in this series was very basic – just the title of the film in bold type and quotes at the top, and cut (track) numbers and times on the bottom. This stereo disc used album extracts with specially recorded spoken pieces by Mothers members Howard Kaylan, Mark Volman, and Frank Zappa. All four commercials were included (with subtitles not listed on the promo single) on the second CD of Rykodisc's "Frank Zappa's 200 Motels" (RCD 10513/14) on October 14, 1997. Since FZ did not own the soundtrack, licensing was required to reissue any of its previously released components.

"Cut 1" was subtitled "Coming Soon!..." and used drag racing as the theme of Kaylan and Volman's voice-overs. Clips of "Strictly Genteel" and "I'm Stealing The Towels" were used. "I'm Stealing The Towels" was part of the soundtrack but was not in the film. "Cut 2" was subtitled "The Wide Screen Erupts…". Flo & Eddie did the opening and closing sales pitches, and an unknown pro announcer spoke over clips of "I'm Stealing The Towels," "Strictly Genteel," and "Does This Kind Of Life Look Interesting To You?". "Cut 3" (subtitled "Coming Soon!...") is an alternate take of the Kaylan/Volman drag racing theme with no music bed. Finally, "Cut 4" (subtitled "Frank Zappa's 200 Motels...") was a drastic edit of Cut 1 using just Kaylan's recitation of the film title and a small bit of "I'm Stealing The Towels." All four spots concluded with FZ using his broadcaster voice to give the R-rating of the film. These spots were included in a 50th anniversary set.

* * *

FRANK ZAPPA: What Will This Evening Bring Me This Morning/ Daddy, Daddy, Daddy (7" 45 rpm single)
Planned for US release on October 18, 1971 as United Artists 50857, but cancelled
The A-side was replaced by "Magic Fingers" with the same catalog number and released on November 8, 1971 (see that listing below)
Released November 26, 1971 as United Artists UP 35319 (England)

A-side
What Will This Evening Bring Me This Morning (3:27) (Frank Zappa) • Master #: none • STEREO
Recorded: Late August 1970 at Whitney Studios, Glendale, CA (basic track), and November 1970 at Whitney Studios, Glendale, CA (bass overdub)
Personnel: Frank Zappa (guitar); Mark Volman (co-lead vocal); Howard Kaylan (co-lead vocal); Ian Underwood (keyboards, woodwinds); Aynsley Dunbar (drums); George Duke (trombone); Jeff Simmons (bass)
Producer: Frank Zappa
Engineer: Barry Keene

B-side
Daddy, Daddy, Daddy (3:11) (Frank Zappa) • Master #: none • STEREO
Recorded live on January 28 – February 5, 1971 at Pinewood Studios, London, England, and April 1971 at Whitney Studios, Glendale, CA (overdubs)
Personnel: Frank Zappa (guitar); Mark Volman (co-lead vocal, backing vocals); Howard Kaylan (co-lead vocal, backing vocals); Ian Underwood (keyboards, woodwinds); Jim Pons (backing vocals); Aynsley Dunbar (drums); George Duke (trombone); Martin Lickert (bass); Ruth Underwood (orchestra drum set)
Producer: Frank Zappa
Engineer: Bob Auger (Pinewood); Barry Keene (Whitney)

This was another MOI single credited just to Frank Zappa, but United Artists could not decide on what to do with it. "What Will This Evening Bring Me This Morning" (without the bass overdub present here) was the 1970 demo that Zappa presented to attract funding for the "200 Motels" film project. Flo & Eddie's vocals were both in real time and sped up. The song's genesis was "What Will This Morning Bring Me This Evening," which kicked off the seven-song "groupie opera" performed during the June-December 1970 Mothers tour. Both "What Will…" songs share some musical content. Live versions of "What Will This Morning…" can be heard on "The Mothers 1970" (Spokane, WA on September 17, 1970), "Beat The Boots II: Tengo Na Minchia Tanta" (a New York City show that November 13) and in the film "200 Motels," but not on the soundtrack. "What Will This Evening Bring Me This Morning" is known to have been performed on August 21, 1970 (Civic Auditorium, Santa Monica, CA) and at the late show on November 29, 1970 (The Coliseum, London, England).

United Artists had second thoughts about whether "What Will This Evening Bring Me This Morning" was the best A-side candidate from "200 Motels." The full-length album track was slated for the single, and the "what will I say the next day" section took up the last two minutes of the nearly 3½-minute song. It was also one of many Zappa tracks which referenced gonorrhea: "Groupie Bang Bang," "Who Needs The Peace Corps?," "Our Bizarre Relationship," "Road Ladies," "The Clap," "Dinah-Moe Humm," and "Why Does It Hurt When I Pee?". The headquarters of United Artists elected to cancel the North American release of the single with "What Will This Evening…" and "Daddy, Daddy, Daddy" as the B-side, but they offered it for release to their European counterparts. The single was released in England and the Netherlands in late November 1971, with the latter packaged in a picture sleeve. British promotional and stock copies were manufactured with pushout centers, and some stock copies were issued with solid centers. The French issue of this single (United Artists UP 35 319) had a picture sleeve, while the Dutch release (United Artists 5C 006-93125) had an art sleeve. "Daddy, Daddy, Daddy" was one side of an Italian promo single (United Artists YD 303) with Spinach's "Action Man" on the flip.

"Daddy, Daddy, Daddy" was the fifth entry in the "groupie opera" performed by the Flo & Eddie lineup from June to December 1970. "The Mothers 1970" used the Pepperland (San Rafael, CA) take from September 26. "Beat The Boots II: Tengo Na Minchia Tanta" contained a November 13 performance. As noted earlier, "Daddy, Daddy, Daddy" used the "Tell Me You Love Me" guitar riff. "Daddy" was quoted in the Fillmore East released performance of "Bwana Dik." It was also played at the Bridges Auditorium at Pomona College in Claremont, CA on May 18, 1971. "Daddy" was revived during the fall 1976 and fall 1977 tours. "Philly '76" captured the song during the October 29, 1976 show at the Spectrum Theater. Flo & Eddie guested on vocals at the November 19, 1976 gig at Cobo Hall in Detroit, MI. The 1984 band performed "Daddy, Daddy, Daddy" during the European and North American tours.

* * *

FRANK ZAPPA AND THE MOTHERS OF INVENTION: Tears Began To Fall/ Junier Mintz Boogie (7" 45 rpm single)
Released October 20, 1971 as Reprise 1052 and Bizarre/Reprise 1052 (both editions)

A-side
Tears Began To Fall (2:50) (Frank Zappa) • Master #: (RCA 0472)S • STEREO
see Junier Mintz single

B-side
Junier Mintz Boogie (2:53) (Frank Zappa) • Master #: (RCA 0473)S • STEREO
see Junier Mintz single

The final shot for Warner Bros.' Reprise label to straighten out the Junier Mintz disaster came almost three months later. This time, the record had the proper crediting and was issued on both Bizarre/Reprise and Reprise itself. It was the only Zappa release that appeared on Straight, Bizarre, and Reprise. Promo copies were stereo and mono versions of the A-side only. Stock copies are again extremely elusive, but they do exist.

"Tears Began To Fall"/ "Junier Mintz Boogie" was also made available in Italy (Bizarre/Reprise K 14100), New Zealand (Reprise RO.1052), and Venezuela (Reprise REP 1052). The French arm of Reprise decided to be different from everyone else by using "Happy Together" as the flipside of "Tears Began To Fall" (Reprise K 14120). That record was issued with a picture sleeve on November 26, 1971.

* * *

FRANK ZAPPA: Magic Fingers/ Daddy, Daddy, Daddy (7" 45 rpm single)
Released November 8, 1971 as United Artists 50857

A-side
Magic Fingers (2:57) (Frank Zappa) • Master #: UAST-8578 • STEREO
Recorded: live on January 28 – February 5, 1971 at Pinewood Studios, London, England, and April 1971 at Whitney Studios, Glendale, CA (overdubs)
Personnel: Frank Zappa (guitar, bass, fuzz bass, rhythm guitar); Mark Volman (co-lead vocal, backing vocals, tambourine); Howard Kaylan (co-lead vocal, backing vocals); Ian Underwood (keyboards, woodwinds); Aynsley Dunbar (drums); George Duke (keyboards, trombone); Martin Lickert (bass); Ruth Underwood (orchestra drum set)
Producer: Frank Zappa
Engineer: Bob Auger (Pinewood); Barry Keene (Whitney)

B-side
Daddy, Daddy, Daddy (3:11) (Frank Zappa) • Master #: UAST-8574 • STEREO
see "What Will This Evening Bring Me This Morning"

United Artists felt that "Magic Fingers" was the correct A-side to promote the "200 Motels" soundtrack. "Magic Fingers" was Zappa's ode to John Joseph Houghtaling's invention, the Magic Fingers Vibrating Bed. Debuting in 1958, the bed could be found at hotels and motels throughout the US and Europe. The single of "Magic Fingers" faded out before Howard Kaylan's monologue. It was included as the last audio track on Rykodisc's double soundtrack CD in 1997. The flipside was the same as the previous United Artists single coupling, and promotional copies again featured stereo and mono versions of the A-side. The only complaint that could be made was that the MOI should have been credited.

"Magic Fingers" is in the background during the "Playground Psychotics" track "The Worst Reviews." "Halloween 73" used a recording of the song from October 21, 1973. "Magic Fingers" was quoted during the November 30, 1974 performance of "Trouble Comin' Every Day" at the Field House, North Central College, Naperville, IL. Live versions of "Magic Fingers" from the August-October 1978 band can be heard on "Beat The Boots I: Saarbrücken 1978," "Chicago '78," and "Halloween."

A "Magic Fingers" recording from the October-December 1980 band is on "Stage, Vol. 6," and it was repeated on the second volume of Steve Vai's "The Secret Jewel Box" set. The song was rehearsed in 1987, but it did not make the cut for the 1988 tour. As mentioned earlier, "Magic Fingers" is one of numerous FZ songs which mention chrome in their lyrics. This single was released in Italy (United Artists UA 35344) with reversed sides and a picture sleeve.

At this point, Argentina decided to release an unusual 33 1/3 rpm promo EP (Music Hall/ Reprise 183) with two extracts of Jethro Tull's "Thick As A Brick" and two extracts of "Holiday In Berlin" (from "Uncle Meat") on the B-side. Once again, the titles were written in Spanish.

To urge radio listeners to vote in the US presidential election on November 7, 1972, the National Association Of Progressive Radio Announcers created a series of public service announcements. Two 33 1/3 rpm 12" stereo records were titled "72 Vote P.S.A.'s" (sic) with the same content. The first was a custom pressing issued with an art sleeve. Although no mention of a record label appeared, the United Artists promo release number SP-79 was assigned to the disc. Frank Zappa's 50-second promo was Track 14 on side 2, and The

Phlorescent Leech & Eddie had Track 5 (60 seconds) and Track 6 (30 seconds) on Side 1. The second pressing was issued on a regular United Artists label with the same promo catalog number.

* * *

THE MOTHERS: Cletus Awreetus-Awrightus/ Eat That Question (7" 45 rpm single)
Released November 6, 1972 as Bizarre/Reprise REP 1127

A-side
Cletus Awreetus-Awrightus (2:55) (Frank Zappa) • Master #: (QCA3289)S • STEREO
Recorded: April-May 1972 at Paramount Recording Studios, Los Angeles, CA
Personnel: Frank Zappa (vocals, guitar); Chunky (aka Ilene Rappaport) (vocals); George Duke (vocals, piano, tack piano, organ); Erroneous (aka Alex Dmochowski) (bass); Aynsley Dunbar (drums); Ernie Watts (C melody saxophone solo); Mike Altschul (soprano saxophone, baritone saxophone); Sal Marquez (trumpet); Ken Shroyer (multiple trombones)
Producer: Frank Zappa
Engineer: Kerry McNabb

B-side
Eat That Question (3:07) (Frank Zappa) • Master #: (QCA3192)S • STEREO
Recorded: April-May 1972 at Paramount Recording Studios, Los Angeles, CA
Personnel: Frank Zappa (guitar, snare drum); George Duke (organ, electric piano); Erroneous (aka Alex Dmochowski) (bass); Aynsley Dunbar (drums); Lee Clement (gong); Mike Altschul (piccolo); Joel Peskin (tenor saxophone); Sal Marquez (trumpet, flugelhorn)
Producer: Frank Zappa
Engineer: Kerry McNabb

The disaster that occurred at the Zappa/MOI early show at The Rainbow Theatre in London on December 10, 1971 would greatly affect the future. The band left the stage after the first encore of The Beatles' "I Want To Hold Your Hand." FZ came out to announce the second encore, and then audience member Trevor Charles Howell pushed Frank off the stage and into the orchestra pit. The band came back on stage without any knowledge of the event. Frank was found unconscious with a broken left leg, rib and ankle, spine damage, a fractured skull, and a crushed larynx. Zappa's spine injury led to temporarily paralysis in one arm, and his damaged larynx lowered his voice pitch by a full third. The late show was naturally cancelled, and Howell was arrested on the spot. Mr. Howell based his actions on jealousy, and he was given one year in prison at his December 30, 1971 trial.

Frank Zappa would not be the same, and neither would his future musical creations. He was taken to Royal Northern Hospital in London and underwent an operation on his leg on December 12, 1971. Frank remained in London for another month while recovering at the Weymouth Street Clinic. Zappa's four-month recuperation began in Hawaii with his leg in a cast. A leg brace was eventually required, and getting around required a wheelchair. Zappa's left leg was a bit crooked and shorter than his right leg once the brace was removed. The last seven tour dates and a "Billy The Mountain" film project were cancelled. Flo & Eddie and the rest of the Mothers explored different musical paths.

Zappa wrote a large quantity of material during his recovery period. The album "Just Another Band From L.A." was assembled and finalized, and Frank created many elaborate instrumental pieces which required a large band to perform and record. The proper execution of these works and all the compositions that followed required a very high level of musicianship. Paramount Recording Studios became Zappa's recording location of choice for this material in April-May 1972, and Kerry McNabb engineered the proceedings. "Waka/Jawaka" (issued on July 5, 1972) was the first project released from this very prolific period.

"The Grand Wazoo" was the next completed project. It was recorded at the same time as "Waka/Jawaka." Exactly three weeks before "The Grand Wazoo" hit the racks, "Cletus Awreetus-Awrightus"/"Eat That Question" was issued as a preview single. It was the last Zappa 45 to be released on Bizarre. "The Grand Wazoo" was accompanied by an elaborate backstory and artwork. Cletus Awreetus-Awrightus was a studio musician character who worked for session contractor Ben Barrett (a real person).

The song devoted to Cletus was a compact, elegant instrumental with wordless vocals and a very catchy, accessible melody. Those vocals (which can be heard starting at about 2:08) were sung by FZ, George Duke, and Ilene Rappaport, the latter going by the nickname Chunky. Rappaport was the lead vocalist of the group Rebecca And The Sunny Brook Farmers, who recorded an album for Musicor in 1969. That group also included Ilene "Novi" Novog, who played with Zappa in the short-lived summer 1975 lineup documented on "Joe's Camouflage." Former Mothers drummer Aynsley Dunbar brought in his former Aynsley Dunbar Retaliation bass player Alex Dmochowski, known as Erroneous because he was in the US illegally due to a visa overstay. In the woodwind department, Ernie Watts played the C melody saxophone solo in the middle of the song, while Mike Altschul played soprano and baritone saxophones. The brass playing involved trumpeter Sal Marquez and Ken Shroyer's overdubbed trombones.

One of the endearing qualities of "Cletus Awreetus-Awrightus" was the manner in which each musician was given a chance to express him/herself within the song context. The single is exactly the same as the album master, and promo copies had stereo and mono mixes of the A-side. No audience tapes exist of rumored performances of "Cletus" by the spring 1973 band. To return the favor of Chunky singing on "Cletus," Zappa whispered at the beginning of "Rosalie" on Chunky, Novi & Ernie's self-titled album (Reprise MS 2146, released February 25, 1974; reissued in Japan twice – Warner Bros. WPCR-10744 on June 21, 2000, and Warner Bros. 5060552 on October 28, 2016).

For the other tracks that Zappa selected for inclusion on "The Grand Wazoo," none of them were short enough to fit comfortably on a single. "Eat That Question" (original title: "Eat That Christian") was trimmed drastically from 6:42 to 3:07 to form the B-side. Both of George Duke's keyboard solos, including his improvised introduction, were cut out. The single master began from the head of the tune, and the integrity of Frank's guitar solo was retained. Edits for the single are audible at 0:30 and 2:10. The jarring single edit at 1:47 is also on the album master, and the single ends at the same place as on the LP. "Eat That Question" used a different combination of musicians than the A-side. The rhythm section of Erroneous and Aynsley Dunbar was intact. Sal Marquez added flugelhorn to his trumpet, and Joel Peskin played tenor saxophone. Mike Altschul played piccolo this time, with Lee Clement playing gong, George Duke on organ and electric piano, and FZ playing snare drum along with lead guitar.

For such a strong instrumental, "Eat That Question" was not played live as often as you might have expected. The 1973 MOI lineups played the song seven times and quoted it once, but the summer and fall 1974 bands only played it once and quoted it once. "Eat That Question" was performed twice during 1980 European soundchecks, rehearsed once during the summer 1981 band, and was quoted once by the 1984 lineup. The 1988 band regularly performed only the intro and head of "Eat That Question" before launching into "Black Napkins." An example of the '88 band's performance can be heard on "Make A Jazz Noise Here."

Once again, Argentina went their own way and issued two 33 1/3 rpm promos that shared Zappa content with another artist. A 4:56 edit of "Waka/Jawaka" was paired with The Doors' "Get Up And Dance" (Music Hall/ Reprise 217), while the single edits of "Eat That Question" and "Cletus Awreetus-Awrightus" were joined by Jethro Tull's "Living In The Past" and "Christmas Song" (Music Hall/ Reprise 40.018). Italy was the only other country that issued the American single, but the sides were reversed. It was released as Bizarre/ Reprise K 14228.

* * *

RUBEN AND THE JETS: If I Could Be Your Love Again/ Wedding Bells (7" 45 rpm single)
Released May 14, 1973 as Mercury 73381

A-side
If I Could Be Your Love Again (3:33) (Frank Zappa) • Master #: 2-50060 • STEREO
Recorded: May 1972 at Paramount Recording Studios, Los Angeles, CA
Personnel: Rubén Ladrón de Guevara (lead vocals); Tony Duran (lead guitar, slide guitar); Robert "Frog" Camarena (rhythm guitar, backing vocals); Johnny Martinez (bass, backing vocals, organ); Robert "Buffalo" Roberts (tenor saxophone); Bill Wild (bass, backing vocals); Bob Zamora (drums); Jim Sherwood (baritone saxophone); Frank Zappa (bass vocals, arranger)
Producer: Frank Zappa
Engineer: Kerry McNabb

B-side
Wedding Bells (2:56) (Robert "Frog" Camarena) • Master #: 2-50064 • STEREO
Recorded: May 1972 at Paramount Recording Studios, Los Angeles, CA
Personnel: Robert "Frog" Camarena (lead vocals); Rubén Ladrón de Guevara (backing vocals); Tony Duran (rhythm guitar, arranger); Johnny Martinez (organ, bass, backing vocals); Bill Wild (bass, backing vocals); Bob Zamora (drums)
Producer: Frank Zappa
Engineer: Kerry McNabb

Rubén Ladrón de Guevara briefly met Frank Zappa at the Shrine Exposition Hall in Los Angeles just after the "Cruising With Ruben & The Jets" album was released. That would have been either December 6 or 7, 1968. Rubén told Frank that he appreciated a group that played in the old R&B and doo-wop style. The first MOI keyboardist named Bob Harris took Rubén to Frank's house after the band finished their touring on July 10, 1971. Harris was replaced by Don Preston when touring began again on August 7, 1971, so Rubén's meeting with Zappa took place between those dates. Frank held a late-night 45s listening session. After getting along well, Zappa and Rubén discussed forming a genuine Ruben And The Jets group for recording and live work opening for The Mothers Of Invention. FZ offered to help Rubén's potential band get their act together.

It took a while for Rubén to assemble a band. By that time in early 1972, Frank was wheelchair-bound. Four demos were cut to attract record companies, with only the Mercury label showing interest. Rubén was joined by lead/slide guitarist Tony Duran, rhythm guitarist and vocalist Robert "Frog" Camarena, bassists Johnny Martinez and Bill Wild, tenor saxophonist Robert "Buffalo" Roberts, drummer Bob Zamora, and former MOI saxophonist Euclid James "Motorhead" Sherwood. They had a nice mix of Los Angeles barrio and city musicians. The Ruben And The Jets LP that Zappa's produced for Mercury was called "For Real." The

"For Real" sessions at Paramount took place while Zappa was working on "Waka/Jawaka" and "The Grand Wazoo." "For Real" was released one year after it was recorded.

To kick things off, Zappa wrote his new song "If I Could Be Your Love Again" (listed as "If I Could Only Be Your Love Again" on the album cover, but not on the LP or 45 labels). Frank's contract with Warner Bros./Reprise allowed him to produce, arrange, and write for, but not perform on, Ruben And The Jets' album. That did not stop Zappa from actively participating on the tracks in an uncredited capacity.

The album credits list FZ as album producer and arranger on "If I Could Be Your Love Again," and co-arranger with Rubén Ladrón de Guevara on "Mah Man Flash" and "Santa Kari." Robert "Frog" Camarena confirmed fan suspicion that Frank Zappa played the guitar solo before Tony Duran's slide solo on "Dedicated To The One I Love." However, it is not generally known that Zappa sang bass vocals on "If I Could Only Be Your Love Again," "Charlena," "Mah Man Flash," and "Santa Kari." The latter track featured FZ's bass tones throughout. Ruben And The Jets had many first-rate vocalists, but they did not have a bass vocalist.

"If I Could Be Your Love Again" was an FZ doo-wop that would not have been out of place on "Cruising With Ruben & The Jets." Unlike "Cruising," this track involved an early '70s approach and sound. Rich vocal harmonies were occasionally joined by Johnny Martinez's falsetto vocals. Zappa's "gotta get your love again" bass vocal began at 2:39 just before the vocal/drum breakdown and continued intermittently until the fade. The single master is exactly the same as the album version released two months earlier. Frank Zappa's later song "Doreen" (on "You Are What You Is") has many lyric, vocal and thematic similarities to "If I Could Be Your Love Again." Variations of the lines "if I could be with you tonight" and "everything would be alright" appear in both songs to show the pursuit of a girl and how great things would be if they got together.

The B-side "Wedding Bells" revolved around Robert "Frog" Camarena's throaty, double-tracked lead vocal and Johnny Martinez's organ. The middle section featured spoken parts repeating what had just been sung. The spare backing of this slow ballad did not require the saxophone players Sherwood and Roberts. It is a duplicate of the LP master. Promotional copies of the record were the same as stock copies in that both sides were featured.

For some reason, digital offerings of Ruben And The Jets' Mercury masters have been taken from records. The master tapes reside in the same place as the Burt Ward session tape – namely, Universal's tape library in Edison, NJ. Herb Cohen owned the group's output, and his estate controls its current distribution. "For Real" was supposed to be released on CD by the Enigma label in 1989 (catalog number 7 73534-2), but it never appeared. The Edsel label in England issued "For Real" on CD on December 12, 1994 (release number EDCD 406).

A lot happened between the time "For Real" was recorded and it was released. Slide guitarist Tony Duran played on sessions for "Waka/Jawaka," "The Grand Wazoo," and "Joe's Domage." Duran joined Frank Zappa in the Grand Wazoo lineup that toured during September 1972, and he was also part of the Petit Wazoo group from October and December 1972.

The Grand Wazoo lineup can be heard on the "Imaginary Diseases" CD, the "Wazoo" album, the track "Trudgin' Across The Tundra" on "One Shot Deal," the "Little Dots" album, and the "Rollo" single from 2017 which will be listed later on. Tony can also be heard on 1974's "Apostrophe (')" and "The Crux Of The Biscuit." Ruben And The Jets opened for The Grand Wazoo lineup during December 8-10, 1972. To promote "For

Real" (released March 12, 1973), Ruben And The Jets opened for The Mothers on March 23 and 24, 1973.

* * *

RUBEN AND THE JETS: Charlena/ Mah Man Flash (7" 45 rpm single)
Released July 23, 1973 as Mercury 73411

A-side
Charlena (3:11) (Manuel Chavez – Herman B. Chaney) • Master #: 2-50908 • STEREO
Recorded: May 1972 at Paramount Recording Studios, Los Angeles, CA
Personnel: Rubén Ladrón de Guevara (lead vocals, tambourine, percussion); Tony Duran (lead guitar, slide guitar); Robert "Frog" Camarena (rhythm guitar, backing vocals); Johnny Martinez (bass, backing vocals, organ); Robert "Buffalo" Roberts (tenor saxophone); Bill Wild (bass, backing vocals); Bob Zamora (drums); Jim Sherwood (baritone saxophone); Frank Zappa (bass vocals)
Producer: Frank Zappa
Engineer: Kerry McNabb

B-side
Mah Man Flash (3:20) (Rubén Ladrón de Guevara) • Master #: 2-50067 • STEREO
Recorded: May 1972 at Paramount Recording Studios, Los Angeles, CA
Personnel: Rubén Ladrón de Guevara (lead vocals, co-arranger); Tony Duran (lead guitar, slide guitar, piano); Robert "Frog" Camarena (rhythm guitar, backing vocals); Johnny Martinez (bass, backing vocals); Robert "Buffalo" Roberts (tenor saxophone); Bill Wild (bass, backing vocals); Bob Zamora (drums); Jim Sherwood (baritone saxophone); Frank Zappa (bass vocals, co-arranger)
Producer: Frank Zappa
Engineer: Kerry McNabb

"If I Could Be Your Love Again" did not receive sufficient airplay and sold poorly. "Charlena" and "Mah Man Flash" were selected as the follow-up 45. "Charlena" was written while Manuel Chavez and Herman Chaney were in The Jaguars in 1959, but they split before the song was recorded. Chavez's group The Sevilles released "Charlena" in December 1960 on the J.C. label (release number: 116). "Charlena" was covered by numerous groups. As the '60s progressed into the '70s, versions of "Charlena" moved from vocal group arrangements to heavier, rock-based treatments such as Ruben And The Jets' take.

The 5:54 length of "Charlena" on the "For Real" album would require a great deal of editing to create a single version. We know that Frank Zappa was very familiar with cutting tape (see "Lonely Little Girl" above), so he made many elaborate edits to the album master to create the single. The edits occur on the single at 0:35, 0:42, 1:34, 1:38, 1:58, 2:13, 2:21, 2:28, and 2:46. On the album version, Zappa's bass vocals began just before the vocal breakdown and they lasted from 2:55-3:43. Those vocals started on the single at 1:38, and about half of Frank's vocal contribution was edited out.

Rubén composed the roots rocker "Mah Man Flash" (original title: "Flash Gordon") and arranged it with Frank Zappa. It was spiced with rock and roll namechecks, Spanish asides, and sax and guitar licks and solos. Tony Duran banged away on the piano. Zappa's bass vocal can be heard during the last four seconds.

Promotional copies were the same as stock copies except that promos mentioned the editing of the A-side. One track listed on studio session sheets, "Spirit Of Love," does not appear to have been released. Ruben

And The Jets broke up after recording the album "Con Safos" without Zappa and Jim Sherwood.

Instead of "Charlena," the Italian and Dutch divisions of Mercury elected to go with two other Zappa-produced tracks as their single: "All Nite Long"/ "Spider Woman." Both singles had different picture sleeves. The 45s were both released on July 27, 1973 with Mercury catalog number 6052 334. The tracks were direct transfers from the album masters. The A-side was a cover of the Joe Houston Orchestra instrumental A-side "All Night Long" (the correct spelling; released as Money 203-45 in October 1954), and the flip was written by Zappa equipment tech Paul Hof with Lonnie Scott, Tony Duran, and Rubén Ladrón de Guevara. Ruben And The Jets' "All Nite Long" was also issued the same day as a promotional Italian jukebox single backed by Bionic Boogie's "Dance Little Dreamer" (Mercury AS 5000 438). The "All Nite Long"/ "Spider Woman" single was reissued in Italy on October 28, 1977, using the same catalog number and a different picture sleeve. It was re-released because the Italian TV program "L'altra Domenica" ("Another Side Of Sunday") used "All Nite Long" as its theme. "L'altra Domenica" was a Sunday afternoon variety show on Rai 2 hosted by Renzo Arbore. All pressings of the single incorrectly list "All Nite Long" as 3:20, but it is 2:20. "Spider Woman" was correctly listed as 3:58.

Rubén Ladrón de Guevara, Robert "Frog" Camarena and Johnny Martinez sang at a Mothers show at the Shrine Auditorium in Los Angeles on February 23, 1974. The "Apostrophe (')" and "Roxy & Elsewhere" albums featured vocals by Rubén and Camarena. Rubén can also be heard on "Zoot Allures," and Camarena is also on "Bongo Fury" and "Joe's Camouflage," the latter of which documented his short time in Zappa's summer 1975 band.

* * *

THE MOTHERS: I'm The Slime/ Montana (7" 45 rpm single)
Released October 29, 1973 as DiscReet REP 1180
Reissued April 20, 2013 as Barking Pumpkin BPR 1222 (Record Store Day numbered green marbled 7" 45 rpm single)

A-side
I'm The Slime (both editions – 3:02) (Frank Zappa) • Master #: DiscReet – (RCA3843)S; Barking Pumpkin – none • STEREO
Recorded: mid-March 1973 (basic tracks) and May 31, 1973 (vocal overdubs) at Bolic Sound, Inglewood, CA
Personnel: Frank Zappa (lead vocal, guitar, arranger, conductor); Ralph Humphrey (drums); Sal Marquez (trumpet, vocals); George Duke (clavinet, ARP synthesizer, Fender Rhodes); Tom Fowler (bass); Bruce Fowler (trombone); Ruth Underwood (marimba, vibes, percussion); Ian Underwood (alto saxophone); Kin Vassy (announcer); The Ikettes – Tina Turner, Debbie Wilson, Linda "Lynn" Sims (backing vocals)
Producer: Frank Zappa
Engineer: Barry Keene

B-side
Montana (DiscReet – 4:39; Barking Pumpkin – 5:04) (Frank Zappa) • Master #: DiscReet – (RCA3342V1)S; Barking Pumpkin – none • STEREO
Recorded: March 20, 1973 (basic tracks) and May 26, 1973 (overdubs) at Bolic Sound, Inglewood, CA
Personnel: Frank Zappa (lead vocal, guitar, arranger, conductor); Ralph Humphrey (drums); George Duke (Fender Rhodes, clavinet); Tom Fowler (bass); Bruce Fowler (trombone); Ruth Underwood (marimba, vibraphone, tambourine, drums); Jean-Luc Ponty (baritone violin); Kin Vassy (backing vocals); The Ikettes

– Tina Turner, Debbie Wilson, Linda "Lynn" Sims (backing vocals)
Producer: Frank Zappa
Engineer: Barry Keene

The extensive Grand Wazoo and Petit Wazoo lineups featured top-rate musicians who were up to the task of successfully performing Zappa's complicated, mostly instrumental pieces. Frank's new material required a variety of vocal approaches within the musical surroundings. A new Mothers lineup was created by FZ to continue the high level of musicianship, but with vocal wild cards like Kin Vassy and Ricky Lancelotti. The vast majority of the album recording for what became "Over-Nite Sensation" took place at Ike Turner's Bolic Sound studio in Inglewood, CA, with the remainder being done at Paramount and Whitney. Recording at Bolic enabled FZ to work with The Ikettes, who comprised Ike's then-wife, the powerful Tina Turner, along with Debbie Wilson and Linda "Lynn" Sims. Ike Turner would not allow any crediting of The Ikettes on Zappa's records.

The Bizarre and Straight labels were put to rest. Frank Zappa and Herb Cohen replaced those labels with a new imprint, DiscReet. The new label was a play on discrete quadraphonic (aka quadrophonic) audio reproduction, in which four separate audio channels were played through four speakers. Zappa recorded the band instrumentation in quad, and his intent was to release his future output on quad and stereo discs. Reproducing quadraphonic content required listeners to obtain new equipment, and the various incompatible quad formats led to the format's commercial failure. Frank Zappa ended up releasing quadraphonic versions of two albums: "Over-Nite Sensation" and his solo album "Apostrophe (')."

The first DiscReet album release was "Over-Nite Sensation" on September 7, 1973. It was Warner's A&R man Ron Saul who asked FZ to release "I'm The Slime" as a single. "I'm The Slime"/ "Montana" was released at the end of October. Frank proceeded to create an edited remix with no vocal echo and an alternate ending solo. The conclusion of Zappa's guitar intro on "I'm The Slime" contained feedback which was edited out of the album mix. As for the song itself, Frank spoke three verses about the manipulative power of television. Kin Vassy's subsequent spoken line "That's right, folks...Don't touch that dial" was adapted from "Blondie" radio series announcer Howard Petrie's introduction during that show's run from 1939-1950. The Ikettes then took over, leading into FZ's ending solo. The "obsessed 'n deranged" lyric would be used at a December 31, 1974 gig at Long Beach Arena (Long Beach, CA) during a performance of "That Arrogant Dick Nixon" which used the music of "The Idiot Bastard Son." The only way to obtain a digital copy of the "I'm The Slime" single master is as a downloadable bonus track from iTunes and other digital retailers.

"I'm The Slime" was part of The Mothers' live set at the start of their North American tour in February 1973. The backing tracks were laid down in mid-March after the first run of shows, and vocal overdubs were recorded in late May after that tour leg was completed. "Slime" can be heard by the fall 1973 band on "Halloween 73," "Stage, Vol. 1" (the December 9, 1973 late show), and that performance was also included on "The Roxy Performances" and "Roxy – The Movie." The 1974 tour has not been represented on record yet, but "Denny & Froggy Relate" from "Joe's Camouflage" has a 1975 quote of "I'm The Slime." The December 1976 lineup performed "I'm The Slime" for "Zappa In New York" and the 40th anniversary deluxe edition, and their "Saturday Night Live" TV performance with NBC announcer Don Pardo can be heard on "Beat The Boots III: Disc Six." The winter 1977 band performed the song, and the 1981 band played "Slime" without an FZ solo (such as on "Halloween 81"). An April 1982 rehearsal of "Carolina Hard-Core Ecstasy" quoted "Slime." The aforementioned "Beat The Boots III" volume also has a 1984 version, and "Slime" was soundchecked during 1988.

"Montana" completed the "I'm The Slime" single. Zappa's song dealt with cornering the dental floss market in Montana, a state he never performed in. Except for variations of the chorus lines "movin' to Montana soon" and "gonna be a dental floss tycoon," Frank's subtly humorous vocals were spoken, and the repeat of his sung lines from 1:44-1:52 were slowed down a third. The Ikettes' backing vocals embellished the ends of each verse. Zappa's guitar solo was cut out at 1:55. This led into the rapid fire Ikettes vocals (sped up a minor third) during the complicated middle section. Tina Turner had trouble learning this part. Either Debbie Wilson or Linda "Lynn" Sims figured it out on tape first and Tina and the other girl recorded their parts afterward. The end of the song used repeats of the chorus lines with Frank and The Ikettes, answered by Kin Vassy's "Yippy-Ty-O-Ty-Ay" responses before fading. "Montana" was started at Bolic Sound on March 20, 1973 and was completed there on May 26.

The "I'm The Slime"/"Montana" single pairing was reissued on Record Store Day in 2013 with a picture sleeve and a 25-second longer edit of the B-side. The original "Montana" single edit can be found on "Strictly Commercial." Zappa's original reference to dental floss was in "A Nun Suit Painted On Some Old Boxes" from "200 Motels." Oral health was covered by another "200 Motels" work – "Dental Hygiene Dilemma." Another floss reference appeared in "Titties & Beer" on "Zappa In New York" and the deluxe edition. Zircon-encrusted tweezers were part of the lyrics for "Montana," "Dinah-Moe Humm" (another "Over-Nite Sensation" track) and "The Poodle Lecture" which preceded live versions of "Stink-Foot."

The enduring message of "Montana" got the attention of the American Dental Association. In 1981, the association asked Frank Zappa to record some radio spots promoting dental health and flossing as part of the ADA's public service radio campaign during 1981 and 1982. Frank recorded three 30-second spots for the ADA's custom label. The spots naturally used "Montana" as the music bed. The first spot was part of the ADA's spring/summer 1981 single (record number DWP928A/B). The last commercial on side one (Track 11) was the FZ spot "Dental Floss Tycoon." The autumn/winter 1981 disc (DWP930A/B) featured the Zappa ad "Trick Or Treat" as the third track on side one. The spring/summer 1982 release (DWP933A/B) was a more deluxe affair. It came with a picture sleeve with photos of the narrators on one side and their ad copies on the other. The Zappa ad on this disc was "Keep Your Teeth." It is interesting to note that Frank Zappa's ad was Track 6 on side one, and Track 7 was Steve Allen's spot "Toothbrush Wears Out."

"Montana" was a long-running live favorite. The horn-fortified Petit Wazoo lineup during the fall of 1972 was the first to play it live. This early arrangement of "Montana" lacked the middle section. The song was consistently performed in 1973, with "Road Tapes, Venue #2" (from August 24) and "Halloween 73" being the earliest live versions released. Parts of the early shows on December 9 and 10, 1973 were first released on "Stage, Vol. 4" before their complete inclusion on "The Roxy Performances" in 2018. In addition, the December 9 early show featured "Dupree's Paradise" with a "Montana" quote. The videos and subsequent CDs of "The Dub Room Special!" and "A Token Of His Extreme" include a live take of "Montana" from Los Angeles TV station KCET on August 27, 1974.

The live "Montana" pinnacle was reached during the Helsinki, Finland "Stage, Vol. 2" version recorded on September 22, 1974. This was the show at which a fan requested The Allman Brothers' "Whipping Post." That performance, "Montana (Whipping Floss)," was later released as a CD single, the later discussion of which covers the entire story. This version was also on the "Stage Sampler."

The next gig that contained a released version of "Montana" was the December 28, 1976 performance on "Zappa In New York 40th Anniversary Deluxe Edition." The June 11, 1980 concert at Palais des Sports in Paris, France included "Montana" as one of numerous quotes within "A Pound For A Brown On The Bus." The

Halloween 1981 takes of "Montana" are on the video "The Torture Never Stops" and the "Halloween 81" set. Finally, the December 23, 1984 tour ending concert in Los Angeles featured "Montana" on "Stage, Vol. 4."

* * *

FRANK ZAPPA: Cosmik Debris/ Uncle Remus (7" 45 rpm single)
US commercial release planned for release on May 20, 1974 as DiscReet DIS 1203, but cancelled
Released May 20, 1974 as DiscReet PRO 586 (7" 45 rpm promo single)
Reissued August 23, 1974 as DiscReet K 19201 (England)

A-side
Cosmik Debris (both editions – 4:10) (Frank Zappa) • Master #: US promo – (RCA3998)S; England – K 19201 A • STEREO
Recorded: May 28, 1973 (basic tracks) and June 1973 (vocal overdubs) at Bolic Sound, Inglewood, CA
Personnel: Frank Zappa (lead vocal, guitar, arranger); George Duke (Fender Rhodes, clavinet, Hammond organ, ARP synthesizer); Sal Marquez (trumpet); Tom Fowler (bass); Bruce Fowler (trombone); Ian Underwood (tenor saxophone); Ruth Underwood (percussion); Jean-Luc Ponty (violin); Ralph Humphrey (drums); The Ikettes – Tina Turner, Debbie Wilson, Linda "Lynn" Sims (backing vocals)
Producer: Frank Zappa
Engineer: Barry Keene

B-side
Uncle Remus (US promo – 2:49; England – 2:54) (Frank Zappa – George Duke) • Master #: US promo – (QCA3287)S; England – K 19201 B • STEREO
Recorded: May 24, 1972 at Paramount Recording Studios, Los Angeles, CA (basic tracks), and May-June 1973 at Bolic Sound, Inglewood, CA (guitar and vocal overdubs)
Personnel: Frank Zappa (lead guitar, lead vocal, arranger); George Duke (piano, ARP synthesizer); Alex Dmochowski (bass); Aynsley Dunbar (drums); The Ikettes – Tina Turner, Debbie Wilson, Linda "Lynn" Sims (backing vocals)
Producer: Frank Zappa
Engineer: Kerry McNabb (Paramount); Barry Keene (Bolic)

The album "Apostrophe (')" was released on March 22, 1974. "Apostrophe (')" very quickly became Frank Zappa's fastest selling album and first gold record, peaking at #10. One thing was missing, though: no single was available to maximize the sales potential of the album. "Cosmik Debris"/ "Uncle Remus" was the first attempt by DiscReet to supply that necessary single. Both tracks were the same as the stereo album masters. The commercial release was assigned the number DiscReet DIS 1203, but it was cancelled in favor of a promo single. Warner Bros./Reprise executives Mo Ostin and Joe Smith created the PRO series in 1969 to service radio stations and fans with label material that needed a little extra push to reach their desired audiences. This single fell into that category. The commercial British single came three months later. Portugal was the other country which elected to issue this single (Warner Bros. N-S-63-75).

Recording for "Cosmik Debris" began while vocal overdubs for The Mothers' "Over-Nite Sensation" were being completed at Bolic Sound. Like the previous single, Zappa's vocals were mostly spoken and close-miked. The Ikettes once again provided backing vocals on the choruses and bridge. The lyrics dealt with how FZ debunked fake guru The Mystery Man and his claims of taking Zappa to Nervanna ("Nirvana") – the ultimate state of happiness. Each part of "Cosmik Debris" was decorated by fills and flourishes that spotlighted various members of the band. The second verse referred to "The Grand Wazoo." Frank's guitar solo was just over half a minute long. The bridge section starting at 3:03 used the guitar riff of Jimi Hendrix's "Who Knows" and used sped up Ikettes backing vocals (3:05-3:33) and Zappa's slowed down vocal from 3:33-3:39. Both speed variations were by one step. Like his song "Camarillo Brillo," FZ asked whether The Mystery Man was wearing a real poncho or a Sears poncho. The ending vocals of "Om shanti" combined Om, the Hindu sacred syllable used at the start of mantras or chants, and Shanti, the Sanskrit word for peace.

The stereo/quad album and single masters of "Cosmik Debris" omitted a six-second introduction that was later released on "The Crux Of The Biscuit" in 2016. The album mix was also part of the "Strictly Commercial" and "ZAPPAtite" compilations.

"Cosmik Debris" was a solid part of live sets by many Zappa bands. The Petit Wazoo lineup premiered the song during their October-December 1972 tour. The "Little Dots" album has one example of this band. Lyrics and vocals were not finalized in this embryonic version, but the fact that "Cosmik Debris" was an excellent FZ guitar solo showcase was very much in evidence. The next released version of the song was the 2014 Mother's Day digital download of the August 23, 1973 late show in Helsinki, Finland. "Halloween 73" sported yet another live take. The early show on December 9, 1973 was captured on "The Roxy Performances" and "Roxy – The Movie," with a longer version on "Roxy – The Soundtrack." The early show on December 10 was also on "The Roxy Performances."

"The Dub Room Special!" video and subsequent CD included the August 27, 1974 KCET version of "Cosmik Debris." Dweezil Zappa used Frank's vocals and guitar from an unidentified 1974 performance of the song to accompany the backing by the 2008 edition of Zappa Plays Zappa. That track from Los Angeles was part of the 2011 birthday bundle. Improvisations from "Cosmik Debris" (September 26, 1974 in Paris, France) were called "Bathtub Man" on the "One Shot Deal" collection in 2008. The song was not performed between December 1974 and January 1978, but it was consistently played afterward through 1988.

The early 1979 band represented "Cosmik Debris" on "Beat The Boots I: Anyway The Wind Blows." "Buffalo" featured the fall 1980 lineup, and "Halloween 81" used the next year's band. Edited live performances of "Cosmik Debris" from different 1984 locales were issued on "Stage, Vol. 3," the "Stage Sampler," and the "Does Humor Belong In Music?" video. The 1988 band's performance of "Cosmik Debris" was on "The Best Band You Never Heard In Your Life."

The basic tracks of "Uncle Remus" were recorded at Paramount as part of a Zappa-produced George Duke demo along with "Psychosomatic Dung" and "For Love (I Come Your Friend)." The first two songs were re-recorded by Duke for his 1975 album "The Aura Shall Prevail," and the last was recorded for "Faces In Reflection" (1974). The title "Uncle Remus" came about after Frank told George that he liked the backing track and wanted to write lyrics for it. Zappa's lyric set was inspired by Joel Chandler Harris' "Uncle Remus," the title character and narrator of a book originally published in 1881. George Duke's piano intro led into Zappa and The Ikettes jointly singing throughout. The last 30+ seconds until the fade consisted of FZ's guitar solo with Ikettes backing.

The complete recording was issued as "Uncle Remus (Mix Outtake)" on "The Crux Of The Biscuit" in 2016. Three sections were edited out to create the single and stereo album masters, and the quad mix lost an additional two measures. The song's final lyric, "Down In De Dew," was the title of an instrumental that was on "Läther" and a posthumous single listed later.

"Uncle Remus" was rarely performed in concert. The March 7, 1973 concert at Veterans Memorial Hall in Columbus, OH featured George Duke working in "Uncle Remus" after his keyboard intro of "Dupree's Paradise." During the May 2, 1973 gig at the Coliseum (Indianapolis, IN), the concert opener "Fifty-Fifty" used the main "Uncle Remus" vamp. The spring 1975 band slotted "Uncle Remus" into "Echidna's Arf (Of You)." After years of neglect, the 1988 band performed "Uncle Remus" at least three times.

* * *

FRANK ZAPPA: Don't Eat The Yellow Snow/ Cosmik Debris (7" 45 rpm single)
Released October 7, 1974 as DiscReet DSS 1312

A-side
Don't Eat The Yellow Snow (3:26) (Frank Zappa) • Master #: (RCA4739)S • STEREO
Recorded: December 12, 1973 at Bolic Sound, Inglewood, CA (basic tracks), and January 1974 at Paramount Studios, Los Angeles, CA (overdubs)
Personnel: Frank Zappa (lead vocal, guitar, arranger); George Duke (Hohner clavinet, ARP Odyssey, electric piano, backing vocals); Tom Fowler (bass); Bruce Fowler (trombones); Sal Marquez (trumpet); Ruth Underwood (percussion); Ralph Humphrey (drums); Napoleon Murphy Brock (tenor saxophone, backing vocals); Rubén Ladrón de Guevara (backing vocals); Robert "Frog" Camarena (backing vocals); Ray Collins (backing vocals)
Producer: Frank Zappa
Engineer: Bob Hughes (Bolic); Kerry McNabb (Paramount)

B-side
Cosmik Debris (4:10) (Frank Zappa) • Master #: (RCA3998)S • STEREO
see previous single

The 1922 silent documentary "Nanook Of The North" was the influence on the Eskimo-themed pair of songs "Don't Eat The Yellow Snow" and "Nanook Rubs It" which began the "Yellow Snow" suite. The first iteration of the suite debuted at the end of April 1973 during the North American tour with a revised Mothers lineup: Jean-Luc Ponty was gone, and Napoleon Murphy Brock was in. As the live suite developed, it would incorporate three large modules: 1) "Don't Eat The Yellow Snow" (with that song and "Nanook Rubs It"), 2) "St. Alfonzo's Pancake Breakfast" (with that song, "Rollo Interior," "Father O'Blivion," and a "Mar-Juh-Rene" discussion bookended by reprises of both songs in the module, and the late '70s addition "Rollo Goes Out"), and 3) the similarly titled but unrelated instrumental "Farther O'Blivion" (with "Join The March And Eat My Starch," "The Steno Pool At Big Swifty's," a transitional section, "The Be-Bop Tango," a drum solo, and the song "Cucamonga").

The suite was thoroughly road-tested throughout 1973, and it was ready for recording at Bolic Sound in December. For recording purposes, the "Don't Eat The Yellow Snow" suite was trimmed to the "Yellow Snow" song, "Nanook Rubs It," "St. Alfonzo's Pancake Breakfast," and "Father O'Blivion." Overdubs were added in January 1974 at Paramount. Zappa asked Ruben And The Jets vocalists Rubén Ladrón de Guevara and Robert "Frog" Camarena to sing backing vocals, and former MOI vocalist Ray Collins did the same.

Zappa and The Mothers promoted "Apostrophe (')" via three US tour jaunts between mid-February (a month before its release) and mid-July 1974. Three California dates in August would precede the month-long European leg of the tour in early September 1974. Unknown to Zappa, radio was promoting the studio version of "Don't Eat The Yellow Snow" while Frank was building the song's live reputation.

During the summer of 1974, Pittsburgh, PA radio station WKTQ-AM (affectionately known as 13Q to its listeners) started playing an edit of the "Don't Eat The Yellow Snow" suite. 13Q program director Dennis Waters took it upon himself to edit "Yellow Snow" so that it could be played during his 10AM-2PM slot. Waters came to WKTQ in 1973 after a stint in Washington, DC. His edit took parts of "Don't Eat The Yellow Snow," "Nanook Rubs It" and "St. Alfonzo's Pancake Breakfast" to run about 3½ minutes. Waters' handiwork was a hit with 13Q listeners, and word of its success reached other radio stations and Frank Zappa. Frank made a professional edit that followed Waters' template. On WKTQ, "Apostrophe (')" entered the station's chart at #19 for the week ending May 25, 1974. The edit followed afterward, and "Apostrophe (')" peaked at #7 at the station. WKTQ's year-end chart indicated that "Don't Eat The Yellow Snow" was their 80th most popular single for 1974.

"Don't Eat The Yellow Snow" became Zappa's first charting single by entering the Billboard chart at #97 for the week ending October 19, 1974. The next two weeks, the record inched up to #93 and hit its peak of #86 before falling off the chart. Frank Zappa personally thanked Dennis Waters in front of the crowd at the November 6, 1974 concert at the Syria Mosque concert in Pittsburgh. Promos once again just featured stereo and mono mixes of the A-side.

The overwhelming success of "Apostrophe (')" was accompanied by a 30-second television commercial with animation by Cal Schenkel. It was Zappa's intent for this commercial to be aired during monster movie broadcasts. The commercial had short clips of album tracks and the narration promoted "Don't Eat The Yellow Snow" and "Cosmik Debris."

The single master of "Don't Eat The Yellow Snow" began with two ARP Odyssey wind sweeps over the rhythm track. The song's lyrics and musical asides were engaging throughout, such as the quote of Lionel Hampton's "Midnight Sun" from 0:07-0:09. Only Frank Zappa could easily incorporate doo-wop vocals within a modern context. The "Nanook Rubs It" portion of the track had both real-time and sped up Bruce Fowler trombone parts. The term "strictly commercial" was used between 0:50-0:55, and a mention of Fido the dog was made between 2:00-2:05. Other FZ songs mentioning Fido were "Dirty Love" and "Cheepnis." "Great googly moogly" was Zappa's exhortation between 2:20-2:21. The first record that used that phrase in its entirety was Howlin' Wolf's "Going Down Slow," recorded in December 1961. Not surprisingly, the single master of "Yellow Snow" was included on the compilations "Strictly Commercial" (all editions) and "ZAPPAtite." The single version was reissued in 2014 with an alternate mix of "Down In De Dew" as the B-side. That record is mentioned later. The B-side "Cosmik Debris" used the same master tape as the promo single above.

On the live front, two different summer 1973 Australian tour performances of "Yellow Snow" were released on "The Crux Of The Biscuit" and "One Shot Deal." Alternate studio takes of "Yellow Snow" were issued on "The Roxy Performances" (as "Don't Eat The Yellow Snow – In Session") and "The Crux Of The Biscuit." Part of the "In Session" version was in "Roxy – The Movie" during the ending credits. The summer 1978 band used the revised suite arrangement with "Rollo Goes Out" at its end. They can be heard on "Beat The Boots I: Saarbrücken 1978," "Chicago '78," and "Halloween." Part of the February 19, 1979 "Yellow Snow" performance was issued on "Stage, Vol. 1." The 1980 band was the last FZ lineup to play "Yellow Snow," but none of their versions have been released to date.

This single was released in Canada (as DiscReet DSS 1312) and New Zealand (Reprise RO 1312). The B-side of the Canadian issue misspelled the A-side as "Cosmick Debris." The British release of "Don't Eat The Yellow Snow" took place on November 22, 1974. Both sides were credited to Frank Zappa. They went with

"Camarillo Brillo" as the B-side of DiscReet K 19202. It was manufactured twice: with a solid center and with a push-out center. While it may have made sense to promote Zappa's two most recent albums, the B-side should have been credited to The Mothers since it came from the album "Over-Nite Sensation." "Camarillo Brillo" was faded early at 3:54 on the UK 45.

No US single was released from the next album "One Size Fits All," but DiscReet in Germany smartly capitalized on the "OSFA" track "Du Bist Mein Sofa" (aka "Sofa No. 2") which was sung in their language. It was paired with an edit of "Stink-Foot" from "Apostrophe (')." It was originally slated for release on June 29, 1975, but it was eventually released on August 8 of that year. The picture sleeve used the back cover photo of Frank Zappa from "Weasels Ripped My Flesh."

Frank Zappa recorded an interview with Dennis C. Benson before the November 7, 1975 gig at Civic Arena in Pittsburgh, PA. Benson, an ordained Presbyterian minister, aired the interview in Pittsburgh on his 9pm-midnight Sunday radio program "Pinpoint" on KQV (1410AM). Benson wrote the book "The Rock Generation," which was copyrighted on March 4, 1976. His book included two 8" 33 1/3 rpm Evatone Soundsheets (flexidiscs) of interviews. The first disc (101075AX/101075BX) featured the Zappa interview segment "Decorating Time" (2:25) as the second track on side one. The records were produced by Dennis Benson at the Cork Cellar, and audio assistance was provided by Abingdon Audio-Graphics.

* * *

GRAND FUNK RAILROAD: Can You Do It/ 1976 (7" 45 rpm single)
Released July 26, 1976 as MCA-40590

A-side
Can You Do It (2:46) (Richard Street – Thelma Gordy) • Master #: (MC5379E) • STEREO
Recorded: June-July 1, 1976 at The Swamp, Parshallville, MI (basic tracks), and July 1976 at The Record Plant, Los Angeles, CA (vocal overdubs)
Personnel: Mark Farner (lead vocal, backing vocals, guitar); Don Brewer (backing vocals, drums, percussion); Mel Schacher (bass, backing vocals); Craig Frost (keyboards, backing vocals)
Producer: Frank Zappa
Engineer: Frank Zappa with assistant Mark Stebbeds (The Swamp); Michael Braunstein & Davey Moire (The Record Plant)

B-side
1976 (4:21) (Mark Farner) • Master #: (MC5333) • STEREO
Recorded: June-July 1, 1976 at The Swamp, Parshallville, MI (basic tracks), and July 1976 at The Record Plant, Los Angeles, CA (vocal overdubs)
Personnel: Mark Farner (lead vocal, guitar); Don Brewer (backing vocals, drums, percussion); Mel Schacher (bass, backing vocals); Craig Frost (keyboards, backing vocals)
Producer: Frank Zappa
Engineer: Frank Zappa with assistant Mark Stebbeds (The Swamp); Michael Braunstein & Davey Moire (The Record Plant)

The idea of Frank Zappa even being in the same room with Grand Funk Railroad, let alone producing an album for them, was considered puzzling for most people at the time. FZ and GFR shared managerial and record company issues. Grand Funk fired their manager Terry Knight at the beginning of 1972 because they felt that Knight was pocketing too much of the band's earnings. The legal battle between Grand Funk Railroad and Terry Knight went on and on. The band finally got out of their Capitol label contract in early 1976 and signed a three-album deal with MCA. Strangely enough, EMI International, the parent company of Capitol, would handle the group's British releases moving forward. Zappa was battling with manager Herb Cohen, and he could not wait to end his contractual arrangement with Warner Bros. Frank fired Cohen in May 1976. Litigation relating to this firing led to a temporary reassignment of FZ's DiscReet contract to its parent company Warner Bros.

Despite signing a new contract, Grand Funk Railroad wanted to break up. The Flint, MI group's manager Andy Cavaliere suggested Frank Zappa as the producer of their MCA debut, Grand Funk's 11th studio LP. The group met Frank, and they immediately got along well. They decided to record basic tracks at Mark Farner's farm studio called The Swamp, and overdubs would be done at The Record Plant in Los Angeles. On session sheets, The Swamp's location was shown as Fenton, MI, but Mark Farner lived in nearby Parshallville, MI. Zappa wanted GFR to record their material live with a minimum of overdubs. Frank really enjoyed producing and engineering the straightforward rock and roll that Grand Funk brought into the studio. The group nearly broke up on the first day of overdubs, but FZ talked them out of it.

Part of the problem was a lack of confidence in their abilities. The band members had lost their touch in creating hit singles which drove their album sales. GFR chose the Motown song "Can You Do It" as their first single. The Contours released it on Motown's Gordy label at the end of February 1964 as the fourth follow-up to their big hit "Do You Love Me." At the time, The Contours reached #41 on the Billboard pop chart and #16 on the R&B single listings. Grand Funk's album track had studio banter and a false start, but those 31 seconds were cut out for the single version. Mark Farner double-tracked his vocals and the rest of the band added their well-known harmonies. The group's direct rock approach on "Can You Do It" was paired with some R&B touches. Released on July 26, 1976, "Can You Do It" reached #45 in the US. The riff-based B-side "1976" was one of two songs on the album dealing with America's bicentennial, freedoms that Americans enjoy, and the survival of the nation. Some environmental concerns were also made clear in the lyrics. In a way, GFR's "1976" was similar to Zappa's "200 Years Old." Promos of the single had stereo and mono versions of the edited A-side. The album "Good Singin' Good Playin'" was shipped by MCA a week after the single, but copies were not in stores until August 9, 1976. British promotional copies of the single (EMI International INT 523) listed an August 13 release date, but stock copies were not available until August 20.

During the vocal overdub sessions for the MCA album at The Record Plant in L.A., Zappa asked drummer Don Brewer to play bongos on "Lemme Take You To The Beach." Mark Farner and Eddie Jobson were there to do vocals, but only Jobson's work was included in the final mix. The track was started during the summer 1969 "Hot Rats" sessions. It was first released with the incorrect title "Let Me Take You To The Beach" on "Studio Tan" in 1978, and it also appeared properly credited on "Läther."

* * *

GRAND FUNK RAILROAD: Just Couldn't Wait/ Out To Get You (7" 45 rpm single)
Released November 1, 1976 as MCA-40641

<u>A-side</u>
Just Couldn't Wait (3:29) (Mark Farner) • Master #: (MC5335) • STEREO
Recorded: June-July 1, 1976 at The Swamp, Parshallville, MI (basic tracks), and July 1976 at The Record Plant, Los Angeles, CA (vocal overdubs)

Personnel: Mark Farner (lead vocal, backing vocals, guitar, piano); Don Brewer (backing vocals, drums, percussion); Mel Schacher (bass, backing vocals); Craig Frost (keyboards, backing vocals)
Producer: Frank Zappa
Engineer: Frank Zappa with assistant Mark Stebbeds (The Swamp); Michael Braunstein & Davey Moire (The Record Plant)

B-side
Out To Get You (3:58) (Don Brewer – Craig Frost) • Master #: (MC5639E) • STEREO
Recorded: June-July 1, 1976 at The Swamp, Parshallville, MI (basic tracks), and July 1976 at The Record Plant, Los Angeles, CA (vocal overdubs)
Personnel: Mark Farner (vocals, guitar); Don Brewer (vocals, drums, percussion); Mel Schacher (bass, backing vocals); Craig Frost (keyboards, backing vocals); Frank Zappa (guitar solos)
Producer: Frank Zappa
Engineer: Frank Zappa with assistant Mark Stebbeds (The Swamp); Michael Braunstein & Davey Moire (The Record Plant)

The second A-side from "Good Singin' Good Playin'" had all the hallmarks of Grand Funk's sound, but it was not considered strong enough to receive measurable radio play or record sales. "Just Couldn't Wait" did not appear on Billboard's singles chart after its release on November 1, 1976. Mark Farner did not have any ideas for the guitar solos on "Out To Get You," so he asked Frank if he could play something on it. The last overdub done for the album was by FZ on July 1, and he contributed not one, but three guitar solos which lasted about a minute each for the mostly instrumental track. One of the few lyrics in "Out To Get You" became the album title "Good Singin' Good Playin'." The single contained the first two Zappa solos in their entirety and faded in the middle of the third one. Promotional copies only featured the single edit on both sides, but this time, both sides were in stereo.

EMI International in Europe skipped this single and issued "Pass It Around"/ "Don't Let 'Em Take Your Gun" instead. The British release (EMI International INT 528) was supposed to be released on January 14, 1977, but it did not appear until two weeks later. It was also issued with a picture sleeve in Spain (EMI 10 C006-06.366), and the Spanish translations were "Circula"/ "No Les Dejes Que Te Quiten Tu Revólver." Tracks from the album were also on two various artists discs in Thailand, but those were unlawful releases. "Pass It Around" by Mark Farner and Don Brewer made more sense as a European single, but the full five-minute track was offered rather than an edited version. Farner's "Don't Let 'Em Take Your Gun" was the other song on the album which dealt with the US bicentennial. Its lyrics dealt with the pride that Americans should have, and that citizens should be prepared to bear arms to defend their nation. The song also referred to GFR's #1 hit "We're An American Band." While Zappa was at Mark Farner's farm, Mark taught Frank how to shoot a gun. Frank was thrilled when he aimed the gun at a can and hit it!

Don Brewer took keyboardist Craig Frost along with him for a vacation in Jamaica. After being repulsed by the reception they received there, they returned home within 12 hours. Their experience was captured by Brewer's song "Rubberneck." The song had a sense of humor and was nothing like the rest of the other songs recorded at that time. Zappa helped with the arrangement and provided his patented doo-wop vocals. The band decided to shelve the track. "Rubberneck" was included as a bonus track on the first (and only) CD reissue of the full album (Hip-O HIPD-40144; released January 12, 1999). The album masters of both A-sides were included on the "More Of The Best" CD (Rhino R2 70530; issued June 25, 1991), and "Can You Do It," "Pass It Around" and "Crossfire" were part of the three-CD anthology "Thirty Years Of Funk: 1969-1999" (Capitol/EMI 72434 99523 2; issued June 29, 1999).

Frank Zappa produced GFR's album like it was one of his own. "Good Singin' Good Playin'" was well-recorded, mixed and engineered, and it was a faithful document of tracks which flowed directly into each other. Despite everyone's best efforts, Grand Funk's sales slide continued. The album peaked at #52 in the US during its very brief chart run. The completion of the album was accompanied by the band's breakup. In 1981, Mark Farner and Don Brewer put together another lineup for two more studio albums. Since 1996, Don Brewer and bassist Mel Schacher have led the touring edition of GFR. With all the years that have passed, Grand Funk fans consider "Good Singin' Good Playin'" to be the band's best album from beginning to end.

After Grand Funk Railroad's breakup in 1976, Mark Farner started a solo career and the other three members formed the band Flint (named after their hometown). They signed a contract with the Columbia label. Flint recorded two albums, but only the first one was released in November 1978. Their debut album was self-titled and featured Frank Zappa's guitar on the tracks "Better You Than Me" and "You'll Never Be The Same."

* * *

FRANK ZAPPA: Find Her Finer/ Zoot Allures (7" 45 rpm single)
Released November 29, 1976 as Warner Bros. WBS 8296

A-side
Find Her Finer (3:18) (Frank Zappa) • Master #: (UCA 6495)VIS • STEREO
Recorded: April-June 1976 at The Record Plant, Los Angeles, CA
Personnel: Frank Zappa (lead vocals, guitar, bass, keyboards, synthesizer); Terry Bozzio (drums, backing vocals); Don Vliet (harmonica); Roy Estrada (backing vocals); Rubén Ladrón de Guevara (backing vocals); André Lewis (backing vocals)
Producer: Frank Zappa
Engineer: Michael Braunstein & Davey Moire

B-side
Zoot Allures (4:15) (Frank Zappa) • Master #: (UCA 6498)S • STEREO
Recorded: April-June 1976 at The Record Plant, Los Angeles, CA
Personnel: Frank Zappa (guitar); Terry Bozzio (drums); Dave Parlato (bass); Ruth Underwood (marimba); Lou Anne Neill (harp)
Producer: Frank Zappa
Engineer: Michael Braunstein & Davey Moire

The turbulence in Frank Zappa's career would lead to some changes in the way he did business. The band name The Mothers was retired after their European tour ended in mid-March 1976. Zappa retained Terry Bozzio on drums and vocals. Former band members Roy Estrada, André Lewis and Napoleon Murphy Brock were brought in to vocally sweeten studio tracks: Estrada and Lewis were used right away, and Brock contributed to later projects. Record Plant engineer Davey Moire also contributed vocally. There would be a six-month window until touring began again with a vastly different lineup of Zappa, Bozzio, Eddie Jobson (keyboards, violin), Patrick O'Hearn (bass), Ray White (guitar, vocals), and Lady Bianca (keyboards, vocals).

Starting in April 1976, studio recording for Zappa's next solo project was done in a completely different fashion – namely, by himself. Frank began with Rhythm Ace drum machine patterns and built up the tracks by recording nearly all of the instruments himself. Terry Bozzio recorded his drums using the Rhythm Ace tracks as a guide. The originally planned double album "Night Of The Iron Sausage" from these sessions was trimmed down to the single disc "Zoot Allures" released on October 29, 1976. The album covers featured the incomplete touring band (Zappa, Bozzio, Jobson and O'Hearn) before Ray White and Lady Bianca had been auditioned. Jobson and O'Hearn did not contribute to the single disc version.

FZ fans were accustomed to guitar-powered, full band arrangements on record. For the most part on "Zoot Allures," Frank replaced band interaction by a strong synthesizer presence. The title track and the live "Black Napkins" (from February 3, 1976 in Osaka, Japan) were the only exceptions, offering band performances rather than multiple Zappa layers and Bozzio replacements of drum machine tracks. Despite the recording methodology, the songs on "Zoot Allures" were designed to be played live. Many of the album tracks would have long performance histories. Zappa considered "Black Napkins" and "Zoot Allures" to be two of his three signature works ("Watermelon In Easter Hay" was the other).

The laid-back "Find Her Finer" was an unusual choice for a leadoff single. It was released exactly one month after the album. Frank's lyrics advised acting stupid to get the girl. Stupidity would be a frequent topic of future songs. Captain Beefheart's harmonica opened the track which featured FZ's upfront vocal and backing by Bozzio, Estrada, Rubén Ladrón de Guevara, and Lewis. "Find Her Finer" was faded early on the single, leading to a track 1:03 shorter than its album counterpart. The single did not attract substantial interest from radio or record buyers. Promotional copies had stereo and mono versions of the edited A-side. Stock copies are very scarce. Pre-2012 CDs had a 4:07 edit, and a different edit was on the "Understanding America" collection in 2012.

"Find Her Finer" debuted at the very end of the fall 1975 tour. The earliest live version to be released was from the early 1976 band on "FZ:OZ." The fall 1976 lineup with Bianca can be heard performing the song on "Philly '76." "Zappa In New York 40th Anniversary Deluxe Edition" sported two live versions by the expanded December 1976 band. The fall 1977 band only played the song once. A livelier arrangement of "Find Her Finer" was regularly played by the 1988 band and was represented on "The Best Band You Never Heard In Your Life."

The guitar showcase "Zoot Allures" was recorded by a one-off collection of musicians. Bassist Dave Parlato was in the Grand Wazoo and Petit Wazoo lineups between September and December 1972, and he was also in the Abnuceals Emuukha Electric Symphony Orchestra in September 1975. This was the first of his many Zappa album appearances. Also debuting on a Zappa album was harpist Lou Anne Neill. She was an Abnuceals member and appeared on numerous FZ albums. Completing the instrumentation were Ruth Underwood (marimba) and drummer Terry Bozzio. The single master was the same as the album mix, and the studio track also appeared on the albums "Frank Zappa Plays The Music Of Frank Zappa" and "ZAPPAtite."

The development of "Zoot Allures" started off very innocently in 1974. The chord progression of the song was played during a performance of "Don't You Ever Wash That Thing?" on September 25 at Konserthuset, Göteborg, Sweden. The same chordal pattern was played during "Dupree's Paradise" at the early Halloween show at The Felt Forum in New York City, the late show at the Orpheum Theater in Boston, MA on November 9, and as part of an improvisation at Civic Center Arena (St. Paul, MN) on November 27. The fall 1975 lineup was the first to perform the fully realized "Zoot Allures," and an example of their work was made available on "Joe's Menage."

The early 1976 band represented "Zoot Allures" on "FZ:OZ," "Stage, Vol. 3" (only the first part from Osaka, Japan on February 3, 1976), and a Tokyo, Japan performance from two days later accompanied the studio version on "Frank Zappa Plays The Music Of Frank Zappa." "Zoot Allures" on this tour consisted of three parts: the part before the solo (heard on the just mentioned "FZ:OZ" and "Stage, Vol. 3"), the solo section matching the studio recording, and an experimental section that became "Ship Ahoy" (known best for its inclusion on "Shut Up 'N Play Yer Guitar Some More," "Läther," "QuAUDIOPHILIAc," and the aforementioned Tokyo version on "FZ Plays The Music Of FZ").

The fall 1977 lineup quoted "Zoot Allures" within "Wild Love" at the Uptown Theater in Kansas City, MO (November 11). "Zoot Allures" was rehearsed at the end of the years 1977 and 1978, but it was not played during the 1978 or 1979 tours. It was only played once during the spring 1980 tour (April 20 late show; Atlanta, GA), and was soundchecked on May 31 (Drammen, Norway). During the August 12 rehearsal for the fall 1981 tour, Zappa tried and failed to incorporate "Zoot Allures" into "The Illinois Enema Bandit."

What was successful was FZ's usage of his "Zoot Allures" guitar solos in different contexts. The November 17, 1981 solo from New York City was incorporated into "Truck Driver Divorce" on the 1984 album "Them Or Us." The "Guitar" collection extracted two "Zoot Allures" solos using different titles: the December 7, 1981 solo (Salt Lake City, UT) was called "Chalk Pie," and the May 21, 1982 solo (Cologne, Germany) was entitled "When No One Was No One." The aforementioned "Stage Vol. 3" edition used an edit of Osaka (February 3, 1976) as its front part and led into the guitar solo from Cap D'agde, France (May 30, 1982). "Halloween 81" used a complete take, and the Mother's Day digital download in 2014 (discussed below) issued a composite from three 1982 performances.

"Does Humor Belong In Music?" contained different composite versions of "Zoot Allures" from 1984 on the video and CD editions. "Zoot Allures" performances from the fall 1984 and early 1988 tours have not been represented yet, but the spring 1988 tour can be heard on "The Best Band You Never Heard In Your Life."

* * *

FRANK ZAPPA: Disco Boy/ Ms. Pinky (7" 45 rpm single)
Released March 7, 1977 as Warner Bros. WBS 8342

A-side
Disco Boy (5:28) (Frank Zappa) • Master #: (UCA 6499)S • STEREO
Recorded: April-June 1976 at The Record Plant, Los Angeles, CA
Personnel: Frank Zappa (lead vocals, guitar, bass, keyboards, synthesizer); Terry Bozzio (drums, backing vocals); Davey Moire (backing vocals); André Lewis (backing vocals); Roy Estrada (backing vocals); Linda Sue "Sparky" Parker (backing vocals)
Producer: Frank Zappa
Engineer: Michael Braunstein & Davey Moire

B-side
Ms. Pinky (3:49) (Frank Zappa) • Master #: (UCA 6494)S • STEREO
Recorded: April-June 1976 at The Record Plant, Los Angeles, CA
Personnel: Frank Zappa (lead vocals, guitar, bass, synthesizer); Terry Bozzio (drums); Don Vliet (harmonica); Ruth Underwood (synthesizer); Roy Estrada (backing vocals); unknown (opening scream)
Producer: Frank Zappa
Engineer: Michael Braunstein & Davey Moire

The second single from "Zoot Allures" was a close examination of human behavior. The strange things that people do were frequently covered in Frank Zappa's previous material, but his satirical views of current behavior had more of a laser focus. The A-side "Disco Boy" was based on examples of male vanity that Frank saw in a Danish bathroom. These guys didn't go to the bathroom to "go doody" (defecate) – they spent a lot of time trying to look perfect in the bathroom mirror before going out and finding some female action on the dance floor. The use of a word like "doody" indicates the childish nature of these so-called men. At the end of the song, the disco boy lost the girl he wanted to his friend and he had to resort to masturbation to satisfy his carnal desires until he repeated his bathroom routine the next night.

"Disco Boy" was clearly a rock-based track with a strong twin vocal presence from Zappa and backing from Terry Bozzio, Davey Moire, André Lewis, Roy Estrada, and Linda Sue "Sparky" Parker (Miss Sparky from The GTO's). Lyrical references were made to KC And The Sunshine Band's "Get Down Tonight" ("do a little dance") and Chicken Delight, a fast-food restaurant chain that opened in 1952 along with its main competitor Kentucky Fried Chicken (now known as KFC). Chicken Delight fell behind as KFC's greater attention to food quality and service captured the vast majority of the chicken market.

The Rhythm Ace drum machine track on "Disco Boy" was retained in the final mix, unlike the rest of the album. Pre-2012 CDs deleted the three-second Rhythm Ace intro, a seven-second segment at the 3:00 mark, and faded the track eight seconds early. These album edits were first made when "Zoot Allures" was included as part of "The Old Masters Box Three." The original "Zoot Allures" LP and the 45 have 16 guitar riff repeats at the end and are the same length. The edit was repeated on "Strictly Commercial." An edited, overdubbed remix was part of the "Have I Offended Someone?" collection, and an even shorter edit without overdubs was on "Understanding America."

The single attracted some attention from more adventurous radio stations and reached #105 in the US. Promotional copies had stereo and mono mixes of the A-side. Stock copies are now rare, even though a good number were manufactured. The next commercial single that Zappa would release, "Dancin' Fool," explored the disco phenomenon with FZ as the title character. Despite disco's worldwide popularity, "Disco Boy" was not a regular single release in any other country. An unusual Italian promo 45 (Warner Bros./Atlantic Promo 031) was an unusual release, with "Disco Boy" on one side and Herbie Mann's "Bird Walk" (an Atlantic release) on the flipside.

The early 1976 band was the first to play "Disco Boy" live, but it was played instrumentally after the solo of "Chunga's Revenge." Six performance by the fall 1977 lineup were made available on "Halloween 77" in 2017. The October 30 take was first issued on the "Baby Snakes" video and soundtrack (the CD and the 2012 complete film soundtrack download edition), and "Son Of Cheep Thrills." The performance on Halloween night quoted "Disco Boy" during the track "Halloween Audience Participation" and was first issued in the "Baby Snakes" film before its inclusion on the 2012 soundtrack download and "Halloween 77." "Disco Boy" by the early 1978 band was represented on "Hammersmith Odeon." A late August/ early September 1978 rehearsal in Munich, Germany included a version of "I'm On Duty" which quoted "Disco Boy." "Stage, Vol. 4" had a composite of two German "Disco Boy" performances from June 1982. The 1988 band performed the song, but none of their "Disco Boy" tracks have been officially issued.

Finnish autograph collector Erkki "Uncle Eki" Rapo gave Frank Zappa a copy of Kalle, a pornographic magazine from his homeland. This issue of Kalle had an advertisement for a sex toy called Ms. Pinky. Zappa asked his bodyguard John Smothers if he could locate a Ms. Pinky toy while they were in Amsterdam, Holland. The story of "Ms. Pinky" was captured in the track "Lonely Person Devices" on "Stage, Vol. 6." It was an introduction to "Black Napkins." In the "Baby Snakes" video, a larger version of Ms. Pinky was on hand.

Before its studio recording, "Ms. Pinky" was instrumentally performed by the early 1976 band following the third "Zoot Allures" segment "Ship Ahoy." A completely different but incomplete offshoot of "Ms. Pinky" (informally titled "Song For Pinky") was performed once on March 13, 1976 in Lugano, Switzerland.

On record, "Ms. Pinky" started with a scream that was most likely from the "recreational activities" recorded for "The Torture Never Stops." A heavy synthesizer riff and Frank's dual vocals drove "Ms. Pinky" along. Zappa was accompanied by Terry Bozzio, Captain Beefheart on harmonica, Ruth Underwood on synthesizer, and Roy Estrada on falsetto vocals. Pre-2012 CDs were faded nine seconds early. As far as the single was concerned, it was shorter than the album, as the single repeated the line "you can poot it…you can shoot it" five times instead of six on the LP.

Thematically, "Ms. Pinky" is a lonely person device like "Magic Fingers" (from "200 Motels") or "Little Rubber Girl" ("Stage, Vol. 4"). Its use of pickup lines is similar to "Stick It Out," "What Kind Of Girl Do You Think We Are?," "Dancin' Fool," and "Artificial Rhonda." In the case of "Artificial Rhonda" on "Thing-Fish," that cut used the backing track of "Ms. Pinky" with overdubs.

The spring and summer 1980 bands were the first to perform the complete "Ms. Pinky" in concert. The fall 1980 lineup's takes of "Ms. Pinky" are on "Stage, Vol. 6" (1992) and "Buffalo" (2007). The 1981 band rehearsed "Ms. Pinky" but did not play it, and it was only played on the first date of the spring 1982 tour (May 5 at Vejlby-Risskov Hallen, Århus, Denmark). "Ms. Pinky" was also rehearsed in 1987, but it was not played during the '88 tour.

Frank Zappa did a phone interview for the syndicated Presbyterian radio program "What's It All About?". Producer/host Bill Huie was the director of TV, Radio, and Audio-Visuals (TRAV) for the southern branch of the Presbyterian Church in Atlanta, GA. Huie's approach for this subscription series of stereo 45 rpm records was to present musicians talking about faith (or lack of it), while a selection of their music played in the background. Each artist on "What's It All About?" had one side of the record. The Zappa program dealt with the freedom he enjoyed in doing things his way, and how he related to other people and musicians.

The same Zappa "What's It All About?" program (4:55 in length) was released on four different records. The first was program 418 from April 1978 (master # MA 1157; Firefall was program 417), followed by program 486 from August 1979 (master # MA 1755; Dolly Parton was program 485), program 548 from November 1980 (master # MA 1824; David Bowie was program 547), and program 906 from September 1981 (master # MA-2903; David Bowie was program 907). This last record appears to be the last edition in the "What's It All About?" series. The music segments used on all these programs were "Road Ladies," "Would You Go All The Way?," "Rudy Wants To Buy Yez A Drink" and "Transylvania Boogie" (all from "Chunga's Revenge"), and "Call Any Vegetable" from "Just Another Band From L.A.". All of this music was out of date by the time of the first program in 1978, and the tunes were really out of date by the last airing in 1981.

After Zappa exposed the late 1976 band to New York City's gay nightlife for "research," Frank Zappa made some recordings of grout (voice segments used in-between songs) at The Record Plant in early March 1977. The Gilded Grape and The Pleasure Chest were two of the places they went to. Similar to "Lumpy Gravy," Terry Bozzio, bassist Patrick O'Hearn and engineer/vocalist Davey Moire were recorded underneath a grand piano covered with a blanket and the piano's sustain pedal was depressed. The majority of the recorded grout involved a conversation about leather which reflected their recent club experiences in New York. Grout extracts would appear on numerous Zappa releases moving forward.

With all the legal stuff going on, Frank Zappa's creativity went into overdrive. Zappa would finally reemerge in September 1978 with a new record label (Zappa Records), a new distributor (Phonogram), and a new album called "Martian Love Secrets." The album would be renamed "Sheik Yerbouti" with striking cover photos of FZ.

DiscReet issued "Zappa In New York" in March 1978, and "Studio Tan" followed six months later. They sneaked out "Studio Tan" in mid-January 1979, and they answered "Sheik Yerbouti" with "Orchestral Favorites" in early May 1979. The legal matters ended in 1982 when Frank received a large settlement.

* * *

FRANK ZAPPA: Sheik Yerbouti "Clean Cuts" (some copies list "Limited Zappa Edition") (12" 33 1/3 rpm promo sampler single)
Released March 5, 1979 as Zappa MK-78

A-side – Track 1
Baby Snakes (1:50) (Frank Zappa) • Master #: MK-78 A • STEREO
Recorded live on January 25, 1978 at Hammersmith Odeon, London, England (basic tracks), August 7-8, 1978 at Cherokee Recording Studios, Los Angeles, CA (keyboard and vocal overdubs), and August 16, 1978 at The Village Recorders, Los Angeles, CA (vocal overdubs)
Personnel: Frank Zappa (lead vocals, lead guitar); Adrian Belew (rhythm guitar); Tommy Mars (lead vocals, keyboards); Peter Wolf (keyboards); Patrick O'Hearn (bass); Terry Bozzio (drums); Ed Mann (percussion)
Producer: Frank Zappa
Engineer: Peter Henderson (Hammersmith Odeon); Joe Chiccarelli (Cherokee and The Village Recorders)

A-side – Track 2
Tryin' To Grow A Chin (3:32) (Frank Zappa) • Master #: MK-78 A • STEREO
Recorded live on January 27, 1978 at Hammersmith Odeon, London, England (basic tracks), and August 16, 1978 at The Village Recorders, Los Angeles, CA (overdubs)
Personnel: Frank Zappa (lead guitar); Adrian Belew (rhythm guitar); Tommy Mars (keyboards); Peter Wolf (keyboards); Patrick O'Hearn (bass); Terry Bozzio (drums, lead vocal); Ed Mann (percussion); Napoleon Murphy Brock (backing vocals); André Lewis (backing vocals); Randy Thornton (backing vocals); Davey Moire (backing vocals)
Producer: Frank Zappa
Engineer: Peter Henderson (Hammersmith Odeon); Joe Chiccarelli (The Village Recorders)

A-side – Track 3
City Of Tiny Lites (5:30) (Frank Zappa) • Master #: MK-78 A • STEREO
Recorded live on January 27, 1978 at Hammersmith Odeon, London, England (basic tracks), and August 16, 1978 at The Village Recorders, Los Angeles, CA (overdubs)
Personnel: Frank Zappa (lead guitar, co-lead vocal); Adrian Belew (rhythm guitar, auto horn, co-lead vocals); Tommy Mars (keyboards); Peter Wolf (keyboards); Patrick O'Hearn (bass); Terry Bozzio (drums); Ed Mann (percussion)
Producer: Frank Zappa
Engineer: Peter Henderson (Hammersmith Odeon); Joe Chiccarelli (The Village Recorders)

B-side – Track 1
Dancin' Fool (3:43) (Frank Zappa) • Master #: MK-78 B • STEREO
Recorded live on February 28, 1978 at Hammersmith Odeon, London, England (basic tracks), August 16, 21 and late August 1978 at The Village Recorders, Los Angeles, CA (overdubs), and 1969-August 21, 1978 audio collage from various sources ("The Revenge Of The Knick Knack People" extract)
Personnel: Frank Zappa (lead guitar, lead vocals); Adrian Belew (rhythm guitar, backing vocals); Tommy Mars (keyboards, backing vocals); Peter Wolf (keyboards); Patrick O'Hearn (bass, backing vocals); Terry Bozzio (drums, backing vocals); Ed Mann (percussion, backing vocals); Napoleon Murphy Brock (backing vocals); André Lewis (backing vocals); Randy Thornton (backing vocals); Davey Moire (backing vocals)
Producer: Frank Zappa
Engineer: Peter Henderson (Hammersmith Odeon); Joe Chiccarelli (The Village Recorders)

B-side – Track 2
Flakes (6:41) (Frank Zappa) • Master #: MK-78 B • STEREO
Recorded live on January 25, 1978 at Hammersmith Odeon, London, England (basic tracks), and August 15-16 and August 21, 1978 at The Village Recorders, Los Angeles, CA (Mann overdubs: 15th-16th, Terry Bozzio overdubs: 21st)
Personnel: Frank Zappa (lead guitar, lead vocal); Adrian Belew (rhythm guitar, lead vocal, harmonica); Tommy Mars (keyboards); Peter Wolf (keyboards); Patrick O'Hearn (bass); Terry Bozzio (drums); Ed Mann (percussion); Napoleon Murphy Brock (backing vocals); André Lewis (backing vocals); Randy Thornton (backing vocals); Davey Moire (backing vocals)
Producer: Frank Zappa
Engineer: Peter Henderson (Hammersmith Odeon); Joe Chiccarelli (The Village Recorders)

B-side – Track 3A
What Ever Happened To All The Fun In The World (0:33) (Frank Zappa) • Master #: MK-78 B • STEREO
Recorded: October 1967 at Apostolic Studios, New York, NY (Cuneo voice), January 28 – February 5, 1971 at Pinewood Studios, London, England ("I Have Seen The Pleated Gazelle" extracts), and March 1977 at The Record Plant, Los Angeles, CA (Bozzio, O'Hearn and Moire voices)
Personnel: Terry Bozzio (voice, percussion); Patrick O'Hearn (voice); Davey Moire (voice); Louis "The Turkey" Cuneo (voice); Ruth Underwood (orchestral drum set); The Royal Philharmonic Orchestra – Elgar Howarth, conductor
Producer: Frank Zappa
Engineer: Dick Kunc (Apostolic), Bob Auger (Pinewood), Davey Moire (The Record Plant)

B-side – Track 3B
Rat Tomago (5:15) (Frank Zappa) • Master #: MK-78 B • STEREO
Recorded live on February 15, 1978 at Deutschlandhalle, Berlin, Germany
Personnel: Frank Zappa (lead guitar); Adrian Belew (rhythm guitar); Tommy Mars (keyboards); Peter Wolf (keyboards); Patrick O'Hearn (bass); Terry Bozzio (drums); Ed Mann (percussion)
Producer: Frank Zappa
Engineer: Claus Wiedemann

The construction of "Sheik Yerbouti" was the polar opposite of "Zoot Allures." It was mainly derived from live band recordings with numerous layers of overdubs, and the March 1977 grout connected them all. Live tracks came from the Hammersmith Odeon in London, the Palladium in New York City, and xenochrony from various sources. Overdubs were done in Los Angeles at Cherokee Recording Studios and The Village

Recorders, and in Burbank, CA at Kendun Recorders. The pronunciation of "Sheik Yerbouti" was designed to make fun of KC And The Sunshine Band's 1976 hit "(Shake, Shake, Shake) Shake Your Booty."

The promotional offerings for Phonogram's distributed labels were low-budget affairs with black and white covers and simplistic graphics. The "Clean Cuts" edition of "Sheik Yerbouti" was no exception. A handful of copies of this promo (retitled "Limited Zappa Edition" with a white cover) were sent overseas to promote the album on foreign radio stations. The "Limited Zappa Edition" record labels listed the song titles, but did not have any logos to disguise the fact that Phonogram actually pressed the disc for CBS Records' use in other countries. Despite their relative frugality when compared to Warner Bros., Phonogram's promos had a great effect on Zappa's sales.

The first "Clean Cuts" single began with "Baby Snakes." This very quick song was rehearsed on October 30, 1977 in front of the cameras for the "Baby Snakes" film, and it was also rehearsed on December 29. Its first live performance was on the last day of 1977. The rehearsal was released in that film, with the audio first available on the 2012 soundtrack download. The basis of the "Sheik Yerbouti" version was the Hammersmith Odeon performance on January 25, 1978. Frank Zappa and Tommy Mars double-tracked their vocal parts, with Mars adding various keyboard parts. In between the first and second verses, Frank bent his vocal note down and then up again for the word "snakes." In the past, Frank would have slowed the tape down, but it was done in real time on this occasion. However, the vocals were sped up for the 0:57-1:00 reference to the audio/video/medical standards organization SMPTE – "Society of Motion Picture & Television Engineers." "Baby Snakes" was also in the film, the 1983 like-named album, and the film soundtrack download. On this record, as on "Sheik Yerbouti," "Baby Snakes" ran into "Tryin' To Grow A Chin" without any space between the tracks.

A February 28, 1978 live London take of "Baby Snakes" was released in 2010 on "Hammersmith Odeon," and the special Munich performance of the song during the summer of that year was on "Beat The Boots II: At The Circus." "Baby Snakes" was rehearsed in August 1978, but it was not played again.

The energetic "Tryin' To Grow A Chin" was in development since the fall of 1975. It had lots of reference points packed into 3½ minutes. This January 27, 1978 Hammersmith Odeon track used a cadre of studio backing vocalists (Napoleon Murphy Brock, André Lewis, Lewis' friend Randy Thornton and Davey Moire) to accompany Terry Bozzio's lead. The "Hey Joe" bass riff was in full evidence, as was the 0:30-0:40 quote of The Velveteens' aforementioned "Dog Patch Creeper" which followed the lines "Lord, he's my next of kin – he's a Mex-i-kin." A passing reference to former MOI bassist Jeff Simmons at 0:46 was followed by The Who's "Baba O'Riley" riff (1:08-1:19) and the twin lead guitars and chords from The Eagles' "Hotel California" (1:19-1:33). The "Hotel California" quote was an addition to the original "Chin" arrangement, and that Eagles song incidentally used the same chords as Jethro Tull's "We Used To Know" from their "Stand Up" album. Bozzio's "get the picture?" line was previously used in "Billy The Mountain" and would later appear in the "Joe's Garage" arrangement of "A Token Of My Extreme." Another line, "one more time for the world" was adapted from Love's "No Matter What You Do" from their 1966 debut LP.

"Tryin' To Grow A Chin" was normally followed by "City Of Tiny Lites" in a live setting, and that sequence was duplicated on "Sheik Yerbouti" and this "Clean Cuts" edition. The October 29, 1975 gig at the Palace Theatre in Waterbury, CT was a workshop for "Tryin' To Grow A Chin." The song's lyrics were spoken during "Black Napkins" at the early show, and the late show performance of "Chunga's Revenge" included "Sy Borg," the chord progression of "Chin" and The Safaris' "Wipe Out." The Halloween 1975 concert at the Felt Forum in New York included "Chin" within "Any Downers?". Three nights later, the Spectrum Theater gig in

Philadelphia included the chords of "Chin" and "Sy Borg" as part of "Zoot Allures."

The first release of the full "Tryin' To Grow A Chin" was in the 2006 birthday bundle. It was a Sydney, Australia performance from January 20, 1976. "Philly '76" featured "Chin" from October 29, 1976, and "Läther" had a London take of the song from February 16, 1977. Six October 1977 versions of "Chin" from New York were part of the "Halloween 77" collection. Out of those six, the Halloween night version had been previously issued on "Stage, Vol. 6." "Hammersmith Odeon" included the February 28, 1978 recording.

When Zappa's childhood friend Denny Walley came into the band during the summer of 1978, Walley took over Bozzio's vocal role for "Tryin' To Grow A Chin." Denny's legendary inability to remember its lyrics led to many humorous moments for the band and for fans. Examples of Walley singing "Chin" with the early 1979 band can be heard on "Stage, Vol. 1" (the late show on February 18) and "Beat The Boots I: Anyway The Wind Blows" (February 24). "Tryin' To Grow A Chin" was quoted within "City Of Tiny Lites" at the Civic Arena Bowl in St. Paul, MN on November 18, 1980. The fall 1981 band played "Chin," with "Halloween 81" being the first representative sample of that band's take on the song.

"City Of Tiny Lites" was a live staple for Zappa's bands from its debut in October 1976 to the 1988 band. Ray White was the first to sing it with FZ, as evidenced by the fall 1976 band takes on "Philly '76" and "Beat The Boots II: Conceptual Continuity." Adrian Belew took over the lead vocal mantle after Ray White's departure in the first quarter of 1977. "Halloween 77" contains six complete live versions of "City Of Tiny Lites." Parts of the October 30 and 31 shows were in the "Baby Snakes" movie and soundtrack download. The performance from the night before the "Sheik Yerbouti" take was part of the 2010 birthday bundle, and "Hammersmith Odeon" housed a February 28, 1978 version.

For the "Sheik Yerbouti" take of "City Of Tiny Lites" on this "Clean Cuts" edition, Adrian Belew made the song his own. Belew squeaked a miniature auto horn in response to the lyric at 0:28-0:30 and 4:00-4:01. This version went into "Dancin' Fool" on the album, but this disc faded the track at 5:28 (just before its end) for radio programmers. Frank sang the bridge vocal leading into a guitar solo. The expansiveness of the solos would be increased in time. Fans consider the fall 1980 solos on "City Of Tiny Lites" to be the peak of the song's development.

Denny Walley took over the lead vocal on "City Of Tiny Lites" in the summer of 1978 and throughout 1979. Examples of his vocal abilities on the tune are on "Beat The Boots I: Saarbrücken 1978" and "Beat The Boots I: Anyway The Wind Blows." Both shows on March 31, 1979 were the sources of the "City Of Tiny Lites" Zappa guitar solo segments which were xenochronized into "Outside Now" on "Joe Garage Acts II & III." Parts of FZ's solo from that night's late show were also xenochronized for "Keep It Greasey" on the same "Joe's Garage" double LP, and the full solo was used for the "Guitar" album and billed as "Outside Now (Original Solo)."

Ray White returned to the band in early 1980 and became the "City Of Tiny Lites" vocalist once again. The fall 1980 band can be heard playing the song on "Buffalo." Two guitar solos from the song were extracted for other collections. The solo from October 30, 1980 was called "Another Variation Of The Formerly Secret" in the 2011 birthday bundle. The best-known solo from that band was called "Variations On The Carlos Santana Secret Chord Progression" on "Shut Up 'N Play Yer Guitar Some More." The Halloween 1981 take of the song was on the video "The Torture Never Stops." The Salt Lake City, UT solo from December 7, 1981 was first used on "The Guitar World According To Frank Zappa" under the title "Things That Look Like Meat." A longer version of that solo with a synthesizer overdub was included on the "Guitar" collection.

The summer 1982 band can be heard performing "City Of Tiny Lites" in different forms. The June 24, 1982 solo from Zurich, Switzerland was called "That Ol' G Minor Thing Again" on "Guitar." "Stage, Vol. 5" had a composite version of the entire song from London, Cap d'Agde, France, and Bolzano, Italy.

The only released remnant of the 1984 band performing "City Of Tiny Lites" is the opening fragment at the end of "Tinsel Town Rebellion" on the "Does Humor Belong In Music?" video. "Make A Jazz Noise Here" includes a full 1988 performance on the song as well as a quote within "Fire And Chains." The April 16, 1988 guitar solo from Brighton, England was called "Scratch & Sniff" on the album "Trance-Fusion." Bobby Martin was the vocalist for "City Of Tiny Lites" during the 1988 tour, as evidenced on "Zappa '88: The Last U.S. Show."

Side two of the "Clean Cuts" edition opened with the classic "Dancin' Fool." Its basic track was from the February 28, 1978 Hammersmith Odeon show. Based on the same environment as "Disco Boy," "Dancin' Fool" dealt with the dancing aspect of the disco lifestyle rather than the primping and the preening of the disco darlings. Frank Zappa double-tracked his vocals, and the same quartet of backing vocalists on "Tryin' To Grow A Chin" were present here. From the 3:14 mark to its 3:41 end, Zappa spoke some cliched pick-up lines over the repeated Japanese phrase "Ki-ni-shinai" (meaning "don't worry about it") and part of the "Läther" track "Revenge Of The Knick Knack People." "Revenge Of The Knick Knack People" was finished on August 21, 1978 at The Village Recorders in L.A., so the completion of "Dancin' Fool" must have taken place just after that date. This particular promo record is unusual in that the grout of Patrick O'Hearn saying "Heh heh heh ye-yes!" (3:41-3:43 on the album) is not present, as the track ends abruptly. That grout was originally included in the "Läther" track "Duck Duck Goose."

"Dancin' Fool" was given a nervous premiere on October 30, 1977 in New York. It can be found on "Halloween 77." The only other time that "Dancin' Fool" was played by the fall 1977 band was on New Year's Eve. "Hammersmith Odeon" is the only released example of "Dancin' Fool" from early 1978. The August-October '78 band is well represented on "Beat The Boots II: At The Circus," "Beat The Boots I: Saarbrücken 1978," "Chicago '78," and the "Saturday Night Live" TV appearance (a "Halloween" video track and in lesser quality audio on "Beat The Boots III: Disc Six"). Most people who were not familiar with Frank Zappa first took notice of "Dancin' Fool" through its "SNL" performance on October 21, 1978.

Every band until 1988 had their opportunity to play "Dancin' Fool," but its regularity decreased as time went on. The February-April 1979 lineup represented the song on "Beat The Boots I: Anyway The Wind Blows." The "Buffalo" album included the fall 1980 band doing the song on its own and with the vamp behind "The 'Real World' Thematic Extrapolations." "Dancin' Fool" was also on "Halloween 81." Except for the outro, the "Dancin' Fool" version from the July 1, 1982 gig was on "Stage, Vol. 5." The video "Does Humor Belong In Music?" had an NYC Pier performance from August 26, 1984. More details about the commercial single editions of "Dancin' Fool" follow in the next listings.

"Flakes" was FZ's admission that California was (and still is) loaded with lazy, self-centered people that never follow through with anything. The basic track came from yet another Hammersmith Odeon gig, this time from January 25, 1978. A lot of vocal and instrumental touch-ups were done in the middle of that summer. The same quartet of backing vocalists (Brock, Lewis, Thornton and Moire) was used again. The fall 1977 band debuted "Flakes," and five versions from that time can be heard on "Halloween 77." At that point, the song did not have all the vocal and instrumental elements which ended up on "Sheik Yerbouti."

It is well known that Frank Zappa could not play guitar and sing at the same time. Frank made the mistake of doing both when showing "Flakes" to Adrian Belew. Adrian thought that FZ sounded like a sick folk singer, so Belew worked in a complete Bob Dylan impression with harmonica (1:23-2:38) to contrast Zappa's lead vocal. During 1:46-1:48 of that section, Frank referred to Mandies, British slang for Mandrax, the UK brand name for methaqualone and known as Quaalude in the US. A 3:09-3:14 reference was made to the 1977 Pillsbury Frosting Supreme TV commercial that told us that their frosting was so creamy that it could be applied with a paper knife. Another Belew contribution was the pair of comical "one-two-three-four" countoffs (4:30-4:32 and 5:07-5:09) in the "Sheik Yerbouti" version and subsequent arrangements. Frank's reference to unions on "Flakes" was also present on "Rudy Wants To Buy Yez A Drink," "Lonesome Cowboy Burt," "Stick Together," and "Yo Cats."

On "Sheik Yerbouti," "Flakes" went right into "Broken Hearts Are For Assholes," which also had a "one-two-three-four" countoff. On this "Clean Cuts" record, "Flakes" fades at 6:41 to play this track separately. The "Sheik Yerbouti" basic track of "Flakes" was offered with different overdub components in the "Baby Snakes" film and download soundtrack under the title "The Way The Air Smells…". The February 28, 1978 Hammersmith take of "Flakes" was on "Hammersmith Odeon." After Adrian Belew left the band, Ike Willis sang "Flakes." The September 3, 1978 version with Ike can be heard on "Beat The Boots I: Saarbrücken 1978." The fall 1980 band played "Flakes" regularly, but nothing from that band has been released. The Halloween 1981 lineup with Ed Mann's "Flakes" vocal is on "Halloween 81" and the videos "The Torture Never Stops" and "The Dub Room Special!". The May-July 1982 lineup has not been represented on disc, especially since it only performed "Flakes" twice.

The third band of side two consisted of "What Ever Happened To All The Fun In The World" and "Rat Tomago." "What Ever…" consisted of grout and music fragments from three different time periods: 1967, 1971, and 1977. The first three seconds featured Davey Moire speaking the track title, followed by a leather conversation between Terry Bozzio and Patrick O'Hearn and laughing from Louis "The Turkey" Cuneo. Interspersed with the conversation were two sped up clips of The Royal Philharmonic Orchestra playing "I Have Seen The Pleated Gazelle" from "200 Motels." "Punky's Whips" on "Läther" had the same first three seconds of "What Ever…," and the same album had the rest of this edited conversation at the conclusion of "Filthy Habits."

The grout went right into "Rat Tomago," as it did on "Sheik Yerbouti." "Rat Tomago" (named by Ahmet Zappa) was an edited, four-track Berlin, Germany guitar solo from "The Torture Never Stops" from February 15, 1978. "Torture" was regularly performed from April 1975 to June 1988 except for 1979 and 1982. Unlike its album presentation, "Rat Tomago" was featured on this record without the Patrick O'Hearn grout ("Oh-ooh-h, listen to him go!") at its end. "Rat Tomago" was a Grammy nominee for "Best Rock Instrumental Performance," but it lost to the star-powered "Rockestra Theme" by Paul McCartney's group Wings. "Rat Tomago" was repeated on "Zappa Picks By Jon Fishman Of Phish."

Frank Zappa was told that "Sheik Yerbouti" sold more than 1.6 million copies by 1992, so it can be said that this "Clean Cuts" edition did its job very well. It peaked at #21 in the US.

* * *

FRANK ZAPPA: Dancin' Fool/ Baby Snakes (7" 45 rpm single)
Released April 2, 1979 as Zappa Z-10
FRANK ZAPPA: Dancin' Fool/ Dancin' Fool (12" 33 1/3 rpm promo single)
Released April 23, 1979 as Zappa MK-83
FRANK ZAPPA: Dancin' Fool/ Baby Snakes (12" 33 1/3 rpm single)
Released April 27, 1979 as CBS 7261 (The Netherlands)

A-side
Dancin' Fool (7" – 3:45; both 12" editions – 6:15) (Frank Zappa) • Master #: 7" – 2-55095; 12" – none • STEREO
Recorded live on February 28, 1978 at Hammersmith Odeon, London, England (basic tracks), August 16, 21 and late August 1978 at The Village Recorders, Los Angeles, CA (overdubs), 1969-August 21, 1978 audio collage from various sources ("The Revenge Of The Knick Knack People" extract), and March 1977 at The Record Plant, Los Angeles, CA (O'Hearn voice)
Personnel: Frank Zappa (lead guitar, lead vocals); Adrian Belew (rhythm guitar, backing vocals); Tommy Mars (keyboards, backing vocals); Peter Wolf (keyboards); Patrick O'Hearn (bass, backing vocals, ending voice); Terry Bozzio (drums, backing vocals); Ed Mann (percussion, backing vocals); Napoleon Murphy Brock (backing vocals); André Lewis (backing vocals); Randy Thornton (backing vocals); Davey Moire (backing vocals)
Producer: Frank Zappa
Engineer: Peter Henderson (Hammersmith Odeon); Joe Chiccarelli (The Village Recorders); Davey Moire (The Record Plant); various (audio collage recordings)

B-side
Baby Snakes (7" – 1:50; Dutch 12" – 1:45) (Frank Zappa) • Master #: 7" – 2-55025; 12" – none • STEREO
see previous single

It was clear before "Sheik Yerbouti" was released that "Dancin' Fool" would be a single A-side. The subject of "Dancin' Fool" was Frank himself, and he spent the whole song poking fun at his inadequacies in the disco world. Like "Disco Boy," "Dancin' Fool" had a heavy guitar presence at its start. It was not what you would have expected for a disco-themed tune. The song's third line "one of my legs is shorter than the other" referred to the Rainbow Theatre incident in late 1971. The choruses of "Dancin' Fool" featured full-bodied vocals with a hint of humor and Zappa's typically eclectic instrumentation. The bridge section of "The beat goes on and I'm so wrong" started out in a dissonant fashion but was smartly built up into the chorus with the words "I may be totally wrong but I'm a…" crammed into a short time frame. At 2:05, FZ says "Yowsah, Yowsah, Yowsah," which made fun of Chic's dance hit "Dance, Dance, Dance (Yowsah, Yowsah, Yowsah)." Chic revived 1920s jazz violinist Ben Bernie's phrase in their song, and Frank put the phrase into his own context. The following chorus led into another "I may be totally wrong" section, this time with Ed Mann's percussion only.

The pick-up line section of "Dancin' Fool" with the aforementioned "Ki-ni-shinai" vocals and "Revenge Of The Knick Knack People" backing spanned the 3:14-3:41 segment of the track. Zappa's mention of "Looking For Mr. Goodbar" (3:21-3:22) referred to the 1977 film about a woman's ill-fated search for love in nightclubs. The rest of Frank's pick-up lines dealt with the empty comments that desperate disco guys used to feign interest in a woman's ethnicity, religion, manicure, or zodiac sign. This section concluded with Frank's last line, "Your place or mine?" and the previously discussed grout from Patrick O'Hearn. Similar pick-up lines can be heard in "Stick It Out," "What Kind Of Girl Do You Think We Are?," and "Artificial Rhonda."

People responded strongly to Zappa's self-deprecating humor and the song's depiction of silliness of the disco lifestyle. Album-oriented radio stations in the US went all-in for "Dancin' Fool," but there was some resistance from Top 40 radio stations who only played "serious" disco songs. That resistance led to a #45 single placing in Billboard, which was Zappa's best showing at the time. Like "Rat Tomago," "Dancin' Fool" was also nominated for a Grammy award – this time, in the "Best Rock Vocal Performance, Male" category. The winner of that award was "Gotta Serve Somebody" by Bob Dylan, who also used some sly humor in his lyrics.

Both sides of this single were exactly like the album masters, which was a rarity. Promotional copies featured the stereo mix of "Dancin' Fool" on both sides. Canadian singles were issued with the same label and catalog number as the US release. The UK, German and Dutch 7" releases of this single (release date: April 27, 1979) had variations of the CBS catalog number S 7261, with the German and Dutch 45s sporting different picture sleeves. No sleeves were made for the Australian and New Zealand editions (CBS BA 222516). For those interested in minutia, the British release forgot the apostrophe on the word "Dancin'"! "Dancin' Fool" did not chart in any other country. The song was also included on the compilations "Strictly Commercial" (outside of Japan) and "ZAPPAtite."

The Netherlands was the only country that issued a commercial 12" edition of "Dancin' Fool" in 1979. That picture sleeve release featured an exclusive, 6:15 disco mix of the A-side with the brief "Baby Snakes" on the flip. The extended mix was not credited as such on the A-side. The American disco-mixed 12" (listed above) was a promotion-only issue for radio stations, and it was included years later on the Japanese CD and vinyl editions of "Strictly Commercial" and the 2008 birthday bundle. Typical for Phonogram, the US 12" was given typically cheesy packaging. It is not known why this mix was not commercially released, especially since the 7" sold reasonably well and the 12" promo received a sizable amount of airplay in the US.

For the 12" version of "Dancin' Fool," the first 1:11 was an instrumental loop of the pick-up "Ki-ni-shinai" module with some phasing. The album master followed from 1:11-4:27, with the pick-up section returning along with the "Revenge Of The Knick Knack People" backing until 5:09. At that point, a different loop of the pick-up section continued until 5:29. The final "I may be totally wrong" section continued into the vocal mix of the pick-up lines to its conclusion with the Patrick O'Hearn grout. The real timing of the track is 6:16.

* * *

FRANK ZAPPA: Bobby Brown/ Baby Snakes (7" 45 rpm single/ 12" 33 1/3 rpm single)
Released July 6, 1979 as CBS 7485 (7")/ CBS 12.7485 (12") (The Netherlands)

A-side
Bobby Brown (2:43) (Frank Zappa) • Master #: none • STEREO
Recorded live on January 27, 1978 at Hammersmith Odeon, London, England (basic tracks), and August 8-9, 1978 at Kendun Studios, Burbank, CA (keyboard and vocal overdubs), and August 10-11, 1978 at The Village Recorders, Los Angeles, CA (Ed Mann overdubs), and August 17-18, 1978 at The Village Recorders, Los Angeles, CA (Tommy Mars overdubs)
Personnel: Frank Zappa (lead vocals, guitar); Adrian Belew (rhythm guitar); Tommy Mars (keyboards); Peter Wolf (keyboards); Patrick O'Hearn (bass); Terry Bozzio (drums); Ed Mann (percussion); Napoleon Murphy Brock (backing vocals); André Lewis (backing vocals); Randy Thornton (backing vocals); Davey Moire (backing vocals)
Producer: Frank Zappa
Engineer: Peter Henderson (Hammersmith Odeon); Joe Chiccarelli (The Village Recorders)

B-side
Baby Snakes (1:50) (Frank Zappa) • Master #: none • STEREO
see Sheik Yerbouti "Clean Cuts"

The lyrical content of many tracks on "Sheik Yerbouti" precluded the release of a second US single. Just imagine a meeting of record company executives at CBS in The Netherlands asking, "So, why don't we release one of Zappa's dirty songs in our country, where English is not our first language? Great idea!" It was indeed a stroke of brilliance. "Bobby Brown" was not a hit in The Netherlands, but many copies made their way into Norway and Sweden. The record was played in Scandinavian discos, and "Bobby Brown" became a #1 gold record hit in both Norway and Sweden. Thanks to "Bobby Brown," "Sheik Yerbouti" became Frank Zappa's most successful international album. "Bobby Brown" was later included on the "Strictly Commercial" and "ZAPPAtite" compilations. A remixed version appeared on "Have I Offended Someone?". After its inclusion on "Sheik Yerbouti," the song was usually titled "Bobby Brown Goes Down."

Both editions came in a picture sleeve. The 12" edition was a bit ridiculous for two reasons: it contained two very short songs (especially the 1:50 B-side), and the record played at 33 1/3 rpm. "Bobby Brown" did not include the Patrick O'Hearn grout at the end of the album master.

"Bobby Brown" came to light after FZ met with two male interviewers whose girlfriends brainwashed them with women's lib ideas to the point that they felt the necessity to be submissive to be successful. Zappa ran with the idea of creating a title character whose life changes after having sex with a lesbian nicknamed Freddie. Bobby Brown becomes a gay radio promo man. His desire to succeed reaches the point of S&M activity. Bobby's favored method of submissive pleasure is penetrating his anus on a spindled stool (the Tower Of Power) while his partner urinates on him ("golden showers"). Despite Bobby's inability to perform properly afterward, he is thankful of the experience with Freddie because he now feels successful.

The recording of "Bobby Brown" was a typical "Sheik Yerbouti" track in that it came from a London gig with tons of overdubs. Frank Zappa recorded three vocal tracks, and the usual quartet of backing vocals created a strong vocal blend. For most fans, the most fascinating thing about the song was that the lyrics continued to build in a surprising and humorous manner until the very end.

"Bobby Brown" was a firm fixture in Frank Zappa live sets even before it appeared on a record. Every Zappa band lineup performed the song at one time or another. The New York City crazies at The Palladium in 1977 responded ecstatically to the five Halloween week performances of "Bobby Brown," as evidenced on "Halloween 77." The film "Baby Snakes" and the soundtrack download featured the Halloween night take. From its inclusion in the film, the reputation of "Bobby Brown" grew rapidly.

The early 1978 band can be heard playing "Bobby Brown" on "Hammersmith Odeon." "Beat The Boots II: At The Circus" and "Beat The Boots I: Saarbrücken 1978" have two versions from the summer '78 group. The 1979 lineup does not have a released version, but the fall 1980 band can be heard doing the song on "Buffalo." "Halloween 81" was the first recorded evidence from that band, but we still have nothing from the 1982 and 1988 groups. The summer 1984 tour featured "Bobby Brown" on the video of "Does Humor Belong In Music?," and the fall band from that year can be heard on "Stage, Vol. 3" and "Cheap Thrills."

The extremely important German edition of "Bobby Brown" was released in February 1980. It will be discussed a bit later.

* * *

FRANK ZAPPA: Joe's Garage/ Central Scrutinizer (12" 33 1/3 rpm promo single/ 7" 45 rpm single/ Record Store Day numbered 7" picture disc single)
12" Released September 3, 1979 as Zappa MK-107
7" Released October 29, 1979 as Zappa Z-31
Record Store Day 7" Released April 16, 2016 as Barking Pumpkin BPR 1224

A-side
Joe's Garage (12" promo – 6:10; 7" [Zappa] – 4:06; 7" [Barking Pumpkin] – 4:18) (Frank Zappa) • Master #: 12" – 2-55389; 7" – 2-55679; Barking Pumpkin 7" – none • STEREO
Recorded: April 21-22, 1979 (basic tracks), April 27, 1979 (saxophone overdubs), and May 28-29, 1979 (Cuccurullo guitar overdubs) at The Village Recorders, Los Angeles, CA
Personnel: Frank Zappa (lead guitar, co-lead vocal, arranger, conductor); Warren Cuccurullo (rhythm guitar); Denny Walley (slide guitar, backing vocals); Ike Willis (co-lead vocal, backing vocals); Peter Wolf (keyboards); Tommy Mars (keyboards); Arthur Barrow (guitar, bass); Ed Mann (percussion); Vinnie Colaiuta (drums); Jeff Hollie (tenor saxophone); Marginal Chagrin (aka Earle Dumler) (baritone saxophone); Bill "Stumuk" Nugent (bass saxophone); Al Malkin (vocals on 12" version only); Craig "Twister" Steward (harmonica)
Producer: Frank Zappa
Engineer: Joe Chiccarelli

B-side
Central Scrutinizer (3:27 [all editions]) (Frank Zappa) • Master #: 12" and 7" – 2-55388; Barking Pumpkin 7" – none • STEREO
Recorded: April 25-26, 1979 (basic tracks) and June 7, 1979 (percussion overdubs) at The Village Recorders, Los Angeles, CA
Personnel: Frank Zappa (lead vocal, guitar, arranger, conductor); Warren Cuccurullo (rhythm guitar); Denny Walley (slide guitar); Peter Wolf (keyboards); Arthur Barrow (bass); Ed Mann (percussion); Vinnie Colaiuta (drums)
Producer: Frank Zappa
Engineer: Joe Chiccarelli

Frank Zappa was playing around with the live album ideas "Warts & All" and "Shut Up 'N Play Yer Guitar" during 1979. The tracks on "Warts & All" would be scattered throughout the next few albums. "Shut Up" would undergo additional refinements before its eventual mail-order release in 1981. However, Frank's most immediate concern was to record a standalone, studio-based single – "Joe's Garage"/ "Catholic Girls" – as his summer 1979 product.

Zappa took his band into The Village Recorders on April 11, 1979. It took until April 21-22 to finalize backing tracks for the song "Joe's Garage." Recording for "Catholic Girls" would have to wait for nearly two weeks. As work progressed, Zappa brought in recent tour-tested songs, a few unrecorded older ones, and the new "Crew Slut." The working title for the album was "Arrogant Mop."

It became clear after recording the songs "Joe's Garage," "Crew Slut" and "Keep It Greasey" between April 21-25 that the underlying lyrics lent themselves to a rock opera treatment. Before the next overnight session (April 25-26), Frank had the initial continuity written for the track "The Central Scrutinizer." Zappa's megaphone-voiced character The Central Scrutinizer connected the lyrical and musical dots. Credited as "Rap" on the session sheet, "The Central Scrutinizer" was tracked using a much slower arrangement of "My Guitar Wants To Kill Your Mama" as its musical backdrop. The Central Scrutinizer's role was two-fold: to enforce existing and future anti-music laws, and to introduce the "Joe's Garage" album as a warning against playing music. As additional songs were recorded, further Central Scrutinizer links were cut and interspersed between the tracks.

Twelve tracks were in the can by the end of May, and a total of 19 cuts were completed during the round-the-clock sessions at The Village Recorders that lasted until June. Kendun Recorders in Burbank, CA was used for final touch-ups. After everything was assembled, there was enough material for three LPs. A depression in the music industry prevented the release of all three albums at once. Zappa issued the first act of the "Joe's Garage" rock opera as a single album on September 17, 1979, and the second and third acts followed on two LPs on November 19. In this way, the closeness of the release dates would not disturb the continuity of the opera's message.

The song "Joe's Garage" came together from distinct sources in March 1979. FZ came up with a guitar part during a French soundcheck, and he wrote the rest of the music at the Hotel Römischer Kaiser in Dortmund, Germany on March 25. The song was presented instrumentally as "So Garage" at the Dortmund gig that night. The lyrics for the title song came to Frank after his musicians shared their garage band roots with him.

After the Central Scrutinizer character sets the stage, the tale of "Joe's Garage" begins unfolding when we hear from Larry Fanoga (voiced by FZ). Larry was a former garage bandmate of the teenaged Joe (Ike Willis' role) in the Canoga Park neighborhood of L.A. His comment of "It makes its own sauce…if you add water" was another dog reference, this time to Gravy Train dog food commercials. Joe sang about the garage his band played in along with his Fender guitar/amp combo. Larry described the band's desire to perfect their song, despite complaints from Joe's parents and neighbors. Their improvement was marked by female worshippers and a gig at a go-go bar. A record company guy promised the world and delivered nothing, resulting in the end of the band. Joe reminisces about the old days and musical trends that passed his group by, and he dreams of playing his song today. Neighbor Ms. Sy Borg (voiced by Denny Walley) calls the police. The Central Scrutinizer interrupts with "The white zone is for loading and unloading only" (a repeated announcement at Los Angeles International Airport until September 11, 2001). Amid Ms. Borg's exhortations, Officer Butzis arrives and has Joe arrested in his garage. One of Ms. Borg's comments, "He used to cut my grass…he was a very nice boy" was also used in the song "He Used To Cut The Grass." The Central Scrutinizer interrupts again and tells us that Joe received a donut and a recommendation to get involved with his local church. In the early rock and roll days, parents thought that rock music was the work of the devil and religion was the only cure.

As for the American single release of "Joe's Garage"/ "The Central Scrutinizer," a promotional 12" was used to attract radio play and to determine if a commercial single was warranted. Radio stations were warned about the album's lyrics, but neither of these tracks were in the least bit offensive. The 12" used the full album track on the A-side. The B-side used the album master, but it was quickly faded as it went into the "Joe's Garage" cymbal intro. "Joe's Garage" received considerable airplay in some markets, but not in the New York metropolitan area. Despite this, the commercial single was issued almost two months after the 12". Promotional 7" copies had 4:06 stereo and mono edits of the A-side. The album version of "Joe's Garage" was also made available on "ZAPPAtite."

The commercial 7" was a completely different product. "Joe's Garage" on the single had a cymbal intro without the Central Scrutinizer dialog on top of it. Ike Willis' opening vocal had a large amount of reverb that was not on the album mix. The first two FZ chorus vocals (0:38-1:38 on the album version) were edited out. Zappa's lead vocal and the following backing vocals were much louder in the single mix compared to the LP. In addition, the reverb on the clapping following the verse about the girls dancing was toned down for the single. The single's remaining vocal sections (including The Central Scrutinizer's intrusion) were also mixed differently. Officer Butzis' first line ("This is the police") was mixed out before the last two words of Ms. Borg's line "I'm not joking around anymore!" were cut off at 4:06. The quotes of The Surfaris' "Wipe Out" and Tony Allen & The Champs' "Nite Owl" respectively occurred on the single from 1:55-1:58 and 2:39-3:00. The album version on the 12" has those quotes respectively from 2:54-2:57 and 3:38-3:59. "Wipe Out" was engineered by Paul Buff at Pal in 1962. This was the second quote of Tony Allen's 1955 song, as "Nite Owl" was also quoted in "Memories Of El Monte."

The track on "Strictly Commercial" which was credited as the single version of "Joe's Garage" is missing the cymbal intro. It started with the bass note which followed the cymbal. Otherwise, the rest of the track matches the single with a 4:06 length. The 2016 Record Store Day picture disc reissue of the US single does have the full intro and runs longer at 4:18 rather than 4:06. The sound quality of the picture disc is less than stellar, but it is the only place to obtain this extended mix.

"Central Scrutinizer" on the American single is also a unique mix, as the track is presented completely on its own without the segue. To be precise, the single matches the album master except for the end, when the megaphone vocal continues through the line "We take you now to a garage in Canoga Park" without the music of "Joe's Garage" underneath it. The Record Store Day picture disc has the B-side same mix as the original US single. To complete the picture, "Understanding America" has a shorter mix of "Central Scrutinizer."

After its modest instrumental presentation in 1979, "Joe's Garage" was part of FZ's repertoire for every tour after that. The only released live versions of "Joe Garage" were on "Buffalo" (from October 25, 1980), "Halloween 81," and "Stage, Vol. 3" and "Cheap Thrills" (from the same November 23, 1984 Chicago take).

Both tracks on this single did not involve xenochrony, as they did not have guitar solos. All the other "Joe's Garage"-era tracks with guitar solos except for "Crew Slut" and "Watermelon In Easter Hay" had live guitar solos from the 1980 tour flown over studio backing tracks. The isolated guitar solos were recorded by Claus Wiedemann on a two-track Nagra recorder.

* * *

L. SHANKAR: Dead Girls Of London/ Dead Girls Of London (12" 33 1/3 rpm promo single)
Released September 24, 1979 as Zappa MK-114

A-side
Dead Girls Of London (5:21) (Lakshminarayana Shankar – Frank Zappa) • Master #: 2-55298 • STEREO
Recorded: Late January-early February 1979 at Advision Studios, London, England (basic tracks), early February 1979 at AIR Studios, London, England (overdubs), and April 1979 at The Village Recorders, Los Angeles, CA (Frank Zappa and Ike Willis vocals)
Personnel: L. Shankar (acoustic and 5-string Barcus Berry electric violin, vocals, string orchestra); Frank Zappa (vocals, arrangement, orchestration); Ike Willis (vocals); Phil Palmer (mandolin, acoustic guitar, electric guitar); Dave Marquee (bass); Simon Phillips (drums); James Lascelles (Fender Rhodes, organ, acoustic piano, synthesizer); Vicky Blumenthal (backing vocals)
Producer: Frank Zappa
Engineer: Geoff Young (Advision); Steve Nye (AIR); Joe Chiccarelli (The Village Recorders)

B-side
same as A-side

Frank Zappa met Indian violinist Lakshminarayana Shankar at an open-air festival concert at Ludwigsparkstadion in Saarbrücken, Germany on September 3, 1978. At the festival, L. Shankar was playing with John McLaughlin's group The One Truth Band after a stint in McLaughlin's previous group Shakti. Shankar and FZ jammed briefly backstage and Frank invited Shankar to play in New York. Before that happened, Shankar joined Zappa's band in Berlin four days after they met. Their New York plans came to fruition, as Shankar appeared at all of Zappa's Halloween week concerts except for October 29. Shankar was slated to be in the 1979 band, but it was not to be. However, Frank wanted to produce a rock-based Zappa Records album for Shankar before some UK dates began on February 10, 1979.

Recording for L. Shankar's album "Touch Me There" began at London's noted Advision Studios in late January 1979. Shankar wrote three songs that required lyrics, so Frank created words for " Dead Girls Of London," "Knee Deep In Heaters," and the title track. Zappa was in the middle of writing lyrics when Van Morrison unexpectedly called looking for work. Van was still signed to Warner Bros. (Zappa's enemy) in the US, but his recordings outside North America were handled by Phonogram. Frank asked Van to come in and sing "Dead Girls Of London," which he did in 15 minutes.

The Warner Bros. nonsense turned up again when Zappa was assembling the album for release. WB did not want Van Morrison's vocal on the album. On top of that, Van's manager wanted half of the publishing proceeds despite the fact that Morrison did not write the song. FZ and Ike Willis replaced Van Morrison's vocal for "Dead Girls Of London" during the recording for the "Joe's Garage" project two months later. To disguise their participation, the pseudonym Stucco Homes was used to credit Frank and Ike's joint vocals. That pseudonym was not used when the album was later released on CD. The Van Morrison version was finally released in the 2011 birthday bundle.

Before things went sour with Warner Bros. and Van Morrison, Zappa played "Dead Girls Of London" with his February-April 1979 band. Two examples of their work are part of the 2006 birthday bundle (London; February 19, 1979) and "Beat The Boots I: Anyway The Wind Blows" (Paris; February 24, 1979). The fall 1980 band also played the song, which can be heard on "Buffalo." For that tour, the arrangement involved making fun of designer jeans that were very popular at the time. The mid-1982 band offered the song regularly, as evidenced by the "Stage, Vol. 5" version.

"Touch Me There" (Zappa SRZ-1-1602) was released on September 24, 1979 and was promoted by this 12" single for radio play. Both sides of the record featured the stereo album master. Radio station program directors did not show any interest. The album was reissued on August 18, 1992 as Barking Pumpkin D2 74243 and in the UK on Zappa Records CDZAP 50.

L. Shankar played violin at both Upper Darby, PA concerts on May 10, 1980. He co-wrote and played on "Thirteen" ("Stage, Vol. 6"). Shankar was also on the albums "Halloween" and "Everything Is Healing Nicely," and he was part of the January 8, 1993 UMRK soiree with many others.

* * *

FRANK ZAPPA: Joe's Garage (12" 33 1/3 rpm promo sampler single)
Released November 19, 1979 as Zappa MK-129

<u>A-side – Track 1</u>
Joe's Garage (6:10) (Frank Zappa) • Master #: MK-129 A • STEREO
see Joe's Garage/ Central Scrutinizer

A-side – Track 2
Wet T-Shirt Nite (5:26) (Frank Zappa) • Master #: MK-129 A • STEREO
Recorded: April 25-26, 1979 (basic tracks), May 26-27, 1979 (Cuccurullo sitar overdubs), June 1979 (Ed Mann overdubs) at The Village Recorders, Los Angeles, CA, and live on March 21, 1979 at Rhein-Neckar-Halle, Eppelheim, Germany (guitar solo fragment from the track "Toad-O Line" [aka "On The Bus"])
Personnel: Frank Zappa (vocal, guitar, arranger, conductor); Ike Willis (lead vocals); Warren Cuccurullo (electric sitar); Denny Walley (slide guitar); Peter Wolf (keyboards); Arthur Barrow (bass); Ed Mann (percussion); Vinnie Colaiuta (drums); Dale Bozzio (vocal)
Producer: Frank Zappa
Engineer: Joe Chiccarelli

A-side – Track 3
Lucille Has Messed My Mind Up (7:17) (Frank Zappa) • Master #: MK-129 A • STEREO
Recorded: April 30, 1979 (basic tracks) and May 29-30, 1979 (Cuccurullo guitar overdubs) at The Village Recorders, Los Angeles, CA
Personnel: Frank Zappa (vocal, guitar, arranger, conductor); Ike Willis (lead vocal); Warren Cuccurullo (rhythm guitar); Denny Walley (slide guitar); Peter Wolf (keyboards); Arthur Barrow (bass); Ed Mann (percussion); Vinnie Colaiuta (drums)
Producer: Frank Zappa
Engineer: Joe Chiccarelli

B-side – Track 1
A Token Of My Extreme (5:28) (Frank Zappa) • Master #: MK-129 B • STEREO
Recorded: May 3-4, 1979 (basic tracks) and May 28-29, 1979 (Cuccurullo sitar overdubs) at The Village Recorders, Los Angeles, CA
Personnel: Frank Zappa (co-lead vocal, guitar, arranger, conductor); Ike Willis (co-lead vocal); Warren Cuccurullo (electric sitar); Denny Walley (slide guitar, backing vocals); Peter Wolf (keyboards); Arthur Barrow (bass, backing vocals); Ed Mann (percussion, backing vocals); Vinnie Colaiuta (drums)
Producer: Frank Zappa
Engineer: Joe Chiccarelli

B-side – Track 2
He Used To Cut The Grass (8:34) (Frank Zappa) • Master #: MK-129 B • STEREO
Recorded live on March 23, 1979 at Liebenau Stadion, Graz, Austria (guitar solo), and May 11-June 4, 1979 at The Village Recorders, Los Angeles, CA (guitar, bass and keyboard overdubs)
Personnel: Frank Zappa (vocal, guitar, arranger, conductor); Ike Willis (lead vocal); Warren Cuccurullo (rhythm guitar); Denny Walley (slide guitar, Ms. Borg vocal); Peter Wolf (keyboards); Patrick O'Hearn (bass); Ed Mann (percussion); Vinnie Colaiuta (drums)
Producer: Frank Zappa
Engineer: Claus Wiedemann (Liebenau); Joe Chiccarelli (The Village Recorders)

B-side – Track 3
Watermelon In Easter Hay (10:00) (Frank Zappa) • Master #: MK-129 B • STEREO
Recorded: May 1-2, 1979 (basic tracks) and May 24-26, 1979 (guitar overdubs) at The Village Recorders, Los Angeles, CA
Personnel: Frank Zappa (guitar, vocal, arranger, conductor); Warren Cuccurullo (electric sitar); Denny Walley (slide guitar); Peter Wolf (keyboards); Arthur Barrow (bass); Ed Mann (percussion); Vinnie Colaiuta (drums)

Producer: Frank Zappa
Engineer: Joe Chiccarelli

This promotional 12" was designed to highlight tracks from all three acts of "Joe's Garage." A repeat of the title track from the previous 12" started things off. The second track on side one was "Wet T-Shirt Nite." The song was inspired by the wet T-shirt contest at The Brasserie that Zappa and the band viewed in Miami during some off-days during the second week of September 1978. A rough version of the song was soundchecked on September 15, 1978 at the Jai Alai Fronton in Miami. In a role reversal of "The Big Surfer," Zappa (as sleazy MC Buddy Jones) hosted the wet T-shirt contest with Mary (Joe's girlfriend; voiced by Dale Bozzio) as the contestant.

Ike Willis' double-tracked lead vocal on "Wet T-Shirt Nite" set the scene. The instrumental section from 0:53-1:37 was the standalone FZ composition "#8." The riff from another Zappa work, "Saddle Bags," was used three times in succession from 1:58-1:59, 2:02-2:04, and 2:07-2:09. A quote from the first movement of "Mo 'N Herb's Vacation" (2:12-2:30) partially overlapped with a quote of Richard Strauss' "Also Sprach Zarathustra" (2:24-2:35). In Buddy Jones' conversation with Mary, Zappa mentioned his tour bus Phydeau (Fido) III between 3:04-3:05 – another dog reference. Without the sound effects of water being dumped on her to create the right mood, Dale Bozzio didn't respond enthusiastically enough. This error led to Frank's "ice pick to the forehead" joke which was left in the final mix.

On the first "Joe's Garage" LP, "Wet T-Shirt Nite" went right into "Toad-O Line" (aka "On The Bus" on CD reissues). Since this record was designed to be played on radio, the track incorporated the first 50 seconds of "Toad-O Line." That cut used Zappa's guitar solo from the March 21, 1979 performance of "Inca Roads" from Eppelheim, Germany. A longer version of the same solo was called "Occam's Razor" on "One Shot Deal." The title "Toad-O Line" was a play on the band Toto, whose hit "Hold The Line" was quoted by FZ in the first six seconds, and from 0:29-0:42 and 0:48-0:50 on the faded solo used on this promo 12".

"Wet T-Shirt Nite" has also been called "Fembot In A Wet T-Shirt," "The Wet T-Shirt Contest" or other variations on various releases over the years. The television program "The Six Million Dollar Man" spun off "The Bionic Woman," and in true 1970s TV fashion, a crossover episode involving the two programs was required for promotion. The first episode of the three-part "Kill Oscar" broadcast (first air date: October 27, 1976) featured the creation of female androids called Fembots. "The Six Million Dollar Man" aired the second episode on October 31, and "The Bionic Woman" aired the final part on November 3, 1976.

The "Saddle Bags" riff was used during the intro of "Diseases Of The Band" at the London gig on February 19, 1979 ("Stage, Vol. 1") and the entire "Wet T-Shirt Nite" from Paris (February 24, 1979) can be heard on "Beat The Boots I: Anyway The Wind Blows." The song was announced as "Fembot In A Wet T-Shirt Contest" at the same Eppelheim gig as the aforementioned "Inca Roads" solo.

The "Joe's Garage" LP version of "Wet T-Shirt Nite" can also be found on "Zappa Picks By Larry LaLonde Of Primus" and the "Zappa" film soundtrack. The song was rehearsed on September 29 and October 5, 1980, but it was not played on the subsequent tour.

The last song on side one for this promo 12" was "Lucille Has Messed My Mind Up." This record is missing the initial snare hit before the drum roll. The song contained one of Ike Willis' finest lead vocals on record. "Lucille Has Messed My Mind Up" (originally credited to Zappa's pseudonym La Marr Bruister) was initially released by MOI bassist Jeff Simmons on his album of the same title and on the "Zappéd" sampler. The track timing on this sampler is incorrect, as it does not include the ending Central Scrutinizer commentary (indexed separately on CDs as "Scrutinizer Postlude"). It should have been listed as 5:42. "Lucille" was first played during the fall of 1975, and it returned for the 1980, 1984 and 1988 tours. The only released live version of the song came from the fall 1984 band on "Stage, Vol. 3."

Side two of the sampler began with the track which opened Act II of "Joe's Garage": "A Token Of My Extreme." The song was an essential part of live sets in the last half of 1974. It involved nightly updates about band members and the crew. That late '74 lineup can be heard performing the vamp of "A Token Of My Extreme" on "The Dub Room Special!" The same day's performance of the entire song is on the video of the similarly titled "A Token Of His Extreme." The related "Tush Tush Tush (A Token Of My Extreme)" from Helsinki, Finland in September 1974 is on "Stage, Vol. 2." The 1975 lineup with Captain Beefheart performed the song, but none of their takes have been issued. The 1982 lineup rehearsed the song on March 24 without playing it during their tour. "A Token Of My Extreme" was also soundchecked on February 19, 1988 in Boston.

As for the "Joe's Garage" studio version of "A Token Of My Extreme," Zappa's megaphone commentary was presented by another one of his characters, L. Ron Hoover. That character was a parody of Scientology cult founder and sci-fi author L. Ron Hubbard and Hoover brand vacuums. The cult that L. Ron Hoover ran in "Joe's Garage" was called The First Church Of Appliantology, named by Village Recorders engineer Joe Chiccarelli. Vacuums were also referenced in the albums "Chunga's Revenge," "200 Motels," and "The Perfect Stranger." This was one of many songs mentioned earlier which referred to chrome and used the phrase "Get the picture?". The full album track of "A Token Of My Extreme" was used for this promotional disc.

"Joe's Garage" Act III opener "He Used To Cut The Grass" combined a March 23, 1979 FZ guitar solo from Graz, Austria with a mixture of new and repurposed "Joe's Garage" lyrics from the title song, "Outside Now," and "Crew Slut." The full album master is used on this record. The Central Scrutinizer interrupts more than three minutes into the track and at the end. Zappa's solo quoted both "The Radio Is Broken" (6:30-6:35) and "Thirteen" (6:37-6:48). Segments of "He Used To Cut The Grass" can be heard within "Porn Wars Deluxe" on "Understanding America." Parts of the drum track used on "He Used To Cut The Grass" were also employed on "Outside Now," "While You Were Out," and "Stucco Homes." The song was performed twice in 1980.

FZ's third signature tune "Watermelon In Easter Hay" closed this promo 12". The full album track plus the first 0:52 of The Central Scrutinizer's commentary on "A Little Green Rosetta" was used. It is very clear that this record was not a "Clean Cuts" edition, as The Central Scrutinizer's two utterances of the word "fuck" at the beginning of "Watermelon" and another "fuck" in the pre-"Rosetta" commentary were not suitable for airplay. The "Rosetta" commentary here ended with the line "And every time a nice little muffin comes by on the belt, he poots forth…"

The title of "Watermelon In Easter Hay" referred to Zappa's disgust with musicians who showed off when simple backing was required. A session sheet covering an Ed Mann percussion overdub date on August 15-16, 1978 indicates that Mann came in to work on "Watermelon In Easter Hay" along with "Wild Love" and "Flakes."

For the 9/4-time signatured "Watermelon," Zappa recorded two studio solos. He used a Fender Stratocaster for the first, and a Les Paul for the second. It is generally considered FZ's most expressive and melodic musical work. The song began as an encore during the early 1978 tour. Two live versions from that tour are on "Hammersmith Odeon" and "Frank Zappa Plays The Music Of Frank Zappa," with the latter album containing the "Joe's Garage" version as well. The second part of a "Watermelon" studio version (the one that Ed Mann overdubbed later) was called "Drooling Midrange Accountants On Easter Hay" on "QuAUDIOPHILIAc." The early 1979 band can be heard playing "Watermelon" on "Beat The Boots I: Anyway The Wind Blows." Zappa played the song with every band after that. A November 17, 1981 NYC live version debuted on "The Zappa Movie Limited Edition Soundtrack EP! – Exclusive Backer Reward Edition" in late 2020. The Jones Beach live version (August 16, 1984) on "Guitar" is very commonly known.

The large studio bills that Zappa racked up during the recording of "Joe's Garage" would not be repeated. His home studio, the Utility Muffin Research Kitchen (UMRK), was finished in December 1979 at a cost of about $3.5 million. The initial name of UMRK was Studio Z, which was what he called Pal Recording Studio after he bought it from Paul Buff on August 1, 1964. The first UMRK project was the mixing of the single track "I Don't Wanna Get Drafted" in February 1980. That record will be discussed soon.

This "Joe's Garage" promo contributed to a #27 album peak for Act I, and #53 for Acts II and III. The front covers for both LPs featured FZ in blackface. Frank posed with a mop for Act I, and his blackface makeup was being applied for Acts II & III. The three acts were packaged as a triple LP box set in 1987 before their CD reissues.

* * *

FRANK ZAPPA: Joe's Garage/ Catholic Girls (7" 45 rpm single)
Released January 4, 1980 as CBS S CBS 7950 (England)

A-side
Joe's Garage (4:07) (Frank Zappa) • Master #: S CBS 7950 A* • STEREO
see Joe's Garage/ Central Scrutinizer

B-side
Catholic Girls (4:26) (Frank Zappa) • Master #: S CBS 7950 B* • STEREO
Recorded: May 2-3, 1979 (basic tracks) and May 4-24, 1979 (drum and vocal overdubs) at The Village Recorders, Los Angeles, CA
Personnel: Frank Zappa (guitar, co-lead vocal, arranger, conductor); Ike Willis (co-lead vocal); Warren Cuccurullo (electric sitar, backing vocals); Denny Walley (slide guitar, backing vocals); Peter Wolf (keyboards); Arthur Barrow (bass); Ed Mann (percussion); Vinnie Colaiuta (drums); Dale Bozzio (backing vocals); Al Malkin (Officer Butzis vocal)
Producer: Frank Zappa
Engineer: Joe Chiccarelli

Zappa's intended single when he entered The Village Recorders in April 1979 was widely released outside of North America. Regardless of the timings on the record labels, every European release with the same catalog number used the 4:06 US single version of "Joe's Garage" and a 3:55 edit of "Catholic Girls" which eliminated all but the first two words ("This is...") from The Central Scrutinizer's commentary at the end. European releases had variations of the same picture sleeve design, with the British release lacking a sleeve. Some UK singles mistakenly play Bob Dylan's "When You Gonna Wake Up" on the B-side. Australia (CBS BA 222634) did their own thing, as they used a 3:25 edit of "Catholic Girls" on the flipside. As usual, the Dutch release was exported into Scandinavia. The "Joe's Garage" single went on to reach #4 in Norway and #14 in Sweden.

Using common stereotypes, "Catholic Girls" was FZ's attack on Roman Catholicism (the religion that he abandoned), and specifically, Italian-American girls of that religious persuasion. Catholic priests, such as the Father Riley character that Zappa portrayed in this song, were presented as homosexuals. Young girls with light mustaches were described as going to their local Catholic Youth Organizations (CYOs) to learn how execute blow jobs. When Joe (Ike Willis) came in to the track (0:45-0:48), he quoted the Jimmy Van Heusen/ Sammy Cahn song "All The Way" popularized by Frank Sinatra. Two Italian Catholic band members, Warren Cuccurullo and Vinnie Colaiuta, were offered as boys that Catholic girls like Mary (Dale Bozzio) were interested in. After mentioning Cuccurullo, Mary referred to the line "Kinda young, kinda wow!" from Revlon's TV commercial for Charlie perfume that starred Shelley Hack and pianist Bobby Short. The difficult timing of the following instrumental section was perfected by bassist Arthur Barrow and drummer Vinnie Colaiuta just before they laid it down on tape. The "kinda young, kinda wow!" line was later used in "Charlie's Enormous Mouth" on "You Are What You Is." "Catholic Girls" skewered its subject in very much the same way as "Jewish Princess" on "Sheik Yerbouti."

Warren Cuccurullo offered Carmenita Scarfone as a Catholic girl, and Officer Butzis (Al Malkin) revealed that she gave him a venereal disease. Cuccurullo then mentioned Toni Carbone, who was described as having a tongue like a cow. The comic impact of these lines was increased by the use of New York (Al Malkin) and Boston (Dale Bozzio) accents.

Joe came back in using slang (such as "voot") that jazz singer/songwriter Slim Gaillard used in his "Voot-O-Reenee" dictionary. Larry Fanoga (Zappa) agreed with Joe that Catholic girls liked doing it on their knees. During the chorus outro, an extended quote of "Jewish Princess" (3:17-4:03) was overlaid with three Italian melodies: "Tarantella Calabrese" (3:22-3:25 and 3:31-3:33), "Vest la giubba" (3:35-3:37), and "La donna è mobile" (3:43-4:07). The single faded at 3:55 just after the first two words of The Central Scrutinizer's commentary, so there is no airing of the complete "La donna" quote. The traditional "Tarantella Napoletana" was in 12/8 time and was used by Zappa on "Tinsel Town Rebellion" ("Peaches III"), "Stage, Vol. 3" ("Advance Romance"), "Stage, Vol. 6" ("Catholic Girls"), and "The Best Band You Never Heard In Your Life" ("Stairway To Heaven"). "La donna è mobile" ("Woman Is Fickle") started the third act of Giuseppe Verdi's opera "Rigoletto" from 1851. Ruggero Lencavallo's "Vesti la giubba" ("Put On The Costume") is an aria from the end of the first act of his opera "Pagliacci" (1892). Frank Zappa's use of these melodies linked the infidelities of the Italian females in these operas with Catholicism.

"Catholic Girls" was initially performed as an instrumental within an "Easy Meat" guitar solo from Neunkirchen am Brand, Germany on March 30, 1979. The only live version of "Catholic Girls" to be released to date is the February 12, 1988 performance on "Stage, Vol. 6" and "Cheap Thrills." The "Joe's Garage" version of "Catholic Girls" was repeated on "Have I Offended Someone?." The song was quoted in "Yo Cats" on "Frank Zappa Meets The Mothers Of Prevention" and a remix of "Yo Cats" was also on "Offended."

* * *

FRANK ZAPPA: Bobby Brown/ Stick It Out (7" 45 rpm single)
Released February 22, 1980 as CBS S 8216 (Germany)

A-side
Bobby Brown (2:43) (Frank Zappa) • Master #: none • STEREO
see Bobby Brown/ Baby Snakes

B-side
Stick It Out (4:33) (Frank Zappa) • Master #: none • STEREO
Recorded: April 30, 1979 (basic tracks) and May 25-26, 1979 (overdubs) at The Village Recorders, Los Angeles, CA
Personnel: Frank Zappa (guitar, backing vocals, arranger, conductor); Ike Willis (lead vocals, backing vocals); Warren Cuccurullo (guitar, Sy Borg voice); Denny Walley (slide guitar, backing vocals); Peter Wolf (keyboards); Arthur Barrow (bass); Ed Mann (percussion, Sy Borg voice); Vinnie Colaiuta (drums)
Producer: Frank Zappa
Engineer: Joe Chiccarelli

"Bobby Brown" did the business in Scandinavia, and it was time for Germany to cash in. German CBS decided to promote both "Joe's Garage" releases in a picture sleeve by pairing "Bobby Brown" from Act I with "Stick It Out" from Acts II & III. Releasing a single with multiple profanities on both sides was no problem for the German market or for the Swiss or Austrian markets into which the record was exported. "Bobby Brown" became a gold record in all three markets. The record sold more than 250,000 copies in Germany and peaked at #4, while it hit #2 in Austria and #5 in Switzerland. The Spanish release (CBS 8287) was released three weeks later in a different sleeve. "Bobby Brown" did not have the grout at its end like the earlier Dutch single, and it faded just before the explosion.

"Stick It Out" was originally the fourth segment of the five-part "Sofa" suite in the summer of 1971. It was originally performed that way, as evidenced on "Carnegie Hall." "Beat The Boots II: Swiss Cheese/ Fire!" from the notorious Montreux concert on December 4, 1971 featured "Stick It Out" as part of the "Sofa" suite. After the song was much later placed in its more advantageous "Joe's Garage" context, it received a lot more attention. Its original title was "Short Girls." An example of the fall 1980 band performing "Stick It Out" can be heard on "Buffalo." The 1982 band rehearsed the tune but did not perform it during that tour. The summer '84 lineup only performed the entire song once and quoted it within "Truck Driver Divorce" at The Palace Theater in L.A. on July 22, 1984.

Ike Willis (as Joe) double-tracked a German language vocal during the first part of the "Stick It Out" studio version. The first words by the Sy Borg character (voiced by Warren Cuccurullo and Ed Mann) were "Pick me, I'm clean," which was the title of a song on "Tinsel Town Rebellion." Joe then sang the same verse and chorus in English with some Sy Borg interjections. Sy then went into pick-up lines from "What Kind Of Girl Do You Think We Are?" and "Dancin' Fool." Two of those lines, "What's a nice girl like you doing in a place like this?" and "Do you come here often?," were later in "Artificial Rhonda." Starting at 3:32, Sy Borg used the first words from four successive lines of The Who's "See Me, Feel Me" (see, feel, touch, heal) to make chrome references. The "hoo hoo" backing vocals in this section came from Johnny "Guitar" Watson's March 1959 A-side "The Bear" (Class 246). The mention of a steam roller refers to "Latex Solar Beef" from "Fillmore East – June 1971."

The correct timing for "Stick It Out" should be 4:17, as The Central Scrutinizer's ending commentary was edited out. An extended disco mix was prepared by Frank Zappa and engineer Bob Stone, but it has not been issued. The overwhelming popularity of both sides of this record would warrant a Dutch follow-up single with "Stick It Out" as the emphasis track.

* * *

FRANK ZAPPA: Stick It Out/ Why Does It Hurt When I Pee? (7" 45 rpm single)
Released March 14, 1980 as CBS 8287 (The Netherlands)

A-side
Stick It Out (4:19) (Frank Zappa) • Master #: none • STEREO
see previous single

B-side
Why Does It Hurt When I Pee? (3:22) (Frank Zappa) • Master #: none • STEREO
Recorded live on March 21, 1979 at Rhein-Neckar-Halle, Eppelheim, Germany ("Toad-O Line" guitar solo fragment), and April 25-26, 1979 at The Village Recorders, Los Angeles, CA (backing track and vocals)
Personnel: Frank Zappa (guitar, arranger, conductor); Ike Willis (lead vocals); Warren Cuccurullo (guitar); Denny Walley (slide guitar, backing vocals); Peter Wolf (keyboards); Arthur Barrow (bass, backing vocals); Ed Mann (percussion); Vinnie Colaiuta (drums)
Producer: Frank Zappa
Engineer: Joe Chiccarelli

The B-side title came from the comment that Zappa's road manager Phil Kaufman yelled out while urinating on the tour bus to the Saarbrücken, Germany festival on September 3, 1978. Frank wrote the song straight away and premiered it two nights later at Folkets Park, Malmö, Sweden.

Since "Fembot In A Wet T-Shirt," "Toad-O Line" (aka "On The Bus") and "Why Does It Hurt When I Pee?" were recorded as one continuous piece, it made sense to include the last 58 seconds of "Toad-O Line" before the beginning of "Pee?" for the single. Ike double-tracked his vocal, which humorously described that he contracted gonorrhea from the toilet seat. As mentioned previously, this is one of many songs which dealt with sexual diseases. British prog bands were parodied in the middle section. Richard Emmet's "Zing Tree" chime was used at crucial points in the song.

The summer 1978 band performed "Pee?" in Munich, which can be heard on "Beat The Boots II: At The Circus." The early 1979 lineup is represented on "Beat The Boots I: Anyway The Wind Blows." The song was performed more than 60 times during 1980, and was offered by all the other touring bands through 1988. The only other released performance of "Why Does It Hurt When I Pee?" was the composite fall 1984 track on "Stage, Vol. 3."

This picture sleeve edition was solely issued in Holland. Some of the records have the incorrect timings of 4:33 and 2:35, respectively, but the corrected edition times are shown above.

* * *

FRANK ZAPPA: I Don't Wanna Get Drafted/ Ancient Armaments (7" 45 rpm single)
Released April 28, 1980 as Zappa ZR 1001
Re-promoted April 19, 1985 as Zappa ZR 1001

A-side
I Don't Wanna Get Drafted (3:10) (Frank Zappa) • Master #: WS7-73000A • STEREO
Recorded: February 16, 1980 at Ocean Way Recorders, Hollywood, CA
Personnel: Frank Zappa (guitar, vocals); Ray White (guitar, vocals); Ike Willis (guitar, vocals); Tommy Mars

(keyboards); Arthur Barrow (synthesizer bass); Vinnie Colaiuta (drums); Terry Bozzio (mailman vocal); Dale Bozzio (vocals)
Producer: Frank Zappa
Engineer: Allen Sides

B-side
Ancient Armaments (4:10) (Frank Zappa) • Master #: WS7-73000B • STEREO
Recorded live on October 31, 1978 at The Palladium, New York, NY
Personnel: Frank Zappa (lead guitar, end vocal); Denny Walley (slide guitar); Tommy Mars (keyboards); Peter Wolf (keyboards); Ed Mann (percussion); Arthur Barrow (bass); Patrick O'Hearn (bass); Vinnie Colaiuta (drums)
Producer: Frank Zappa
Engineer: Joe Chiccarelli

After the Soviet Union intervened in Afghanistan on Christmas Eve 1979, US President Jimmy Carter reinstated mandatory draft registration. Frank Zappa was incensed by Carter's move, especially since the next presidential election was a little less than 11 months away. To Frank, Carter's decision smacked of an election time ruse which put Americans of draft age in danger. Zappa shut down a band rehearsal on February 8, 1980 to work on "I Don't Wanna Get Drafted." At the next day's rehearsal, Frank came in with the song. The band worked on it between February 9-11. The recording equipment learning curve at UMRK was still taking place, so Zappa took the band plus Terry and Dale Bozzio to Allen Sides' Ocean Way Recorders in Hollywood to quickly cut his draft-based song. The final mixing of "I Don't Wanna Get Drafted" was the first project completed at UMRK.

The original plan was to release a standalone single through Phonogram, but the label was not interested. Zappa terminated his relationship with Phonogram and signed a one-off distribution deal with the Columbia label in the US. Promo 7" and 12" copies in America had stereo and mono mixes of the A-side. Stock and promo copies came with a picture sleeve.

Frank Zappa's character in "I Don't Wanna Get Drafted" was a teenager hit with a draft notice delivered by mailman Terry Bozzio. This kid and his sister (sung by Dale Bozzio) preferred the simple teenage life rather than going to war, where either he or his sister could be shot in the foxhole. Tommy Mars was the real star of the instrumental interlude. With typical FZ humor, "I Don't Wanna Get Drafted" received a decent amount of airplay and peaked at #103 in the US. The record reached #3 in Sweden, of all places. A different mix of the song was included on "The Lost Episodes." The original mix, however, has never appeared in digital form. A summer 1980 re-recording entitled "Drafted Again" was part of the album "You Are What You Is." That same album featured another draft reference within the track "If Only She Woulda." "I Don't Wanna Get Drafted" was played live throughout 1980, and an example from that tour was released on "Buffalo."

"Ancient Armaments" was a New York City Palladium show-opening Zappa guitar solo from Halloween 1978. It was edited from a longer performance. The single edit was reissued in the 2008 birthday bundle. A considerably longer version was released on "Halloween."

In Canada, this 7" single was released as Zappa ZRP 21 without a sleeve, but a commercial 12" with a duplicate of the US picture sleeve and catalog number was made available. All other non-US releases of this single had a picture sleeve except for Australia (CBS BA 222704) and were issued on June 13, 1980. German releases were available on 7" (CBS S 8625) and 12" (CBS 12.8625). The Dutch and Italian 7" releases used the same catalog number as the German issue. UK and Spanish issues used CBS catalog number 8652. A special

Italian jukebox promo single, issued on June 27, 1980 as CBS JC 15029, combined Bob Dylan's "Saved" with "I Don't Wanna Get Drafted." "Drafted" was also on an Italian promo 12" sampler (CBS 12PRM 016).

The US single was re-promoted on April 19, 1985 using the same catalog number. It was available by mail order from Zappa's Barking Pumpkin label for many years. Other than the London Symphony Orchestra project in early 1983, FZ's studio recordings were made at UMRK.

* * *

FRANK ZAPPA: Tinsel Town Rebellion – Special Clean Cuts Edition (12" 33 1/3 rpm promo sampler single)
Released May 11, 1981 as Barking Pumpkin AS 995

A-side – Track 1
Fine Girl (3:31) (Frank Zappa) • Master #: AS 995 A • STEREO
Recorded: July 28, 1980 (basic tracks) and August 20, 22 and 28, 1980 (vocal overdubs) at UMRK, Los Angeles, CA
Personnel: Frank Zappa (guitar, vocal, arranger, conductor); Ike Willis (guitar, vocal); Ray White (guitar, vocal); Tommy Mars (keyboards); Bob Harris (high vocals); Arthur Barrow (bass); David Logeman (drums)
Producer: Frank Zappa
Engineer: Mark Pinske

A-side – Track 2
Love Of My Life (2:26) (Frank Zappa) • Master #: AS 995 A • STEREO
Recorded live on December 5, 1980 (early show) at Berkeley Community Theater, Berkeley, CA
Personnel: Frank Zappa (lead guitar, lead vocal, arranger, conductor); Ike Willis (rhythm guitar, vocals); Ray White (rhythm guitar, vocals); Steve Vai (rhythm guitar, vocals); Tommy Mars (keyboards, vocals); Bob Harris (keyboards, trumpet, high vocals); Arthur Barrow (bass, vocals); Vinnie Colaiuta (drums)
Producer: Frank Zappa
Engineer: Tom Flye

A-side – Track 3
Peaches III (4:48) (Frank Zappa) • Master #: AS 995 A • STEREO
Recorded live on February 18, 1979 (early and late shows) and February 19, 1979 at Hammersmith Odeon, London, England
Personnel: Frank Zappa (lead guitar, vocal, arranger, conductor); Ike Willis (rhythm guitar); Warren Cuccurullo (rhythm guitar); Denny Walley (slide guitar); Tommy Mars (keyboards); Peter Wolf (keyboards); Ed Mann (percussion); Arthur Barrow (bass); Vinnie Colaiuta (drums)
Producer: Frank Zappa
Engineer: Mick Glossop

B-side – Track 1
Tinsel Town Rebellion (4:49) (Frank Zappa) • Master #: AS 995 B • STEREO
Recorded live on December 5, 1980 (early and late shows) at Berkeley Community Theater, Berkeley, CA
Personnel: Frank Zappa (lead guitar, lead vocal, arranger, conductor); Ike Willis (rhythm guitar, vocals); Ray White (rhythm guitar, vocals); Steve Vai (rhythm guitar, vocals); Tommy Mars (keyboards, vocals); Bob Harris (keyboards, trumpet, high vocals); Arthur Barrow (bass); Vinnie Colaiuta (drums)
Producer: Frank Zappa

Engineer: Tom Flye

B-side – Track 2
Brown Shoes Don't Make It (7:34) (Frank Zappa) • Master #: AS 995 B • STEREO
Recorded live on February 17-19, 1979 (both early and late shows on February 18) at Hammersmith Odeon, London, England
Personnel: Frank Zappa (lead guitar, lead vocals, arranger, conductor); Ike Willis (rhythm guitar, lead vocals, backing vocals); Warren Cuccurullo (rhythm guitar); Denny Walley (slide guitar, backing vocals); Tommy Mars (keyboards, backing vocals); Peter Wolf (keyboards); Ed Mann (percussion); Arthur Barrow (bass, vocals); Vinnie Colaiuta (drums)
Producer: Frank Zappa
Engineer: Mick Glossop

After Frank Zappa worked with Columbia to distribute "I Don't Wanna Get Drafted," he made a new, North American distribution deal with the label. The first album product to be released under that arrangement was the double LP "Tinsel Town Rebellion." It was created out of the ashes of two unreleased albums whose contents had been bootlegged: the live collection "Warts & All" and the studio-based late 1980 LP "Crush All Boxes." Remnants from the "Crush All Boxes" title are faintly visible in the front cover artwork for "Tinsel Town Rebellion." The first song on "TTR," "Fine Girl," was to be the second track on side one of "Crush All Boxes." The rest of "Boxes" was reprocessed and/or remixed for the next album "You Are What You Is." Some tracks from "Warts & All" were placed on other releases ("TTR," "You Are What You Is," "Shut Up 'N Play Yer Guitar," "Stage, Vol. 4," "Stage, Vol. 6," and a longer version of the previous single's "Ancient Armaments"), while the rest was not used. The "TTR" album tracks derived from "Warts & All" were "For The Young Sophisticate," "Bamboozled By Love," "Brown Shoes Don't Make It," "Dance Contest," and "Peaches III." The first, third and fifth titles were included on this promo 12". "Tinsel Town Rebellion" reached #66 in the US.

Zappa's "Clean Cuts" promo sampler concept from the Phonogram era was applied to Columbia-distributed promotional items such as this one for "Tinsel Town Rebellion." The first sampler track "Fine Girl" was the only studio track on the album. Recorded at UMRK during the summer of 1980, it was intended to be the emphasis track for radio. When "Fine Girl" was planned for inclusion on "Crush All Boxes," the song's original title was "Some More Like That." Lead vocals were by Zappa, White and Willis, with Bob Harris' soaring falsettos joining them at the 1:42 mark. On this record, "Fine Girl" is faded just before its natural end. The original mix was later included on "Strictly Commercial" and "Zappa Picks By Larry LaLonde Of Primus." FZ and Bob Stone remixed "Fine Girl" at UMRK on August 20, 1986. That drier remix with an opening countoff was included in the 2006 birthday bundle. Live versions of "Fine Girl" can be found by the fall 1981 band on the video "The Torture Never Stops" (from Halloween in New York City) and "Halloween 81," and by the summer '82 lineup on "Stage, Vol 1."

"Love Of My Life" was the second track on side one of this promo 12". It was recorded at the December 5, 1980 early show at the Berkeley Community Center. For most fans, the only way they would have heard the song before was on "Cruising With Ruben & The Jets." Practically no one knew about the Ron Roman version, and the other two Pal versions had not been rediscovered at the time. FZ sang lead with harmony by Ray White, Ike Willis, and falsettos by Bob Harris. Bob's vocal worked in a brief quote of Sam Cooke's "You Send Me" (1:23-1:26), and his singing of a note which he slid upward from 1:40-1:50 stunned the Berkeley crowd and listeners of this album.

The way that "Love Of My Life" was offered on this record differed from the "Tinsel Town Rebellion" version.

After Bob Harris' falsetto line ended at 1:54 on the 12" version, five chorus lines were sung by FZ, White and Willis with a Bob Harris falsetto response. Unfortunately, the 12" fades out just before FZ's final "Love of my…" line to start the sixth chorus. Since the 2:10-2:22 segment on the 12" has been edited out for the song's presentation on "TTR," the album version has only three repeats and starts a fourth. However, the "TTR" track goes further than the 12". The conclusion is that there is no complete "TTR" version of "Love Of My Life," and the 12" offers a unique alternate edit that has not been reissued.

The "TTR" edit of "Love Of My Life" was also included on "Son Of Cheep Thrills." The song was performed throughout 1980, with "Stage, Vol. 4" featuring a New York City performance from May 8. None of the live versions of "Love Of My Life" from the 1981 and 1988 tours have been officially released.

Side one of this "Clean Cuts" edition ended with "Peaches III." Zappa pieced this track together from three Hammersmith Odeon shows between February 18-19, 1979. The 12" is missing a Colaiuta drum hit before his opening drum roll. The title of the track refers to the third release of "Peaches En Regalia," with "Hot Rats" and "Fillmore East – June 1971" being the other albums featuring Zappa's classic instrumental. The arrangement of "Peaches III" was bizarre and thoroughly entertaining at the same time.

Part of that special "Peaches III" arrangement was the 2:09-2:23 segment which emulated the keyboard stylings of Devo and couple of Butzis (Al Makin) mentions. Guitarist Warren Cuccurullo started playing in Al DiMeola's style at 2:57, and ten seconds later, Zappa began the "Let's hear it for another great Italian" section. In succession, Conlon Nancarrow, Warren Cuccurullo, Al DiMeola and Alvin Lee were named by FZ as great Italians, but only Cuccurullo and DiMeola were of Italian-American heritage. After mentioning Conlon Nancarrow's name, 3:11-3:54 of the recording switched to the end of "Why Does It Hurt When I Pee?" to continue the "great Italian" section. Cuccurullo's impression of Al DiMeola continued throughout this section, and the traditional "Tarantella Napoletana" was quoted from 3:36-3:39. The mention of Alvin Lee's name led to Cuccurullo playing Ten Years After's "I'm Goin' Home"-style playing. When the section ended at 3:54, the track switched to Zappa's commentary at the end of the "Don't Eat The Yellow Snow" suite. Frank introduced the band, Butzis, girlfriends, Al DiMeola and Alvin Lee before saying goodbye.

Side two of this sampler consisted of two Frank Zappa compositions which challenged the "Clean Cuts" title. Steve Vai's scream started off "Tinsel Town Rebellion," which Zappa sang with help from Ray White and Ike Willis. The track ping-ponged between both December 5, 1980 Berkeley, CA shows. Like "Joe's Garage," "TTR" was the story of a band that did whatever was necessary to make it big. For this "Clean Cuts" edition, Zappa censored the words "ass," "cocks" and "balls" in succession from first verse. The next effect was just as humorous and realistic as the song itself. The completion of the first verse led to more screams from Vai.

The mention of S.I.R. (Studio Instrument Rentals) referred to the equipment rental and production facility. At 2:03, Zappa's lyric "Chop a line now" was later used in "Cocaine Decisions." Black Sabbath's song "Black Sabbath" was then quoted between 2:07-2:10. At the end of the second verse, the word "fuck" had to go. Accompanying the censored line "It works for all of those record company pricks who come to skim the cream," a quote of Cream's Sunshine Of Your Love" was played (3:14-3:17) before a mention of The Doors' Jim Morrison.

The concluding section with Bob Harris' falsettos was accompanied by an adapted quote of "Johnny's Theme" from "The Tonight Show" (3:43-4:23). Zappa's question "Is everybody happy?" came from bandleader Ted Lewis' catchphrase. The ending of the "I Love Lucy" TV theme was played from 4:23-4:35. This 12" is unlike the album version as it contains the audience response and fades out.

The song "Tinsel Town Rebellion" would incorporate many more quotes as time went on. A prototype version of the song can be heard on the "Buffalo" CD. The 1981 band was first represented on "Halloween 81," but the 1982 band does not have a released version. The Pier live version from August 26, 1984 can be enjoyed on the video "Does Humor Belong In Music?" and the "Have I Offended Someone?" CD. A fall 1984 composite live version is on the CD "Does Humor Belong In Music?'. An edit of the "TTR" LP version is also on "Understanding America."

"Brown Shoes Don't Make It" concluded the second side of the promo 12". It was taken from four Hammersmith Odeon shows between February 17-19, 1979. The song debuted on the second MOI album "Absolutely Free." Frank sang most of the lead vocals, with Ike Willis doing the "Do it again…" part and Tommy Mars handling the "Time to go home" segment. The mention of a TV dinner in the song's lyrics followed a similar mention on the MOI's "It Can't Happen Here" from "Freak Out!". Two quotes in succession were made of James Brown's song "For Goodness Sakes, Look At Those Cakes" (3:37-3:38) and Otis Redding's "I Can't Turn You Loose" (3:38-3:40).

The "She's a dirty young mind" section used a quote of The Beach Boys' "Little Deuce Coupe" (4:53-5:08). For the revised arrangement played during this tour, the question "What would you do, daddy?" was replaced by "What would you do, Frankie?" for a much greater comedic effect.

The 12" conclusion of "Brown Shoes Don't Make It" used the ending chord from the February 18, 1979 late show – the same ending as on the single "For The Young Sophisticate" (listed next). The giveaway is that on both recordings, you can hear Ed Mann's mallet touching his instrument (7:26 on this disc) and Frank touching his guitar (7:31).

"Brown Shoes Don't Make It" was performed rarely in 1968 and 1969. The summer 1973 band can be heard performing the song on "Road Tapes, Venue #2." Parts of the "TTR" version were included in "Porn Wars Deluxe" on "Understanding America." The early 1979 band can be enjoyed on "Beat The Boots I: Anyway The Wind Blows." On occasion, the 1973 and 1979 bands quoted "Brown Shoes" in their sets.

Also of interest from this time is the "Earth News" 7" demo disc "Weird World Of Sports"/ "That's News." "Earth News" was a subscription news interview program on disc which was hosted by Lew Irwin. This was a trial disc (Demo #1/#2) which serviced radio programs outside of the entertainment industry. The second program "That's News" featured a short piece about Frank Zappa's collection of panties which was mentioned in the "TTR" liner notes. Emily Alana James, who saw FZ at the Fort Collins, CO show on December 2, 1980, sought to make a quilt of these undergarments. The quilt was eventually completed. A clip of "Panty Rap" from "TTR" was used in the background of this news story. "Panty Rap" was done over the vamp for "Black Napkins" at the December 5, 1980 late show at the Berkeley Community Theater. This "Earth News" spinoff was a failure and was not repeated.

* * *

FRANK ZAPPA: Love Of My Life/ For The Young Sophisticate (7" 45 rpm single)
Released June 12, 1981 as CBS A 1241 (The Netherlands)

<u>A-side</u>
Love Of My Life (2:15) (Frank Zappa) • Master #: none • STEREO
see Tinsel Town Rebellion – Special Clean Cuts Edition

B-side
For The Young Sophisticate (3:13) (Frank Zappa) • Master #: none • STEREO
Recorded live on February 18, 1979 (late show) at the Hammersmith Odeon, London, England
Personnel: Frank Zappa (lead guitar, lead vocal, arranger, conductor); Ike Willis (rhythm guitar, backing vocals); Warren Cuccurullo (rhythm guitar); Denny Walley (slide guitar, backing vocals); Tommy Mars (keyboards); Peter Wolf (keyboards); Ed Mann (percussion); Arthur Barrow (bass); Vinnie Colaiuta (drums)
Producer: Frank Zappa
Engineer: Mick Glossop

The only commercial single from "Tinsel Town Rebellion" was initially released in The Netherlands. It was later released in Spain with the same catalog number and a picture sleeve from the second "You Are What You Is" photo session. "Love Of My Life" was identical to the "TTR" LP except that it faded to the exact ending of the album track.

"For The Young Sophisticate" was first recorded at Bolic Sound on March 19, 1973. It was later included on "Läther." The "TTR" version came from the February 18, 1979 late show in London. This was a more lighthearted version with three mentions of Vinnie Colaiuta, Denny Walley's impersonation of cartoon character Woody Woodpecker (1:16-1:18 and 2:32-2:34), and a mention of Butzis (Al Malkin) at the end. Zappa sang the bridge with Denny Walley. "For The Young Sophisticate" on this single closed with the same ending that was tacked onto "Brown Shoes Don't Make It" for the "Clean Cuts" edition (the previous listing).

The early 1979 band played "For The Young Sophisticate" as part of "Beat The Boots I: Anyway The Wind Blows." The song was rehearsed on August 5, 1981, but it was not performed during that tour.

* * *

FRANK ZAPPA: Special Clean Cuts Edition – You Are What You Is (12" 33 1/3 rpm promo sampler single)
Released September 23, 1981 as Barking Pumpkin AS 1294

A-side – Track 1
Harder Than Your Husband (2:37) (Frank Zappa) • Master #: AL 1294 • STEREO
Recorded: July 18 and 29, 1980 (basic tracks) and August 18-22, 1980 (guitar, vocal and harmonica overdubs) at UMRK, Los Angeles, CA
Personnel: Frank Zappa (arranger); Jimmy Carl Black (lead vocal); Ike Willis (rhythm guitar, backing vocals); Ray White (rhythm guitar, backing vocals); Denny Walley (slide guitar); Steve Vai (stunt guitar); Craig "Twister" Steward (harmonica); Tommy Mars (keyboards); Arthur Barrow (bass); David Logeman (drums)
Producer: Frank Zappa
Engineer: Mark Pinske & Allen Sides

A-side – Track 2
Teenage Wind (2:56) (Frank Zappa) • Master #: AL 1294 • STEREO
Recorded: July 18 and 29, 1980 (basic tracks) and August 21 – September 2, 1980 (vocal and guitar overdubs) at UMRK, Los Angeles, CA
Personnel: Frank Zappa (backing vocals, arranger); Bob Harris (lead vocal); Ike Willis (rhythm guitar, backing vocals); Ray White (guitar, backing vocals); Jimmy Carl Black (voice); Steve Vai (stunt guitar); Tommy Mars (keyboards); Arthur Barrow (bass); David Logeman (drums)
Producer: Frank Zappa

Engineer: Mark Pinske & Allen Sides

A-side – Track 3
Doreen (2:58) (Frank Zappa) • Master #: AL 1294 • STEREO
Recorded: July 8-10, 1980 (basic tracks) and August 12 – September 6, 1980 (overdubs) at UMRK, Los Angeles, CA
Personnel: Frank Zappa (lead guitar, backing vocals, arranger); Ray White (lead vocal, rhythm guitar); Ike Willis (rhythm guitar, backing vocals); Bob Harris (backing vocals); Steve Vai (stunt guitar); Tommy Mars (keyboards); Arthur Barrow (bass); David Logeman (drums)
Producer: Frank Zappa
Engineer: Mark Pinske & Allen Sides

A-side – Track 4
Goblin Girl (4:12) (Frank Zappa) • Master #: AL 1294 • STEREO
Recorded: July 18, 1980 (basic tracks) and August 11-28, 1980 (overdubs) at UMRK, Los Angeles, CA
Personnel: Frank Zappa (lead vocal, kazoo, arranger); Ike Willis (backing vocals, kazoo); Ray White (backing vocals, kazoo); Bob Harris (backing vocals); Jimmy Carl Black (voice); Steve Vai (stunt guitar); Tommy Mars (keyboards); Arthur Barrow (bass); David Logeman (drums)
Producer: Frank Zappa
Engineer: Mark Pinske & Allen SIdes

B-side – Track 1
You Are What You Is (4:23) (Frank Zappa) • Master #: BL 1294 • STEREO
Recorded: July 8-10, 1980 (basic tracks) and August 11 – September 10, 1980 (keyboard, vocal and guitar overdubs) at UMRK, Los Angeles, CA
Personnel: Frank Zappa (lead vocal, guitar, arranger); Ray White (lead vocal, rhythm guitar); Ike Willis (rhythm guitar, lead vocal); Bob Harris (vocals); Steve Vai (stunt guitar); Tommy Mars (keyboards); Arthur Barrow (bass); David Logeman (drums)
Producer: Frank Zappa
Engineer: Mark Pinske & Allen SIdes

B-side – Track 2
Mudd Club (3:32) (Frank Zappa) • Master #: BL 1294 • STEREO
Recorded: July 8-10, 1980 (basic tracks) and August 11-19, 1980 (keyboard and vocal overdubs) at UMRK, Los Angeles, CA
Personnel: Frank Zappa (spoken vocals, arranger); Ray White (lead vocal, rhythm guitar); Ike Willis (rhythm guitar, lead vocal); Moon Zappa (voice); Motorhead Sherwood (tenor saxophone, snorks); Tommy Mars (keyboards); Arthur Barrow (bass); David Logeman (drums)
Producer: Frank Zappa
Engineer: Mark Pinske & Allen SIdes

B-side – Track 3
Dumb All Over (4:36) (Frank Zappa) • Master #: BL 1294 • STEREO
Recorded: July 8-10, 1980 (basic tracks) and August 11 – September 1, 1980 (vocal overdubs) at UMRK, Los Angeles, CA
Personnel: Frank Zappa (lead vocal, backing vocals, lead guitar, arranger); Ike Willis (rhythm guitar, lead vocal); Ray White (rhythm guitar, lead vocal); Jimmy Carl Black (voice); Tommy Mars (keyboards); Arthur

Barrow (bass); David Logeman (drums)
Producer: Frank Zappa
Engineer: Mark Pinske & Allen SIdes

The next FZ album, "You Are What You Is," was another double LP released just 4½ months after "Tinsel Town Rebellion." "YAWYI" was accompanied by a "Clean Cuts" 12" sampler that offered some interesting variations. The material on the album was mostly drawn from recently performed live material with the exception of a few older pieces. Most of the recording took place at UMRK between July and September 1980.

Side one of the "Clean Cuts" sampler began with "Harder Than Your Husband." Frank Zappa came up with a country ballad that was vocally perfect for former MOI drummer Jimmy Carl Black. The double entendre of the song title punctuated Jimmy's affair with a married woman. Ray White and Ike Willis provided vocal backing, with Denny Walley's slide guitar and Craig "Twister" Steward's harmonica adding to the overall musical flavor.

On "You Are What You Is," the previous track "Teenage Wind" overlapped with "Harder Than Your Husband." The mix on this sampler has a clean introduction, as does the subsequent Dutch single to be discussed later. The album mix has 3½ repeats of the ending "Harder than yer husband, harder than yer . . . much, much, much" chorus, but the sampler and Dutch single (listed later) fade after five repeats. The "harder than your husband" lyric was worked into the outro of the song "You Are What You Is" (also on this sampler).

"Harder Than Your Husband" was performed by Zappa's bands throughout 1980, as well as in the fall of 1981 and mid-1982. FZ did the lead vocal for all of these except for Jimmy Carl Black's guest appearance in Albuquerque, NM on October 12, 1980. A spring 1980 rehearsal of "Harder Than Your Husband" can be heard on "Beat The Boots III: Disc Two." The Halloween 1981 lineup performed the song on the video "The Torture Never Stops" and the "Halloween 81" set.

The "YAWYI" album opener, "Teenage Wind," was band two of side one on this sampler. Arthur Barrow went to Alamo Heights High School (near San Antonio, TX) with Christopher Charles Geppert, later known as Christopher Cross. Barrow was excited to hear Cross' soon-to-be #2 hit "Ride Like The Wind" on the radio and he played Frank Zappa what he remembered about the song after just hearing it once. Frank captured the essence of Cross' song while taking it into a different direction. The song title was listed (with a dash) as "Teen-age Wind" on the back cover of "YAWYI," but without the dash on the album and sampler record labels.

For "Teenage Wind," Bob Harris vocalized a miserable teenager missing out on a Grateful Dead concert. Ray White, Ike Willis and FZ backed him up vocally. The topic of being free matched up with the track "Absolutely Free" on "We're Only In It For The Money." Harris ranted about his parents and decided to sniff some glue with insistent backing vocals singing "Parents," "Parents…France" (Paris, France), and "sniff it good" (a takeoff on Devo's line "Whip it good"). France was also mentioned in Zappa's songs "Conehead" and "In France." Sniffing glue was lyrically part of "Charva," "Uncle Bernie's Farm," "The Jazz Discharge Party Hats," "Harry-As-A-Boy," and "The Massive Improve'lence."

The second pass through the "A" and "B" sections of "Teenage Wind" used "dipshit" backing vocals in response to Harris' parental rant. So much for playing this song on the radio! This "B" section referred to The Grateful Dead's lead guitarist Jerry Garcia and Harris' interest in seeing FZ's film "200 Motels." Jimmy Carl Black then spouted four lines from that film's "Lonesome Cowboy Burt." Those lines about Opal the waitress were also in the songs "You Are What You Is," "No Not Now," and "Truck Driver Divorce."

"Teenage Wind" on this sampler fades before it goes to its natural end, overlapping with "Harder Than Your Husband" on "YAWYI." The song was performed at all tours from 1980-1988. A studio rehearsal from the summer of 1980 was released on "Beat The Boots II: Disc Two." The Halloween '81 performance is on "Halloween 81" and the video "The Torture Never Stops," and the summer 1982 band is on "Stage, Vol. 4." The first date of the 1988 tour (February 2 in Albany, NY) featured a quote of "Teenage Wind" within "King Kong."

FZ actually taught the band how to play Christopher Cross' "Ride Like The Wind." With Al DiMeola guesting on guitar at a November 17, 1981 Ritz gig in New York City, Zappa had drum roadie Brian Peters sing Cross' hit. It was a surprising inclusion in the live set which was broadcast by WLIR-FM (Garden City, NY) – the only New York metropolitan area station that had the guts to regularly play Zappa on their airwaves.

The next two songs on the sampler, "Doreen" and "Goblin Girl," were in the same order on the "YAWYI" album. In their original forms, both tracks were also sequenced together on side one of "Crush All Boxes." The subject of "Doreen" was promo director Doreen Tracey, an original member of "The Mickey Mouse Club." She helped "Don't Eat The Yellow Snow" gain traction as a single while working for FZ's DiscReet custom label with Warner Bros. Ray White took the lead vocal this time, and he sang in the background with Bob Harris, Ike Willis, and Frank Zappa. Like "Teenage Wind" and "Goblin Girl" to follow, the lead and backing vocals bounced off each other. On this 12", "Doreen" fades very early at 2:58.

The "YAWYI" version of "Doreen" was repeated on "Zappa Picks By Larry LaLonde Of Primus." "Doreen" was quoted within the next track "Goblin Girl." The fall 1980 band played "Doreen" twice in full and quoted it within "Goblin Girl" at the November 28, 1980 gig at the Uptown Theater in Chicago, IL. "Doreen" was played during the fall 1981 band and can be heard on "Halloween 81." A composite version from the mid-1982 band is on "Stage, Vol. 5."

The 12" sampler used a 3:36 edit of "Goblin Girl" which conflicts with the listed 4:12 timing. This time, Zappa took the lead vocal with backing by Harris, White, and Willis. Jimmy Carl Black was having a conversation with Roy Estrada, but Roy was not present. To illustrate the lighthearted nature of this song filled with double entendres, kazoos were part of the instrumental breaks between verses. The reference of lighting director Coy Featherstone does not occur due to the sampler edit, but it can be heard on the album version. Three quotes take place during "Goblin Girl": "Mysterioso Pizzicato" (0:16-0:19), "Doreen" (starting at 2:09), and Donna Summer's "Bad Girls" (beginning at 3:13). An alternate mix running at a different tape speed was included on "Have I Offended Someone?". A piece of the original mix opening can be heard during "Hot Plate Heaven At The Green Hotel" in the video "Does Humor Belong In Music?".

"Goblin" Girl" debuted at an April 25, 1980 concert in Piscataway, NJ when it was sung over the vamp of "Love Of My Life." With the exception of "Halloween 81," none of the live versions of "Goblin Girl" between 1980-1984 have been released, especially since the complicated overlapping vocal section of the song was dropped after the 1980 tour.

Side two of the "YAWYI" sampler got underway with the title track. It was the story of a white man who wanted to be black, and a black man who wanted to be white. The guitar riff of "YAWYI" was first played during the solo section of "Yo' Mama" at Deutschlandhalle, Berlin, Germany on February 15, 1978. The complete song debuted at the late show on May 3, 1980 (Music Hall, Boston, MA), but the final lyrics would be revised by the time the track was recorded at UMRK.

Numerous references were made during "You Are What You Is." The white man thought that singing the blues, speaking like the Kingfish character (from radio and TV's "Amos 'n' Andy"), eating chitlins, and using Nivea lotion and Royal Crown pomade would make him a convincing black man. The Negro man changed his diet, put on Jordache designer jeans, and changed his speech patterns in his quest to become white. Without question, the line "I ain't no nigger no more" (2:14-2:16) was not going to garner airplay in the US. This was supposed to be a "Clean Cuts" edition!

For the main body of "YAWYI," Zappa, Harris, White and Willis sang the verses. For the outro, each line by the quartet was met with a Ray White response. Towards the end, White quoted lyrics from "Wonderful Wino," "Lonesome Cowboy Burt," "Teenage Wind," "Jumbo Go Away," "Harder Than Your Husband," and "Mudd Club." The sampler used the full album version but faded the track to the same point. A music video was made of the song for MTV purposes. The studio version of the song was repeated on "ZAPPAtite" and the filmed programs "Video From Hell" and "The Torture Never Stops." A revised version of "YAWYI" with overdubs was used on "Thing-Fish" and "Cheap Thrills." The mention of "working the wall" within "YAWYI" was also included in "Broken Hearts Are For Assholes," "Sex," "The Jazz Discharge Party Hats," "Mudd Club," and "The Meek Shall Inherit Nothing." After its debut in May 1980, "YAWYI" was performed by every FZ band through 1988. "Buffalo" included a live version from the fall 1980 band, and a December 11, 1980 live take was available in the 2006 birthday bundle. The Halloween 1981 performance was included as part of "Halloween 81" and the video "The Torture Never Stops."

The 12" sampler continued with Zappa's song "Mudd Club," which captured the unique characters and atmosphere of that New York City punk and new wave venue. The Mudd Club was owned by Steve Mass, who opened it on Halloween 1978. The club was located at 77 White Street in Manhattan's Tribeca neighborhood and existed until 1983. The club's black ceiling was adorned with HVAC ductwork, lots of wiring, and pipes. Club attendees like to hang on those pipes and bounce off the walls while the music blared. The Mudd Club was not for Studio 54 disco customers – in fact, Mr. Mass went out of his way to prevent those disco guys and girls from entering his establishment. It certainly helped if you wore serious leather and/or chains when you approached The Mudd Club's entrance.

The full intro of "Mudd Club" was included on the sampler 12". A drum hit preceded a Motorhead Sherwood snork before a second drum hit led into Ray White's opening vocal. The "YAWYI" album mix started from the second drum hit. The club crowd included Frank's daughter Moon Unit among many others. FZ and Ike Willis were the vocalists which responded to White's lines. Using a processed vocal, Frank gave a verbal description of the cast of Mudd Club customers present on a given night. Between 1:04-1:05, Zappa described some audience members as "Fabulous Poodles," which was a British group that flourished during the new wave era. Those characters were described doing "The Peppermint Twist," a #1 hit by Joey Dee And The Starliters in 1961 which replaced Chubby Checker's "The Twist" at the top spot. "The Twist" was also mentioned with The Frug, a lesser known dance fad which peaked in the mid-'60s. The extremely active Frug was ideal for overly stimulated Mudd Club customers. Zappa also mentioned Studio 54, which was shuttered in February 1980 after owners Steve Rubell and Ian Schrager were busted for tax evasion.

At 1:38, Motorhead Sherwood entered the track to provide regular snorks that lasted until 2:19. He also snorked from 2:44-2:50 and 3:11-3:12, and he briefly played tenor saxophone between 2:28 and 2:34. At that point, Frank worked in a mention of Al Malkin. Working the pipe and the floor were unique to the Mudd Club, but FZ's reference to working the wall came from the band's experience at The Gilded Grape on 719 8th Avenue in Manhattan.

The end of "Mudd Club" on the sampler was also different. The track went on 11 seconds after the album mix that segued into "The Meek Shall Inherit Nothing." "Mudd Club" was played by all the lineups from 1980-1984, and it was soundchecked in early 1988. One of the performances of "Mudd Club" was at the club itself on May 8, 1980. The fall '80 band can be heard playing "Mudd Club" on "Buffalo," and the Halloween 1981 show performance is on the video "The Torture Never Stops" and the "Halloween 81" set. An overdubbed version of "Mudd Club" was released on "Thing-Fish."

"Dumb All Over" closed the sampler on another controversial note. Once again, the intro on the sampler was longer than the album version. The sampler has the same drum hit and Motorhead snork before Jimmy Carl Black's yelled "Ayyy!" The "YAWYI" mix had a slightly longer "Ayyy" than the sampler. FZ used a processed vocal again to deliver a rap which skewered organized religion. The 12" used a 4:36 edit, which is more than a minute and half shorter than the album version. Ray White and Ike Willis carried the chorus to the outro. The album mix was repeated on "Zappa Picks By Larry LaLonde Of Primus" and "Understanding America."

All of Zappa's lineups from 1980-1988 performed "Dumb All Over" on an infrequent basis. The Halloween 1981 take was on "Halloween 81," the video "The Torture Never Stops" and "Stage, Vol. 1." "Have I Offended Someone?" featured a New York City live version from August 25, 1984. "Dumb All Over" was soundchecked in early 1988, but it was not performed on that tour.

In terms of airplay and sales, this sampler was not as successful as its predecessor. "You Are What You Is" peaked at #93 during its brief time on the US album chart.

* * *

FRANK ZAPPA: Goblin Girl/ Pink Napkins (12" 45 rpm picture disc single/ 7" 45 rpm promo single)
Released October 26, 1981 as Barking Pumpkin W99 02616 (12")/ AS 1328 (promo 7")

A-side
Goblin Girl (3:36) (Frank Zappa) • Master #: BPRP 1114-A (12"); BPR 1115 A (7") • STEREO
Recorded: July 18, 1980 at UMRK, Los Angeles, CA, and August 11-28, 1980 at UMRK, Los Angeles, CA (overdubs) Personnel: Frank Zappa (lead vocal, kazoo, arranger); Ike Willis (backing vocals, kazoo); Ray White (backing vocals, kazoo); Bob Harris (backing vocals); Jimmy Carl Black (voice); Steve Vai (stunt guitar); Tommy Mars (keyboards); Arthur Barrow (bass); David Logeman (drums)
Producer: Frank Zappa
Engineer: Mark Pinske & Allen Sides

B-side
Pink Napkins (4:32) (Frank Zappa) • Master #: BPRP 1114-B (12"); BPR 1115 B (7") • STEREO
Recorded live on February 17, 1977 at Hammersmith Odeon, London, England
Personnel: Frank Zappa (lead guitar, arranger); Ray White (rhythm guitar); Eddie Jobson (keyboards); Patrick O'Hearn (bass); Terry Bozzio (drums)
Producer: Frank Zappa
Engineer: Alan Perkins

The opportunity to release the Halloween-themed "Goblin Girl" just before Frank's favorite day of the year was too good to pass up. This 12" picture disc smartly marketed the month-old "You Are What You Is" and the mail-order "Shut Up 'N Play Yer Guitar Some More" at the same time. The initial run of 12" singles came with a white sticker. When those sold out, copies with a purple sticker were issued. The stickers did not list the track times, but they were listed on the promo 7" single that matched the 12" content. The picture disc used the "YAWYI" rear cover photo for the A-side, and the flipside had the Barking Pumpkin logo on a purple background.

The A-side was an even shorter edit of the "YAWYI" album track. The flipside "Pink Napkins" was the final track on "Shut Up 'N Play Yer Guitar Some More" and was a "Black Napkins" solo. Drawn from the early 1977 tour that produced numerous fine "Napkins" solos, "Pink Napkins" proved that Zappa's subtle playing could be more emotive than simply wailing away. On this single, "Pink Napkins" was slightly shorter than the LP master.

The theme of "Black Napkins" was an outgrowth of "Sleep Dirt" that was rehearsed with Frank Zappa's short-lived summer 1975 band with Denny Walley, Robert "Frog" Camarena, Novi Novog, Napoleon Murphy Brock, Roy Estrada, and Terry Bozzio. "Black Napkins" and a quote of it within "Phyniox (Take 1)" were released on "Joe's Camouflage." Michael Zearott conducted "Black Napkins" with The Abnuceals Emuukha Electric Symphony Orchestra during a recording session at UCLA's Royce Hall on September 18, 1975. That track was first issued on the 40th anniversary of "Orchestral Favorites."

"Black Napkins" immediately became an essential part of every FZ touring band through 1988. In addition to "Pink Napkins," versions of "Black Napkins" have appeared on "Frank Zappa Plays The Music Of Frank Zappa," "FZ:OZ," "Zoot Allures," "Stage, Vol. 6," the "A Token Of His Extreme" video (from "The Mike Douglas Show"; also on "Beat The Boots III: Disc One"), "Philly '76," "Zappa In New York 40th Anniversary Deluxe Edition," "Halloween 77" (also on the 2012 "Baby Snakes" soundtrack download and edited in the "Baby Snakes" film), "Halloween 81," "Hammersmith Odeon," "Chicago '78," "Halloween," "Tinsel Town Rebellion" (the vamp used for "Panty Rap"), "Beat The Boots I: As An Am," and "Make A Jazz Noise Here." The 1984 band did not play or quote "Black Napkins" very often, and the 1988 take on "Make A Jazz Noise Here" lacks Zappa's solo because he edited it out in favor of solos by the horn section.

* * *

FRANK ZAPPA: Harder Than Your Husband/ Dumb All Over (7" 45 rpm single)
Released October 30, 1981 as CBS A 1690 (The Netherlands)

A-side
Harder Than Your Husband (2:29) (Frank Zappa) • Master #: none • STEREO
see Special Clean Cuts Edition – You Are What You Is

B-side
Dumb All Over (5:50) (Frank Zappa) • Master #: BL 1294 • STEREO
see Special Clean Cuts Edition – You Are What You Is

This was a unique picture sleeved single released only in The Netherlands, but it was exported to Scandinavia. The A-side was exactly the same as on the "Clean Cuts" 12" sampler. The B-side timing on the label is incorrect, as an even shorter 4:31 edit was used. The sampler ran 4:36.

* * *

FRANK ZAPPA: You Are What You Is/ Harder Than Your Husband (7" 45 rpm single)
Released November 6, 1981 as CBS BA 222897 (Australia)
Released February 26, 1982 as CBS A1622 (England)

A-side
You Are What You Is (4:22; both editions) (Frank Zappa) • Master #: MX200818 (Australia); CBS A1622 A (England) • STEREO
see Special Clean Cuts Edition – You Are What You Is

B-side
Harder Than Your Husband (2:29; both editions) (Frank Zappa) • Master #: MX200819 (Australia); CBS A1622 B (England) • STEREO
see Special Clean Cuts Edition – You Are What You Is

The Australian release of this single was the first using this coupling. It did not have a picture sleeve. The record labels indicate that this single is from the forthcoming album, which means that "YAWYI" had not been yet released in Australia.

UK promos have the same catalog number as the stock copies. However, some promos with the matrix number CBS-A-1622-ADJ 1 have the offending word in the line "I ain't no nigger no more" bleeped out. Some promos and all stock copies are uncensored and have the matrix number CBS-S-A-1622-A 1. The censored version came with a white circle with the words "EDITED VERSION" on the bottom left corner of the picture sleeve. For the uncensored releases, the A-side matched up with the album master. The B-side was the same mix as the "Clean Cuts" sampler.

* * *

FRANK ZAPPA: You Are What You Is/ Pink Napkins (7" 45 rpm single)
Released February 26, 1982 as CBS A 1622 (The Netherlands and Spain)
FRANK ZAPPA: You Are What You Is – Pink Napkins/ Harder Than Your Husband – Soup 'N Old Clothes
(12" 45 rpm picture disc single)
Released February 26, 1982 as CBS A 11 1622 (Germany)

A-side (7")/ A-side – Track 1 (12")
You Are What You Is (4:22; all editions) (Frank Zappa) • Master #: none • STEREO
see Special Clean Cuts Edition – You Are What You Is

B-side (7")/ A-side – Track 2 (12")
Pink Napkins (4:32; all editions) (Frank Zappa) • Master #: none • STEREO
see Goblin Girl/ Pink Napkins

B-side – Track 1 (12")
Harder Than Your Husband (2:29) (Frank Zappa) • Master #: none • STEREO
see Special Clean Cuts Edition – You Are What You Is

B-side – Track 2 (12")
Soup 'N Old Clothes (7:40) (Frank Zappa) • Master #: none • STEREO

Recorded live February 3, 1976 at Kosei Nenkin Kaikan, Osaka, Japan (opening drum roll), and December 11, 1980 (late show) at Santa Monica Civic Auditorium, Santa Monica, CA
Personnel: Frank Zappa (lead guitar); Steve Vai (rhythm guitar); Ray White (rhythm guitar); Ike Willis (rhythm guitar); Tommy Mars (keyboards); Bob Harris (keyboards); Arthur Barrow (bass); Vinnie Colaiuta (drums)
Producer: Frank Zappa
Engineer: George Douglas

The Netherlands, Spain and Germany followed the US example of promoting two FZ albums ("YAWYI" and the "Shut Up 'N Play Yer Guitar" series) at once. The main difference was that "You Are What You Is" replaced "Goblin Girl" as the emphasis track. CBS Germany took things one step further and created a 12" picture disc single that looked like the American release but offered different tracks. The Spanish release listed the song titles in English for a change, and the Spanish sleeve differed from the Dutch issue. The 7" issues mentioned that "Pink Napkins" was from the forthcoming "Shut Up" box set. Some copies of the 12" came with a sticker promoting the upcoming German tour stops, with the May 12, 1982 gig in Berlin listed first.

"Soup 'N Old Clothes" was a guitar solo from "The Illinois Enema Bandit." The track started with a Terry Bozzio drum roll which was later used on "Stage, Vol. 3" in the drum solo track "Hands With A Hammer." Bozzio's solo was from an Osaka, Japan performance in early February 1976. "Soup 'N Old Clothes" was slightly edited from the 7:56 album master.

At this juncture, Frank Zappa was assembling the ill-fated "Chalk Pie" double album. It was a fascinating cross-section of live material with just a few touched up with studio overdubs. Some of the material was used on "Ship Arriving Too Late To Save A Drowning Witch," "Them Or Us" and "Frank Zappa Meets The Mothers Of Prevention," but the tracks were remixed for those albums. The rest of the recordings were not released. One of the unreleased cuts was the November 17, 1981 Ritz performance of "Clownz On Velvet" with Al DiMeola. This was the same show that featured Christopher Cross' "Ride Like The Wind." DiMeola did not give permission for its release. Al has since regretted his position on the matter.

* * *

FRANK ZAPPA: The Frank Zappa E.P. (7" 33 1/3 rpm single)
Released May 7, 1982 as CBS XPS 147 (England)

A-side
Shut Up 'N Play Yer Guitar (5:30) (Frank Zappa) • Master #: XPS 147 A* • STEREO
Recorded live on February 17, 1979 at Hammersmith Odeon, London, England
Personnel: Frank Zappa (lead guitar, arranger, conductor); Warren Cuccurullo (rhythm guitar); Denny Walley (rhythm guitar); Ike Willis (rhythm guitar); Tommy Mars (keyboards); Peter Wolf (keyboards); Ed Mann (percussion); Arthur Barrow (bass); Vinnie Colaiuta (drums)
Producer: Frank Zappa
Engineer: Mick Glossop

B-side – Track 1
Variations On The Carlos Santana Secret Chord Progression (3:52) (Frank Zappa) • Master #: XPS 147 B* • STEREO
Recorded live on December 11, 1980 (late show) at Santa Monica Civic Auditorium, Santa Monica, CA, and March 1977 at The Record Plant, Los Angeles, CA (Bozzio voice)

Personnel: Frank Zappa (lead guitar, arranger, conductor); Steve Vai (rhythm guitar); Ray White (rhythm guitar); Ike Willis (rhythm guitar); Tommy Mars (keyboards); Bob Harris (keyboards); Arthur Barrow (bass); Vinnie Colaiuta (drums); Terry Bozzio (voice at end)
Producer: Frank Zappa
Engineer: George Douglas (Santa Monica); Davey Moire (The Record Plant)

B-side – Track 2
Why Johnny Can't Read (4:30) (Frank Zappa) • Master #: XPS 147 B* • STEREO
Recorded live on February 17, 1979 at Hammersmith Odeon, London, England
Personnel: Frank Zappa (lead guitar, arranger, conductor); Warren Cuccurullo (rhythm guitar); Denny Walley (rhythm guitar); Ike Willis (rhythm guitar); Tommy Mars (keyboards); Peter Wolf (keyboards); Ed Mann (percussion); Arthur Barrow (bass); Vinnie Colaiuta (drums)
Producer: Frank Zappa
Engineer: Mick Glossop

This EP was free with first edition British LPs of "Ship Arriving Too Late To Save A Drowning Witch." The record number was part of UK CBS's promotional series, but it was not marked as that type of release due to its inclusion with a commercial album. This LP/single combo was designed to coincide with the Dutch box set release of all three volumes in the "Shut Up 'N Play Yer Guitar" series. The box set received wide distribution throughout Europe. When Frank Zappa found out that American record stores were selling the Dutch box, it was necessary to create a domestic box set to meet the unrelenting demand.

Two of the three recordings on this EP were from London performances on February 17, 1979. The first, "Shut Up 'N Play Yer Guitar," was from that Hammersmith Odeon gig. A longer mix on this "Inca Roads" solo was called "Streets And Roads" when it was planned for inclusion on the unissued album "Warts & All." This EP does not have grout at either end of the track, unlike the "Shut Up" album. The track fades to the point where the grout would have taken place. The guitar phrase that Zappa played between 2:21-2:31 and 3:07-3:13 would be later worked into "Thirteen" and "Canarsie." That phrase was also in another track on this EP, "Why Johnny Can't Read," but it was edited out prior to release.

"Variations On The Carlos Santana Secret Chord Progression," namely G minor to C major, was a late show guitar solo extracted from "City Of Tiny Lites" in Santa Monica, CA on December 11, 1980. Using the edge of the guitar pick to fret notes, Frank Zappa used what is called the Bulgarian bagpipe technique between 3:15-3:38 of this track. At the end of "Variations," there are two seconds of grout with keyboards, percussion, and the Terry Bozzio utterance "Ah…e-hem…"

"Why Johnny Can't Read" was the other Hammersmith Odeon track on this EP. It was a solo from "A Pound For A Brown On The Bus." From 2:10-2:17 on this single, Arthur Barrow subtly quoted the plantation song "Shortnin' Bread."

* * *

FRANK ZAPPA: Valley Girl/ No Not Now (7" 45 rpm single)
Released May 28, 1982 as CBS A 2412 (The Netherlands)

A-side
Valley Girl (4:49) (Frank Zappa – Moon Zappa) • Master #: none • STEREO
Recorded: Fall 1981 – Early 1982 at UMRK, Los Angeles, CA
Personnel: Moon Zappa (lead vocal); Frank Zappa (guitar, backing vocals, arranger); Scott Thunes (bass); Chad Wackerman (drums); Ike Willis (backing vocals); Bob Harris (backing vocals); Ray White (backing vocals); Bobby Martin (backing vocals)
Producer: Frank Zappa
Engineer: Mark Pinske & Bob Stone

B-side
No Not Now (5:50) (Frank Zappa) • Master #: none • STEREO
Recorded: Summer 1981 at UMRK, Los Angeles, CA
Personnel: Frank Zappa (guitar, low vocals, arranger); Arthur Barrow (bass); Chad Wackerman (drums); Ike Willis (backing vocals); Bob Harris (high vocals); Ray White (backing vocals); Roy Estrada (backing vocals)
Producer: Frank Zappa
Engineer: Mark Pinske & Bob Stone

Of all places to initially release "Valley Girl" on a single, it was in The Netherlands, where they had no idea what a valley girl was! The record was in print for only five weeks, when it was replaced by the single listed next. The picture sleeve used the Roger Price "Droodles" artwork from the "Ship Arriving Too Late To Save A Drowning Witch" LP. No mention of Frank's daughter Moon was made on the sleeve or record label in either a co-writing or vocal capacity. Due to the vast importance of "Valley Girl" in the United States, we'll reserve the majority of the discussion about "Valley Girl" for the American release a short time later. The Dutch "Valley Girl" 45 is missing the opening chord and starts with the chorus. The album master was used, but it was faded just before the opening of the next "Ship" track "I Come From Nowhere."

"No Not Now" was the opening track on "Ship Arriving Too Late To Save A Drowning Witch." It's funny that the end of this track on the single has the missing chord of "Valley Girl"! Frank Zappa referred to "No Not Now" as a mongoloid rock and roll song. Roy Estrada can be heard throughout doing all his pachuco vocalizations.

A series of Donny & Marie Osmond television commercials for Hawaiian Punch fruit drink clearly had a profound effect on Zappa. The squeaky-clean Utah natives became a central part of the "No Not Now" lyrics. Frank's allusions to delivering string beans to Utah and the use of the term "really wild" referenced the siblings in those Hawaiian Punch ads as well as Donny's "really wild" comment to Marie at the end of one spot. Lyrics about delivering string beans to Utah were also in "Truck Driver Divorce" and "The White Boy Troubles." The mentions of a transcontinental hobby horse, riding the bull, and the wife are also shared by "No Not Now" and "Truck Driver Divorce." The song "Drowning Witch" referred to people with Hawaiian shirts on – yet another Hawaiian Punch commercial reference. The mention of "Book 'em, Danno" was from the TV program "Hawaii Five-O" and was also in the songs "You Are What You Is" and "The Untouchables" (the latter from "Broadway The Hard Way"). At 5:48-5:49, FZ used John Smothers' pronunciation of Epsom Salts, which he called "Ebzen Sauce."

"No Not Now" was rehearsed on September 16, 1981 but was not performed. The song was overdubbed for inclusion on "Thing-Fish" using the original title and as a backwards version entitled "Won Ton On." That title will turn up later.

* * *

FRANK ZAPPA: Valley Girl/ FRANK ZAPPA: Teenage Prostitute (7" 45 rpm single)
Released July 2, 1982 as CBS A2412 (England)

A-side
Valley Girl (3:47) (Frank Zappa – Moon Zappa) • Master #: CBS A2412 A* • STEREO
see previous single

B-side
Teenage Prostitute (2:40) (Frank Zappa) • Master #: CBS A2412 B* • STEREO
Recorded live on December 11, 1981 (early show) at Santa Monica Civic Auditorium, Santa Monica, CA, and early 1982 at UMRK, Los Angeles, CA (guitar overdubs)
Personnel: Lisa Popeil (lead vocal); Frank Zappa (guitar, arranger); Steve Vai (guitar); Ray White (rhythm guitar, backing vocals); Tommy Mars (keyboards); Bobby Martin (keyboards, saxophone, lead vocal); Steve Vai (overdubbed guitar); Ed Mann (percussion); Scott Thunes (bass); Chad Wackerman (drums)
Producer: Frank Zappa
Engineer: Mark Pinske & Bob Stone

Once again, Moon was not credited on the A-side of the UK edition of "Valley Girl." The record appeared on two different UK CBS label designs. The B-side was incorrectly written as "Teenage Prostitute," but Zappa listed it on the rear album cover and record label as "Teen-age Prostitute."

"Teen-age Prostitute" was recorded live in Santa Monica, CA on December 11, 1981 with Steve Vai overdubbing his guitar part the next month. Vocalist Lisa Popeil's father Samuel was an inventor that ran Popeil Brothers, and her half-brother Ron formed Ronco in 1964. Lisa rehearsed with Frank Zappa's 1981 band but she departed before the tour started. Instead, she guested with Frank at both Santa Monica shows. At the early show, she sang "Teen-age Prostitute" (the version on this single and the "Ship" LP) and "Lisa's Life Story" (on "Stage, Vol. 6"). Lisa's late show contributions were "The Dangerous Kitchen" (parts of which were edited into "Lisa's Life Story") and an unissued version of "Teen-age Prostitute."

"Chalk Pie" was supposed to be the first home of "Teen-age Prostitute." FZ kept the lead vocals by Lisa Popeil and Bob Harris, eliminated most of the other vocals, and jacked up the lead guitar for the "Ship" mix. The start of the single version of "Teen-age Prostitute" used the last four seconds of "Envelopes" as its starting point. The ending audience response was shorter than that on the "Ship" album. Popeil's solitary appearance with Zappa was documented on the video "The Torture Never Stops." Another live version of "Teen-age Prostitute" ended up on "Halloween 81."

The other countries that released this combination of tracks were Canada, Australia, and The Netherlands. The latter two locations issued this single with a picture sleeve that would match the American release. The Canadian 45 (Epic E4-8498) used the full 4:58 mix of the A-side (more on that later) and the 2:30 single length of the flip. The top side was credited to "Frank Zappa featuring Moon Zappa," but the song was incorrectly spelled "Valley Girls" and was attributed just to Frank. The B-side was shown properly. The Australian issue (CBS BA 222971) had the classic picture sleeve with Moon and Frank, but attributed both sides to the pair.

Both sides matched the mixes on the British single and the B-side was correctly spelled. The revised Dutch single used the same catalog number as the previous edition. It was issued this time with the Frank/Moon picture sleeve. On the audio side, the second Dutch "Valley Girl" 45 used the "Ship" album masters for both sides. Moon's name was nowhere to be found on the A-side label, but the B-side was properly displayed.

* * *

FRANK & MOON ZAPPA: Valley Girl/ FRANK ZAPPA: You Are What You Is (12" 45 rpm single)
Released July 5, 1982 as Barking Pumpkin 4W9 03069
FRANK & MOON ZAPPA: Valley Girl/ FRANK ZAPPA: You Are What You Is (7" 45 rpm single)
Released August 30, 1982 as Barking Pumpkin WS9 02972

A-side
Valley Girl (4:59 [12"]; 3:47 [7"]) (Frank Zappa – Moon Zappa) • Master #: AS 1485 A (12"); WS9 02972 A (7")
• STEREO
see Valley Girl/ No Not Now

B-side
You Are What You Is (4:22 [12"]; 3:53 [7"]) (Frank Zappa) • Master #: 4W9 03069 B (12"); WS9 02972 B (7")
• STEREO
see Special Clean Cuts Edition – You Are What You Is

We're now ready for the American edition of the single that broke through Top 40 barriers and earned Frank Zappa an actual hit single with a bullet. "Valley Girl" took a long time to develop. When Moon Zappa was 13, she regularly regaled her family with impressions of Encino, CA girls from the San Fernando Valley. Moon slipped a note under Frank's studio door which suggested that she should record her Encino accent on his album. What she really wanted to do was spend some quality time with her father.

Frank came up with the "Valley Girl" guitar riff during a soundcheck in the middle of 1981. Before the band went on the road in September 1981, FZ finished off an overdub session by recording his workout with drummer Chad Wackerman. Zappa returned to the tape after the tour and jotted down some lyrics before he decided what to do next.

The tape with Wackerman was dressed up with a backing vocal arrangement. A few days went by before Frank woke up Moon at an ungodly hour and invited her in the studio to record her Encino routine. Two of the five monologues that Moon recorded made up about 90% of the finished version, with bits of the other three forming the rest. Just for fun, count how many times you hear the words "like," "so," "totally" and "sure" in Moon's lyrics!

Backing vocals by Frank, Bob Harris, Ray White and Ike Willis were laid down to work around the topics of Moon's monologues. Scott Thunes' bass was the last piece of the "Valley Girl" puzzle. Frank had an acetate of "Valley Girl" cut for Moon to take to an interview at KROQ-FM in Pasadena, CA. Moon left the acetate at the station, and response was enthusiastically overwhelming. Music fans loved what Frank and Moon created, and many people started speaking like "Valley Girl" characters in their daily lives. "Valley Girl" was never performed live, but Moon performed a guest "Valley Girl" dialogue during "King Kong" at Olympiahalle in Munich, Germany on June 26, 1982.

"Valley Girl" managed to get simultaneous play on Top 40 and rock stations. Billboard's Rock Tracks chart listed the radio play of "Valley Girl," which peaked at #12. Interestingly, "Valley Girl" was first released as a 12" single in early July 1982 and charted in that format before its 7" version materialized in late August. Billboard did not have the commercial 12" catalog number, so they listed the promo 12" at #75 (with a bullet) when the record debuted for the week ending July 17, 1982. The next week, the correct 12" catalog number was listed at #62 – again, with a bullet. The record peaked at #32 for the week ending September 11, 1982. "Valley Girl" was also a #18 hit in Canada. Thanks to the single's success, the LP "Ship Arriving Too Late To Save A Drowning Witch" peaked at #23 in the US. The album master was also on "Strictly Commercial," "Have I Offended Someone?," "ZAPPAtite," and the "Zappa" film soundtrack.

The Grammy committee nominated "Valley Girl" in the category of "Best Rock Performance By A Duo Or Group With Vocal." Survivor's "Eye Of The Tiger" from Sylvester Stallone's "Rocky III" won the award. Promotion for "Valley Girl" extended to "The Official Valley Girl Coloring Book" (a paperback) from Frank and Moon in October 1982. A talking Valley Girl doll by LJN Toys never got past the prototype stage. The April 1983 film "Valley Girl" went down the same road that the Zappas paved, but Frank failed in legally stopping the film's production. The seven-minute "Valley Girl" documentary was included as a bonus in "The Dub Room Special!" DVD.

Moon's classic utterance "Gag me with a spoon!" was later used and adapted in the "Thing-Fish" tracks "Artificial Rhonda," "The Crab-Grass Baby," and "Ya Hozña," the latter of which also included outtakes from Moon's "Valley Girl" dialogue. Another Moon comment, "Hurt me, hurt me!," was also in "St. Alfonzo's Pancake Breakfast" (from "Apostrophe [']") and "Briefcase Boogie" on "Thing-Fish."

The profits generated by "Valley Girl" enabled Zappa to realize his orchestral project with The London Symphony Orchestra. Frank's friend, the highly regarded musical luminary Nicolas Slonimsky, had a cat called Grody To The Max, named after a line in Moon's "Valley Girl" monologue.

Radio stations were serviced with special 7" and 12" promotional releases which contained the 3:47 7" edit (an early fade) and the 12" version (which ran 4:58 on the 7", or 4:59 on the 12"). Two pressings of the 12" promo (Barking Pumpkin AS 1485) and one pressing of the 7" promo (Barking Pumpkin AE7 1490) were sent to radio.

Amazingly, both single versions of "Valley Girl" have never been released digitally. The 12" version is the most essential, as it contains the full ending of the track.

"You Are What You Is" was the B-side of the US single. A 3:53 edit was used for the 7", and the full "Ship" album track was on the 12" single. Both versions of the song were uncensored.

* * *

FRANK ZAPPA: Shut Up 'N Play Yer Guitar Sampler (12" 45 rpm promo sampler single)
Released October 18, 1982 as Barking Pumpkin AS 1569

A-side – Track 1
Pink Napkins (4:31) (Frank Zappa) • Master #: AS 1569 AS • STEREO
see Goblin Girl/ Pink Napkins

A-side – Track 2
Why Johnny Can't Read (4:32) (Frank Zappa) • Master #: AS 1569 AS • STEREO
Recorded live on February 17, 1979 at Hammersmith Odeon, London, England, and March 1977 at The Record Plant, Los Angeles, CA (O'Hearn voice)
Personnel: Frank Zappa (lead guitar, arranger, conductor); Warren Cuccurullo (rhythm guitar); Denny Walley (rhythm guitar); Ike Willis (rhythm guitar); Tommy Mars (keyboards); Peter Wolf (keyboards); Ed Mann (percussion); Arthur Barrow (bass); Vinnie Colaiuta (drums); Patrick O'Hearn (voice)
Producer: Frank Zappa
Engineer: Mick Glossop (Hammersmith Odeon); Davey Moire (The Record Plant)

B-side – Track 1
Stucco Homes (9:00) (Frank Zappa) • Master #: AS 1569 BS • STEREO
Recorded: Spring 1979 (drum track) and Fall 1979 (overdubs) at Village Recorders, Los Angeles, CA
Personnel: Frank Zappa (lead guitar, arranger); Warren Cuccurullo (rhythm guitar); Vinnie Colaiuta (drums); Terry Bozzio (voice); Patrick O'Hearn (voice)
Producer: Frank Zappa
Engineer: Joe Chiccarelli (Village Recorders – spring 1979); Steve Nye (Village Recorders – fall 1979)

The unexpected success of the "Shut Up 'N Play Yer Guitar" series forced Frank Zappa to create an American three-record box set that was issued on September 20, 1982. This promo 12" was mastered at 45 rpm for much better sound quality. The front cover simply consisted of a letter from FZ to radio bigwigs on a plain white background. The back cover in black contained the track credits in white print. Side one started with "Pink Napkins," which again was slightly shorter than the LP master. This time, "Why Johnny Can't Read" starts with three seconds of grout from the end of the "Return Of The Son Of Shut Up 'N Play Yer Guitar" track "Pinocchio's Furniture."

"Stucco Homes" was a Village Recorders track on which FZ and Warren Cuccurullo played guitar over Vinnie Colaiuta drum tracks that were already laid down. As mentioned earlier, parts of Colaiuta's drum tracks were also used on "He Used To Cut The Grass," "Outside Now," and "While You Were Out." Frank already had the theme for "Stucco Homes" when he quoted it and "Thirteen" during his opening guitar solo at Hallenstadion in Zurich, Switzerland on April 1, 1979. Zappa's guitar riff from 4:14-4:17 and 4:28-4:30 on this record were later inserted into "The Radio Is Broken." A very subtle quotation of "Dueling Banjos" was played from 6:01-6:04. This sampler fades before the 11 seconds of grout that appeared on the album master. When Frank Zappa and Ike Willis replaced Van Morrison's lead vocal on L. Shankar's "Dead Girls Of London," they billed themselves as Stucco Homes.

* * *

FRANK ZAPPA: The Man From Utopia Sampler (12" 45 rpm promo sampler single)
Released April 4, 1983 as Barking Pumpkin AS 1594

A-side – Track 1
The Man From Utopia Meets Mary Lou (3:19) (Donald Woods – Doris Woods – Obediah "Obie" Jessie – Sam Ling) • Master #: AS 1594 AS • STEREO
Recorded live on December 12, 1981 (early show) at Fox Theatre in San Diego, CA, and Early 1982 at UMRK, Los Angeles, CA (percussion, keyboard and vocal overdubs)
Personnel: Frank Zappa (lead vocal, backing vocals, guitar); Steve Vai (guitar); Ray White (guitar, backing

vocals); Bob Harris (backing vocals); Ike Willis (backing vocals); Bobby Martin (keyboards, saxophone, backing vocals); Tommy Mars (keyboards); Arthur "Tink" Barrow (keyboards, bass, micro-bass, rhythm guitar); Ed Mann (percussion); Scott Thunes (bass); Jay Anderson (string bass); Chad Wackerman (drums); Craig "Twister" Steward (harmonica)
Producer: Frank Zappa
Engineer: Bob Stone & Mark Pinske

A-side – Track 2
We Are Not Alone (3:31) (Frank Zappa) • Master #: AS 1594 AS • STEREO
Recorded: Summer 1981 (basic tracks) and January 4, 1982 (drum overdubs) at UMRK, Los Angeles, CA
Personnel: Frank Zappa (guitar); Arthur Barrow (bass, rhythm guitar); Chad Wackerman (drums); Steve Vai (guitar); Ed Mann (vibraphone, marimba); Dick Fegy (mandolin); Marty Krystall (tenor saxophone, bass saxophone)
Producer: Frank Zappa
Engineer: Bob Stone & Mark Pinske

B-side – Track 1
Cocaine Decisions (2:56) (Frank Zappa) • Master #: AS 1594 BS • STEREO
Recorded: Summer 1981 at UMRK, Los Angeles, CA
Personnel: Frank Zappa (lead vocal, drum programming); Roy Estrada (backing vocals); Craig "Twister" Steward (harmonica); Scott Thunes (bass); Tommy Mars (keyboards)
Producer: Frank Zappa
Engineer: Bob Stone & Mark Pinske

B-side – Track 2
Mōggio (3:05) (Frank Zappa) • Master #: AS 1594 BS • STEREO
Recorded live on December 11, 1981 (early show) at Santa Monica Civic Auditorium, Santa Monica, CA (0:00-2:09 of basic track), and November 27, 1981 (late show) at Uptown Theatre, Chicago, IL (2:09-3:05 of basic track), and Early 1982 at UMRK, Los Angeles, CA (keyboard and percussion overdubs)
Personnel: Frank Zappa (guitar); Steve Vai (guitar); Ray White (guitar); Bobby Martin (keyboards, saxophone); Tommy Mars (keyboards); Ed Mann (percussion); Scott Thunes (bass); Chad Wackerman (drums); Jim Sherwood (snorks)
Producer: Frank Zappa
Engineer: Mark Pinske

Frank Zappa's 1982 tour only lasted from May to July in Europe, but it was very eventful. The band's time in Italy was where all the action occurred. The July 7 gig at Parco Redecesio in Segrate near Milan, Italy featured a swarm of mosquitoes and a crowd disturbance which led to a riot and the dispersal of tear gas. The other Italian concerts went on without incident. After the concert in Rome on July 9, a female journalist named Valentina from Italian comic magazine Frigidaire showed Frank a comic album of the android character RanXerox. Zappa asked his Italian friend Massimo Bassoli to contact RanXerox creators Tanino Liberatore and Stefano Tamburini for a dinner meeting. After the Naples performance on July 12, FZ and Tanino Liberatore discussed the creation of an album cover which incorporated the events in Milan. They discussed a full Zappa comic, but Liberatore ended up creating mockups of the album covers showing FZ as RanXerox, or FrankXerox if you will. "The Man From Utopia" became the album featuring Liberatore's artwork.

The time surrounding the release of "The Man From Utopia" on April 4, 1983 was full of indecision on Frank

Zappa's part. The album sides were reversed at the last moment. As "The Man From Utopia" was issued, Zappa was in the process of remixing the entire album. This sampler 12" is the only record representing the album which uses the original master mixes. There were no commercial singles from "The Man From Utopia" in the US, but the 45s released elsewhere used FZ's revised mixes.

"The Man From Utopia Meets Mary Lou" was a medley of two R&B singles released the same month – June 1955. Both songs also mentioned the character Mary Lou in their lyrics. The track started off the album and this sampler. "The Man From Utopia" was written by Donald Woods and his wife Doris. It was the B-side of the Donald Woods And The Vel-Aires With Ray Johnson Combo single "Death Of An Angel" (Flip 45-306). ("Death Of An Angel" was covered by The Kingsmen of "Louie, Louie" fame as an A-side in September 1964.) Woods' group had been with Vernon Green in The Medallions. Utopia Cleaners was owned by Raymond and Odessa Cox and was located at 1820 East 97th Street in the Watts locale of southern Los Angeles. The line "he was a funny little fella, and, people, I'm not shuckin' ya" was misunderstood by Frank Zappa as "he was a funny little fella with feet just like I showed ya." Zappa also changed the line "he would leave in the morning, don't come home till late at night" to "he would leave in the morning, don't come back till late at night." Frank was the lead vocalist for his own version, with Bob Harris (falsettos), Robert Martin, Ray White and Ike Willis backing him up. Craig "Twister" Steward played harmonica. "The Man From Utopia" spanned the first 1:17 of the medley, and was reprised from 2:44-3:18. On this 12" sampler, the end of the medley overlapped with the first 4½ seconds of the next album track "Stick Together" and was faded out. A mix of the "Utopia"/ "Mary Lou" medley without the segue appeared on the "Barking Pumpkin Goes Digital" 12" sampler and on a British and Dutch single (all to be discussed very soon). The original LP mix of the medley appeared on the EMI "Utopia"/ "Ship" two-fer CD. All subsequent CDs have Zappa's remixed version of this track.

"Mary Lou" was written by Obediah "Obie" Jessie with Sam Ling. It formed the 1:17-2:44 segment of Zappa's medley with evenly distributed vocals. Jessie was with "Louie, Louie" composer Richard Berry in The Flairs. The original release of "Mary Lou" (Modern 45x961) was credited to Young Jessie with Maxwell Davis & Orchestra, but the uncredited vocal group The Cadets were also involved. The "Mary Lou" in question was Mary Ann Thomas, a recording artist in her own right. Thomas recorded the single "Shame On You"/ "Beginning Of Our Love" (Flip 45-307) with Donald Woods. That record, credited to Rosalle & Donell, was issued by the Flip label right after "The Man From Utopia." Bob Seger & The Silver Bullet Band recorded "Mary Lou" for their "Night Moves" LP in 1976.

Zappa premiered "The Man From Utopia Meets Mary Lou" at the early show at the Community Theater in Berkeley, CA on December 10, 1981. The basic track for the "Man From Utopia" master was from the early show two nights later at the Fox Theatre in San Diego, CA. The medley was also performed during the 1982 European tour. From that trek, a live version from Pistoia, Italy can be found on "Stage, Vol. 4." The "Utopia"/ "Mary Lou" combo was also occasionally played during the 1988 tour.

"We Are Not Alone" was a summer 1981 UMRK track with Chad Wackerman drum overdubs which replaced Zappa's Linn drum machine programming. The title came from ads for Steven Spielberg's 1977 sci-fi film "Close Encounters Of The Third Kind." The two themes were very melodic and distinct, and were dominated by different instruments. Marty Krystall provided the first (main) theme on tenor and bass saxophones. The second theme was played by Ed Mann (vibes and marimba) and mandolinist Dick Fegy. The two themes alternated until the first theme brought the track to its conclusion. "We Are Not Alone" was used as the theme for the new Australian music television program "Rock Around The World" in 1982. The song was not performed live, but was rehearsed in the summer of 1981 with Zappa-sung lyrics that were in the same vein as "Stevie's Spanking." Once again, the EMI two-fer CD is the only digital disc with the original LP master mix. Later "The Man From Utopia" CDs and "Cheap Thrills" have the FZ remix, on which Dick Fegy's mandolin has more prominence.

Side two of the sampler began with "Cocaine Decisions." This was Frank Zappa's commentary about people of influence in society doing their jobs under the influence of cocaine while other people's lives were in the balance. This was another summer 1981 UMRK track with very spare instrumentation. This time, FZ's programmed Linn drums were retained in the final version. The roles for Craig "Twister" Steward (harmonica) and Tommy Mars (keyboards) were very prominent. Zappa's vocals were double-tracked, and Roy Estrada provided falsettos. Scott Thunes recorded his bass on the first day of his audition for the touring band. The opening line "Chop a line now" and its variations turned up in various versions of the song "Tinsel Town Rebellion."

The sampler and album mixes of "Cocaine Decisions" were slightly shorter than the track on the "Barking Pumpkin Goes Digital" sampler. The original album mix is also on "Understanding America." "Man From Utopia" CDs from 1993 onward and "ZAPPAtite" use Zappa's "Cocaine Decisions" remix that is about a minute longer.

A live Halloween 1981 performance of "Cocaine Decisions" from New York City can be seen and heard on "The Dub Room Special!" video and the "Halloween 81" set. "Stage, Vol. 3" has the only other released live take of the song, and it is a composite of Chicago (November 23, 1984 – first part) and Palermo, Italy (July 14, 1982 – second part).

"Mōggio" was inspired by Frank Zappa's daughter Diva. The character Mōggio was the father of a family (including daughter Chana) that lived in Diva's clothes pocket. A different guitar-based mix of "Mōggio" (along with "Man From Utopia" tracks "The Dangerous Kitchen" and "The Jazz Discharge Party Hats") was originally meant for the "Chalk Pie" album. "Mōggio" was the first part of the 1981 tour rehearsal tune "The Mystery Studio Song" (aka "Furnished Singles" or "Ne Pas Deranger" ["Do Not Disturb" in French]), and "What's New In Baltimore?" formed the second part. On this sampler, the 2:09-2:23 cadenza of "Mōggio" functions as the 1:45-1:59 segment of "What's New In Baltimore?".

The basic track of "Mōggio" was constructed from live performances in Santa Monica, CA and Chicago, IL, and overdubs were done in early 1982 at UMRK. The song was performed right after "What's New In Baltimore?" on the fall 1981 and mid-1982 tours. Two live versions of the songs were on "Halloween 81," and live versions of the pair from Geneva, Switzerland on July 1, 1982 was released on "Stage, Vol. 5" and the second volume of Steve Vai's "Secret Jewel Box." "Mōggio" was soundchecked by the summer 1984 lineup and rehearsed in 1987, but neither lineup performed it live on tour. The 1988 tour featured a quote of Ravel's "Bolero" and "Mōggio" within "Big Swifty" (March 23, 1988 at Towson Center, Towson, MD).

Frank Zappa was not happy with the LP mix of "Mōggio" and replaced it on CD reissues with a revised remix featuring lots of reverb and Chad Wackerman drum overdubs from January 4, 1982. The first use of the revised remix was on the EMI two-fer CD issued on May 9, 1988. The tail end of the track (just before Motorhead's snorks) is slightly longer than CDs released in 1993, 1995, and 2012. "The Man From Utopia" peaked at #153 on Billboard's album chart.

* * *

FRANK ZAPPA: Barking Pumpkin Goes Digital (title on labels: Frank Zappa Album Sampler) (12" 45 rpm promo sampler single)
Released May 16, 1983 as Barking Pumpkin AS 1670

A-side – Track 1
The Man From Utopia Meets Mary Lou (3:19) (Donald Woods – Doris Woods – Obie Jessie) • Master #: AS 1670 RE-1 AS • STEREO
see The Man From Utopia Sampler

A-side – Track 2
Cocaine Decisions (2:56) (Frank Zappa) • Master #: AS 1670 RE-1 AS • STEREO
see The Man From Utopia Sampler

B-side – Track 1
Mo 'N Herb's Vacation (Third Movement) (12:56) (Frank Zappa) • Master #: AS 1670 RE-1 BS • STEREO
Recorded: January 12-14, 1983 at Twickenham Film Studios, London, England
Personnel: The London Symphony Orchestra – conductor: Kent Nagano, concert master: Ashley Arbuckle; Ashley Arbuckle (1st violin); Lennox Mackenzie (1st violin); Michael Humphrey (1st violin); Robin Brightman (1st violin); Sydney Colter (1st violin); Gillian Findley (1st violin); Dennis Gaines (1st violin); Colin Renwick (1st violin); Robert Retallick (1st violin); Cyril Reuben (1st violin); David Goodall (1st violin); Norman Clarke (1st violin); Neil Watson (2nd violin); Ian McDonough (2nd violin); Samuel Artis (2nd violin); Stanley Castle (2nd violin); Geoffrey Crese (2nd violin); Terence Morton (2nd violin); Tom Swift (2nd violin); David Williams (2nd violin); Nicholas Maxted-Jones (2nd violin); Stephen Rowlinson (2nd violin); Sue Kinnersley (2nd violin); Ina McKinnon (2nd violin); Alexander Taylor (viola); Brian Clarke (viola); Peter Noriss (viola); Patrick Hooley (viola); Michael Mitchell (viola); Clarence Atkinson (viola); David Hume (viola); Duff Burns (viola); Jonathan Welch (viola); John Forrester (viola); Ian Rowbotham (viola); Brian Evans (viola); Douglas Cummings (cello); Rod McGrath (cello); Ray Adams (cello); Jennifer Brown (cello); Noel Bradshaw (cello); Ken Law (cello); Francis Saunders (cello); Douglas Powrie (cello); James Potter (cello); Gillian Thoday (cello); Martin Jackson (cello); Keith Glossop (cello); Bruce Mollison (bass); Paul Marrion (bass); Arthur Griffiths (bass); John Cooper (bass); Gerald Newson (bass); Paul Lawrence (bass); John Hill (bass); Simon Hetherington (bass); Paul Davies (flute, piccolo); Frank Nolan (flute, piccolo); Lowry Sanders (flute, alto flute); Michael Hirst (flute); Christopher Nicholls (flute, alto flute); Barry Davis (oboe); Roger Lord (oboe); John Lawley (oboe, cor anglais); Jim Douglas (oboe); Roy Jowitt (clarinet); Ronald Moore (clarinet, Eb clarinet); Michael Angress (clarinet); John Stenhouse (clarinet, bass clarinet); Stephne Trier (clarinet, contrabass clarinet); Robert Burton (bassoon), Nicholas Hunke (bassoon, contrabassoon); Dominic Weir (bassoon, contrabassoon); David Miles (bassoon); James Brown (horn); Terence Johns (horn); Anthony Chidell (horn); Richard Bissill (horn); Colin Horton (horn); John Rooke (horn); Frank Ryecroft (horn); John Butterworth (horn); Maurice Murphy (trumpet, flugelhorns, piccolo); Malcolm Smith (trumpet, flugelhorn); Malcolm Hall (trumpet, flugelhorn); William Lang (trumpet, flugelhorn); Alan Dowley (trumpet, flugelhorn); Eric Crees (trombone); Roger Groves (trombone); Frank Mathison (trombone); Roger Brenner (trombone); Ray Brown (trombone); Stephen Wick (tuba); Kurt-Hans Goedicke (timpani); Michael Frye (percussion); Ray Northcott (percussion); Russell Jordan (percussion); Jack Lees (percussion); Ben Hiffnung (percussion); Ray Parmigiani (percussion); Renata Scheffel-Stein (harp); Robert Noble (piano, celeste); David Ocker (solo clarinet); Chad Wackerman (drums); Ed Mann (featured percussionist)
Producer: Frank Zappa
Engineer: Mark Pinske

This 12" sampler was the first evidence that Frank Zappa was unhappy with the mixes on "The Man From Utopia," but it also contained good news. The photo of Frank on the sampler's front cover was on the back of the first LP from the "London Symphony Orchestra" project. The rear cover blurb on the 12" noted that all future products from Barking Pumpkin would be digital, thanks to the new equipment installed at UMRK. CD releases would be made when the consumer prices for CD players were affordable. The compact disc format had been in development since 1974 and was belatedly introduced to North America in March 1983.

The two tracks on the first side of the sampler were remixes from "The Man From Utopia." According to the sampler's notes, both tracks were "re-tweezed with the digital machinery." "The Man From Utopia Meets Mary Lou" was presented in a digital remix with additional reverb and a cold ending. It should be noted that this mix was reused for the UK and Dutch singles to follow, and it was not the remix that appeared on CDs from 1993 onward. "Cocaine Decisions" is slightly longer with additional reverb. This same remix was also used on a Spanish single, and the tape has not been used since. Despite the reverb added for these mixes, the integrity of the tracks remained intact. The same could not be said about the remix of "Mōggio," whose reverb-laden sound obscured the intricacies of the arrangement.

The nearly 13-minute track on side two, "Mo 'N Herb's Vacation (Third Movement)," was a preview of the "LSO" album released on June 9, 1983. "Mo 'N Herb's Vacation" was an assemblage of musical ideas and works that were originally used for different purposes. The first piece of the puzzle was a guitar phrase that Zappa came up with during Christmas week 1976 for the big band Palladium concerts in New York. Clarinetist and copyist David Ocker started working for Frank Zappa in 1977. Ocker commissioned Frank to write an unaccompanied clarinet piece. The piece, originally called "Blow Job," featured that guitar phrase on clarinet as its opening salvo. A John Bergamo percussion piece with the same title led to the piece being renamed "Mo's Vacation" after former Warner Bros. honcho Mo Ostin.

The arrangement for clarinet was not where Frank Zappa wanted to go with "Mo's Vacation," so he worked in simultaneous rhythm section parts for bass and drums. Those parts were called "Herb's Vacation," titled after former manager Herb Cohen. Mo Ostin and Herb Cohen were in litigation with Frank Zappa at the time. Zappa road-tested "Mo's Vacation" in mid-February 1978 by quoting it within numerous songs. While still occasionally quoting the piece, FZ regularly played "Mo's Vacation" on its own during shows in September and October 1978.

At around the same time as the David Ocker commission in 1977, Frank Zappa was writing the composition "Wøöööĩ" for The Vienna Symphony Orchestra. The main theme of "Wøöööĩ" was a guitar phrase from "The Sheik Yerbouti Tango" that Zappa recast as a violin motive. It was meant to be performed in mid-1979 before negotiations for the performance broke down. To protect his work, Zappa copyrighted "Wøöööĩ" on October 10, 1978. Ocker's solo clarinet performance of "Mo's Vacation" at the University of Southern California on January 19, 1979 went ahead and did not go well. Frustrating wastes of time and money took place with The Residentie Orchestra (The Netherlands), The Syracuse Orchestra (New York), and The Krakow Philharmonic Orchestra (Poland). In every case, money issues and/or politics scuttled plans to perform programs of FZ orchestral music.

Frank started to view the Ocker piece and "Wøöööĩ" as the respective first and second movements of a larger work. In the middle of his aggravating orchestral experiences, Zappa wrote a third movement which tied together and resolved "Vacation" and "Wøöööĩ." The entire three-movement work was called "Mo 'N Herb's Vacation." The entire work was copyrighted on February 24, 1981. A session sheet from April 13, 1981 indicates that the first movement of "Mo 'N Herb's Vacation" was recorded at Studio Z (pre-UMRK) by

David Ocker, John Steinmetz, and Vinnie Colaiuta. This unissued recording featured Ocker playing three clarinet parts and one bass clarinet part, Steinmetz playing three bassoon parts and one contrabassoon part, and Colaiuta playing drums. An early unreleased recording of "Stevie's Spanking" with Colaiuta and bassist Arthur Barrow was tracked in the afternoon before Ocker and Steinmetz's session.

Using the profits from "Valley Girl," FZ had the opportunity to record a full program of his orchestral works with a universally recognized orchestra. A small window of time was available with The London Symphony Orchestra and young conductor Kent Nagano. The rehearsal and recording time were insufficient, leading to numerous performance errors that FZ and Mark Pinske had to fix at UMRK. Like the tracks on the other side of the sampler, Zappa's original "LSO" LP mix (reissued on the remastered LP and the 1986 Rykodisc CD) had a great deal of digital reverb. Bob Stone mixed the tracks that were not on the first "LSO" volume. UMRK engineer Spence Chrislu remixed the entire "LSO" sessions in 1993 without employing the reverb level that Frank Zappa added. Chrislu's mixes were used for the 2012 CD reissue. So, the only place to obtain the original mix of this sampler track is on Rykodisc's CD release.

The London Symphony Orchestra performed the entire album program in London at Barbican Hall on January 11, 1983. The concert was required due to union rules. The next three days were spent in London recording the album on 24 tracks at Twickenham Film Studio. David Ocker played clarinet on "Mo 'N Herb's Vacation." Ed Mann (percussion) and Chad Wackerman (drum set) were part of the entire program.

The third movement of "Mo 'N Herb's Vacation" was used in the video "The Amazing Mr. Bickford." Quotes of the first movement can be found on "Zappa In New York 40th Anniversary Edition" in the tracks "The Purple Lagoon/ Any Kind Of Pain" and "Cruising For Burgers (1977 Mix)." "Burgers" is also on the 1991 CD edition of "Zappa In New York." "Beat The Boots III: Disc One" features the first movement from Poughkeepsie, NY on September 21, 1978. The same movement was quoted in "Wet T-Shirt Nite" on "Joe's Garage Act I," and was rehearsed by the 1980 and 1982 bands. The September 11, 1984 gig at Eissporthalle in Berlin, Germany included "Mo's Vacation" quoted within "The Black Page."

The Berkeley Symphony Orchestra performed a program called "A Zappa Affair" at the University of California's Zellerbach Auditorium in Berkeley, CA on June 15-16, 1984. This ballet performance involved dancers, some of which manipulated puppets. Kent Nagano conducted the orchestra, and David Ocker performed the first clarinet part of "Mo 'N Herb's Vacation." This program marked the American premiere of "Bob In Dacron/ Sad Jane," "Mo 'N Herb's Vacation" and "Pedro's Dowry," and it was also the world premiere of "Sinister Footwear." Neither the ballet performances of these "LSO" works nor the orchestral "Sinister Footwear" have been repeated to date.

In the conceptual continuity sweepstakes, Herb Cohen was also mentioned in "Uncle Meat Film Excerpt Part I," "Does This Kind Of Life Look Interesting To You?," "The Be-Bop Tango (Of The Old Jazzmen's Church)," "Dupree's Paradise," and "Carolina Hard-Core Ecstasy."

* * *

FRANK ZAPPA: The Man From Utopia Meets Mary Lou (Medley)/ Sex (7" 45 rpm single)
Released May 20, 1983 as CBS A 3397 (The Netherlands)

A-side
The Man From Utopia Meets Mary Lou (Medley) (3:19) (Donald Woods – Doris Woods – Obediah "Obie" Jessie – Sam Ling) • Master #: none • STEREO
see The Man From Utopia Sampler

B-side
Sex (3:00) (Frank Zappa) • Master #: none • STEREO
Recorded: Summer 1981 (basic tracks) and January 4, 1982 (drum overdubs) at UMRK, Los Angeles, CA
Personnel: Frank Zappa (lead vocal, guitar); Bob Harris (backing vocals); Ike Willis (backing vocals); Arthur Barrow (bass); Tommy Mars (keyboards); Chad Wackerman (drums)
Producer: Frank Zappa
Engineer: Bob Stone & Mark Pinske

CBS in The Netherlands always seemed to be ahead of the curve when it came to FZ singles. They were the only record division of CBS which released this single, and it was their last product for Zappa. The front of the picture sleeve used Tanino Liberatore's "The Man From Utopia" album drawing. Despite what was listed on the record labels, both sides were not the mixes from the LP. Instead, both sides had additional digital reverb, which FZ became enamored with once he discovered its capabilities. This mix of "The Man From Utopia Meets Mary Lou" debuted on the "Barking Pumpkin Goes Digital" sampler, but the reverbed "Sex" single mix with its complete ending appeared only on this record and the Spanish 45 below. In the UK, "The Man From Utopia Meets Mary Lou" was issued promotionally (CBS XPS 180) with that song on both sides. There was no commercial release in that country.

"Sex" was another summer 1981 track from FZ's home studio. Frank took the lead, with Bob Harris and Ike Willis singing backup. Chad Wackerman replaced Zappa's drum programming in early January 1982. The original version, even in this reverbed mix, lacks the two additional verses that appeared on CDs starting in 1993. An extract of the original mix was part of "Porn Wars Deluxe" on "Understanding America." The longer, remixed edit was on "Have I Offended Someone?".

In terms of conceptual continuity, "Sex" dealt with three topics: bongos, working the wall, and the local jones. Other songs dealing with bongos are "Flower Punk," "Dog Breath," "Uncle Meat," "Sam With The Showing Scalp Flat Top," and "Lemme Take You To The Beach." Working the wall was also talked about in "Broken Hearts Are For Assholes," "The Jazz Discharge Party Hats," "You Are What You Is," "Mudd Club," and "The Meek Shall Inherit Nothing." The other jones involved was in "Jones Crusher."

* * *

FRANK ZAPPA: Cocaine Decisions/ Sex (7" 45 rpm single)
Released May 20, 1983 as CBS A 3400 (Spain)

A-side
Cocaine Decisions (2:56) (Frank Zappa) • Master #: none • STEREO
see The Man From Utopia Sampler

B-side
Sex (3:00) (Frank Zappa) • Master #: none • STEREO
see previous single

CBS Spain's last opportunity to release a Frank Zappa single was similar to the Dutch release, but "Cocaine Decisions" was chosen as the A-side instead. The sleeve design again used Tanino Liberatore's work as its basis. The lyrics of "Cocaine Decisions" were shown in English on the other side. Again, the special mix of the A-side on this single can also be found on the promo 12" "Barking Pumpkin Goes Digital," and this revised B-side mix was also on the Dutch single listed above this one.

* * *

FRANK ZAPPA & THE BARKING PUMPKIN DIGITAL GRATIFICATION CONSORT: The Girl In The Magnesium Dress/ Outside Now, Again (12" 33 1/3 rpm promo single)
Released August 23, 1984 as Angel SPRO-9207 (A-side)/ SPRO-9208 (B-side)

A-side
The Girl In The Magnesium Dress (3:27) (Frank Zappa) • Master #: S600840 • STEREO
Recorded: February-April 1984 at UMRK, Los Angeles, CA
Personnel: The Barking Pumpkin Digital Gratification (Frank Zappa composition on Synclavier)
Producer: Frank Zappa
Engineer: Bob Stone

B-side
Outside Now, Again (4:06) (Frank Zappa) • Master #: S600841 • STEREO
Recorded: February-April 1984 at UMRK, Los Angeles, CA
Personnel: The Barking Pumpkin Digital Gratification (Frank Zappa composition on Synclavier)
Producer: Frank Zappa
Engineer: Bob Stone

In his quest to locate an orchestra which ended with the LSO, Frank Zappa sent in-progress editions of "Mo 'N Herb's Vacation," "Bob In Dacron/ Sad Jane" and "Pedro's Dowry" to legendary French conductor/ composer Pierre Boulez in 1979. Boulez was very interested in having Zappa compose some fresh pieces for his chamber music collective Ensemble InterContemporain. FZ presented Boulez and musical director Peter Eötvös with one brand new piece, "The Perfect Stranger," plus "Naval Aviation In Art?" (originally on "Orchestral Favorites"), and the newly orchestrated "Dupree's Paradise," which had been played in a rock arrangement since 1973. They had a record deal with EMI's Angel classical label. The plan was to combine Ensemble InterContemporain's performances with Synclavier works created by Zappa. The album was titled "Boulez Conducts Zappa: The Perfect Stranger." In addition to its release on LP, "The Perfect Stranger" would be FZ's first compact disc product. Zappa's relationship with EMI continued after this album, as his Barking Pumpkin output was distributed by EMI's Capitol imprint in North America and EMI proper elsewhere.

Pierre Boulez and Ensemble InterContemporain performed these three FZ works at Thèâtre de la Ville in Paris, France on January 9, 1984. The concert also included works by Charles Ives, Carl Ruggles, and Elliott Carter. The same three pieces were recorded at IRCAM, Paris the next two days. Over the next three months, Frank Zappa completed the album with four Synclavier works: "The Girl In The Magnesium Dress," "Love Story," "Outside Now, Again," and "Jonestown." The first and third of these pieces were on this promotional single.

The synthesized sounds used on the original Synclavier versions were based on Fender Rhodes electric piano and vibraphone. Zappa's program notes said that "The Girl In The Magnesium Dress" was about a man-hating girl that killed men with her special dress. The original Angel releases on LP and CD are the only places to locate Zappa's original version of this piece, as well as the other original versions/mixes. Later on, FZ produced a faster-paced version of "Magnesium Dress" using a marimba sample and additional notes in the arrangement. In September 1992, Ensemble Modern performed Ali N. Askin's arrangement of "The Girl In The Magnesium Dress" during eight concerts – some of which were attended by Zappa. Their performances were released as "The Yellow Shark."

"Outside Now, Again" was a slower arrangement of a Frank Zappa guitar solo from "City Of Tiny Lites" which was recorded at the March 31, 1979 early show in Munich, Germany. The solo was used for the well-known track "Outside Now" on "Joe's Garage Acts II & III." The first 3:32 of the Synclavier track's 4:06 length was derived from this Steve Vai-transcribed solo, and three repeats of the theme concluded the piece. Once again, Zappa later revised and remixed "Outside Now, Again" by using different voicing.

* * *

FRANK ZAPPA: Baby, Take Your Teeth Out/ Stevie's Spanking (7" 45 rpm single)
Released October 5, 1984 as EMI 5499 (England)

A-side
Baby, Take Your Teeth Out (1:54) (Frank Zappa) • Master #: EMI 5499A • STEREO
Recorded live on June 11-12, 1982 during soundcheck at Alte Oper, Frankfurt, Germany (basic tracks), and 1982-1984 at UMRK, Los Angeles, CA (vocal overdubs)
Personnel: Ike Willis (lead vocal); Bob Harris (harmony vocal); Thana Harris (harmony vocal); Ray White (harmony vocal); Steve Vai (guitar); Tommy Mars (keyboard solo); Bobby Martin (keyboards); Ed Mann (percussion); Scott Thunes (bass); Chad Wackerman (drums)
Producer: Frank Zappa
Engineer: Mark Pinske & Bob Stone

B-side
Stevie's Spanking (5:24) (Frank Zappa) • Master #: EMI 5499B • STEREO
Recorded live on November 17, 1981 at The Ritz, New York, NY, November 28, 1981 at Northrop Auditorium, Minneapolis, MN, June 26, 1982 at Olympiahalle, Munich, Germany, plus at least one unidentified concert (all basic track components), and 1982-1984 at UMRK, Los Angeles, CA (vocal and Dweezil Zappa guitar overdubs)
Personnel: Frank Zappa (rhythm guitar); Bobby Martin (lead vocals); Ray White (rhythm guitar, backing vocals); Ike Willis (backing vocals); Roy Estrada (backing vocals); Steve Vai (first guitar solo); Dweezil Zappa (second guitar solo); Tommy Mars (keyboards); Ed Mann (percussion); Scott Thunes (bass, mini-Moog); Chad Wackerman (drums)
Producer: Frank Zappa
Engineer: Mark Pinske & Bob Stone

EMI's first Zappa single was a strange combination of tracks from the album "Them Or Us." FZ wrote the A-side, but he's not on it. "Baby, Take Your Teeth Out" was about Zappa's bodyguard John Smothers' false teeth and the malaprops Smothers was known for. Ike sang lead, with backing vocals by Ray White, Bob Harris and his wife Thana. Another song about Smothers was "Dong Work For Yuda," which also shared the lyric "praketing richcraft" with this one. The line "eat the label" referred to the song "Wonderful Wino." Baby, Take Your Teeth Out" was one of many songs which featured Zappa's nonsense "moo-ahh" vocals. The others were "Didja Get Any Onya?," "Dinah-Moe Humm" (on "Baby Snakes"), "Tinsel Town Rebellion" (on "Does Humor Belong In Music?" and "Have I Offended Someone?"), "Be In My Video," "He's So Gay," and "Secular Humanism" (on "Civilization Phaze III"). "Baby, Take Your Teeth Out" was not performed in 1982, but it was played in 1984 with a Zappa guitar solo.

"Stevie's Spanking" was FZ's interpretation of an event which took place after the November 14, 1980 show at Notre Dame University's Athletic & Convention Centre in South Bend, IN. The protagonists were guitarist Steve Vai and fan Laurel Fishman, and lots of insertions supposedly took place! Bobby Martin double-tracked his vocal with Ray White, Ike Willis and Roy Estrada joining in. Frank's son Dweezil recorded his guitar solo in the studio to replace his father's original solo.

The main "Stevie's Spanking" riff was unveiled during the solo of "If Only She Woulda" at Kiel Opera House in St. Louis, MO on November 23, 1980 (late show). The song was worked on at the pre-UMRK Studio Z by Zappa, bassist Arthur Barrow and drummer Vinnie Colaiuta at an April 13, 1981 afternoon session. The full "Stevie's Spanking" debuted after that and usually resulted in a Vai/FZ guitar competition. A Halloween 1981 live excerpt can be seen and heard in "The Dub Room Special!" video, but the "Dub" and "Halloween 81" CDs and the video "The Torture Never Stops" have more complete versions. The guitar battles continued into 1982. That band is on "Stage, Vol. 4" in a composite of three concerts, and the Rome guitar solo is on "Video From Hell." After Steve Vai left the band, "Stevie's Spanking" was rarely performed in 1984 and 1988. The '88 band played the song on "Make A Jazz Noise Here."

The UK single was issued with a black and white picture sleeve of Frank wearing an oven mitt as on the "Them Or Us" back cover photo. The mitt was green, but the sleeve was not able to show that! Two different UK pressings were made, and the 45 was released with the same tracks and sleeve in The Netherlands as EMI 1A 006-20 0388 7.

* * *

FRANK ZAPPA: True Glove (12" 45 rpm single)
Released October 12, 1984 as EMI 20 0387 6 (Germany)

A-side – Track 1
In France (3:30) (Frank Zappa) • Master #: none • STEREO
Recorded: 1981-1984 at UMRK, Los Angeles, CA
Personnel: Johnny "Guitar" Watson (lead vocal); Ike Willis (backing vocals); Napoleon Murphy Brock (backing vocals); Ray White (guitar, backing vocals); Bobby Martin (harmonica solo); Tommy Mars (keyboards); Arthur Barrow (bass); Chad Wackerman (drums)
Producer: Frank Zappa
Engineer: Mark Pinske & Bob Stone

A-side – Track 2
Be In My Video (3:40) (Frank Zappa) • Master #: none • STEREO
Recorded: 1984 at UMRK, Los Angeles, CA
Personnel: Frank Zappa (vocal insinuations, backing vocals, arranger); Ike Willis (backing vocals); Ray White (backing vocals); Napoleon Murphy Brock (backing vocals); Bobby Martin (tenor saxophone, falsetto vocals);

Brad Cole (piano); Scott Thunes (bass); Chad Wackerman (drums)
Producer: Frank Zappa
Engineer: Mark Pinske & Bob Stone

B-side – Track 1
He's So Gay (2:45) (Frank Zappa) • Master #: none • STEREO
Recorded: 1981-1984 at UMRK, Los Angeles, CA
Personnel: Frank Zappa (Synclavier, backing vocals, arranger); Ike Willis (lead vocal); Bob Harris (backing vocals); Ray White (backing vocals); Arthur Barrow (synthesizer bass programming); Chad Wackerman (drums)
Producer: Frank Zappa
Engineer: Mark Pinske & Bob Stone

B-side – Track 2
Won Ton On (5:48) (Frank Zappa) • Master #: none • STEREO
Recorded: late 1981-1984 at UMRK, Los Angeles, CA
Personnel: Frank Zappa (guitar, backing vocals, arranger); Steve Vai (guitar); Ray White (guitar, backing vocals); Tommy Mars (keyboards); Arthur Barrow (bass); Chad Wackerman (drums); Bob Harris (backing vocals); Ike Willis (backing vocals); Roy Estrada (backing vocals); Johnny "Guitar" Watson (vocal commentary); Dale Bozzio (voice); Terry Bozzio (voice)
Producer: Frank Zappa
Engineer: Mark Pinske & Bob Stone

With "True Glove," German EMI came up with a 12" that represented "Them Or Us" (side one) and "Thing-Fish" (side two) in an interesting fashion. The bonus was an alternate version of "Won Ton On" which was considerably different than its "Thing-Fish" counterpart released the next month. The covers drew upon the back cover of "Them Or Us" and were in color, unlike the cheaply manufactured UK single above.

Side one of "True Glove" began with "In France." The song started as a takeoff of Gary Numan's "Cars" which was instigated by bassist Arthur Barrow's quotes all throughout the June 22, 1980 concert (Hallenstadion, Zurich, Switzerland). Frank Zappa was inspired to make up some lyrics about France during that concert, and "In France" developed from there. Eventually, the music changed into something that was not derivative of Numan's song. "In France" was rehearsed on September 29, 1980 and was played occasionally in 1982. "In France" was put together entirely in the studio and had more of a blues feel. With that in mind, Zappa asked one of his R&B idols, Johnny "Guitar" Watson, to do the lead vocal. Frank did not play on "In France." Instead, Ray White played guitar and joined Napoleon Murphy Brock and Ike Willis on backing vocals. The line "I said they got a mystery blow job, turn your peter green" is a reference to former Fleetwood Mac guitarist Peter Green. The scatological humor throughout poked fun at what non-French people thought of what French people did in their lives. Johnny "Guitar" Watson played with Zappa at the Hollywood Palladium on July 22, 1984, and yes, "In France" was part of his act. "Beat The Boots III: Disc Two" has that performance. The version on "Stage, Vol. 3" was from 1984 and is missing FZ's guitar solo.

A remix of "In France" was included on "Have I Offended Someone?". In terms of conceptual continuity, France was also mentioned in the songs "Conehead" and "Teenage Wind." The harmonica reference and its variants were also in "Trouble Comin' Every Day," "The Downtown Talent Scout," "Prelude To The Afternoon Of A Sexually Aroused Gas Mask," "Harmonica Fun," and "Diptheria Blues."

The utter stupidity which was passed off as music videos in the MTV heyday of the early to mid-1980s was a prime topic for FZ to cover in a song. "Be In My Video" blasted every music video cliché that MTV viewers were subjected to on a regular basis. This studio cut used group vocals and Zappa's running commentary to skewer David Bowie's "Let's Dance" and "China Girl," as well as Peter Gabriel's "Shock The Monkey" and Spinal Tap's "Smell The Glove." The opening had a vocal intro similar to The Diamonds' "Little Darlin'." The song also referred to astronomer Carl Sagan, who did not say the word "billions" as often as mentioned here! The line "Reent-toont-teent-toont-teent-toont-teenooneenoonee" was also in "Outside Now," and "Be In My Video" was another "moo-ahh" specimen.

This track was the only recorded appearance by pianist Brad Cole, who quit the band prior to the 1984 tour to make a lot more money in Phil Collins' band. Australian keyboardist Allan Zavod replaced him. Another person who quit was Napoleon Murphy Brock, who left two weeks into the '84 tour. "Be In My Video" was used on the albums "Strictly Commercial" and "Understanding America." The New York City performance from August 26, 1984 was on the "Does Humor Belong In Music?" video and "Stage, Vol. 1." An unknown 1984 live source was part of "Beat The Boots III: Disc Six."

Side two of "True Glove" was devoted to "Thing-Fish." "He's So Gay" started the action in humorous style. This record had the original mix without the Johnny "Guitar" Watson vocal insinuations which were added for later CD releases. The backing for "He's So Gay" was spare, with Zappa's Synclavier, Arthur Barrow's synthesizer bass and Chad Wackerman forming the entirety of the instrumental accompaniment. Lead vocals were jointly handled by Zappa, Willis and White, with Bob Harris doing the Estrada-like falsettos. The end of the song featured a quote of The Culture Club's "Do You Really Want To Hurt Me" to make note of vocalist Boy George's sexual orientation. This was yet another song with "moo-ahh" content.

The only CD that has the original LP mix of "He's So Gay" (and the rest of the album) is the British EMI disc of "Thing-Fish" that is extremely difficult to locate. The 1982 band rehearsed the tune on April 6, but it was not performed live. A remix of "He's So Gay" was included on "Have I Offended Someone?," and the August 26, 1984 New York take of the song is on the video "Does Humor Belong In Music?" and the "Stage, Vol. 6" double CD. A live version of "He's So Gay" from an unknown source was part of "Beat The Boots III: Disc Six."

"Won Ton On" was the most surprising track on this single. It was more than the "Ship" LP track "No Not Now" played backwards. Arthur Barrow and Chad Wackerman respectively played regular bass and drum tracks on top of the backwards madness. Almost all of Johnny "Guitar" Watson's vocal insinuations from the revised version of "He's So Gay" were superimposed on the "Won Ton On" track starting at 3:27. This was the first time that anyone had heard what Watson contributed to "He's So Gay" because the revised track was not released until some Rykodisc CDs from 1986 contained that version.

* * *

FRANK ZAPPA: Thing-Fish/ Them Or Us (12" 33 1/3 rpm promo sampler single)
Released November 21, 1984 as Barking Pumpkin SPRO-9261 (A-side)/ SPRO-9262 (B-side)

<u>A-side – Track 1</u>
Be In My Video (3:39) (Frank Zappa) • Master #: SPRO-9261 • STEREO
see True Glove

<u>A-side – Track 2</u>
He's So Gay (2:47) (Frank Zappa) • Master #: SPRO-9261 • STEREO

see True Glove

<u>A-side – Track 3</u>
Won Ton On (5:53) (Frank Zappa) • Master #: SPRO-9261 • STEREO
see True Glove

<u>B-side – Track 1</u>
The Closer You Are (2:58) (Morgan "Bobby" Robinson – Earl Lewis) • Master #: SPRO-9262 • STEREO
Recorded: 1982-1984 at UMRK, Los Angeles, CA
Personnel: Frank Zappa (lead vocal, arranger); Ray White (backing vocals); Ike Willis (backing vocals); Bobby Martin (backing vocals); Tommy Mars (keyboards); Arthur Barrow (bass); Chad Wackerman (drums)
Producer: Frank Zappa
Engineer: Mark Pinske & Bob Stone

<u>B-side – Track 2</u>
Whipping Post (7:32) (Gregory Allman) • Master #: SPRO-9262 • STEREO
Recorded live on December 11, 1981 (late show) at Santa Monica Civic Auditorium, Santa Monica, CA, and December 12, 1981 (late show) at Fox Theater, San Diego, CA, June 11, 1982 (early show) at Alte Oper, Frankfurt, Germany, and 1982-1984 at UMRK, Los Angeles, CA (drum overdubs)
Personnel: Frank Zappa (guitar solo, arranger); Bobby Martin (lead vocal, keyboards); Steve Vai (rhythm guitar); Ray White (rhythm guitar); Tommy Mars (keyboards); Ed Mann (percussion); Scott Thunes (bass); Chad Wackerman (drums)
Producer: Frank Zappa
Engineer: Mark Pinske & Bob Stone

<u>B-side – Track 3</u>
Planet Of My Dreams (1:40) (Frank Zappa) • Master #: SPRO-9262 • STEREO
Recorded: December 1974 at Caribou Ranch, Nederland, CO (piano track), December 1976 at The Record Plant, Los Angeles, CA (bass overdubs), and 1981-1984 at UMRK, Los Angeles, CA (drum and vocal overdubs)
Personnel: Bob Harris (lead vocal); Ray White (backing vocals); Ike Willis (backing vocals); Thana Harris (backing vocals); George Duke (piano); Patrick O'Hearn (bass); Chad Wackerman (drums)
Producer: Frank Zappa
Engineer: Kerry McNab (Caribou); Michael Braunstein (The Record Plant); Mark Pinske (UMRK)

The US 12" sampler for "Them Or Us" and "Thing-Fish" was belatedly released and was a bit misleading. According to the front cover, side one was supposed to have only "Thing-Fish" tracks, with side two reserved for "Them Or Us." The only "Thing-Fish"-related tracks on this record were side one's "He's So Gay" and "Won Ton On." Since this sampler ran at 33 1/3 rpm, its sound quality was inferior to the commercial German release. The first side of this sampler had three of the four tracks on "True Glove." This mix of "Won Ton On" is five seconds longer than the German 12". For completists, the US sampler is the one to get for that track.

Frank Zappa delved into his R&B singles collection to revive The Channels' "The Closer You Are." The original version was written in 1956 by 15-year-old Earl Lewis with Morgan "Bobby" Robinson. The Channels released their version in August of that year (Whirlin Disc 100). Zappa took the lead on this studio track, with backing by Bobby Martin, Ray White, and Ike Willis. The bands in fall 1981, 1982, the second half of 1984 and 1988 performed the song live. "Stage, Vol. 4" has the only released live version as a composite of Florida and Michigan performances.

The Allman Brothers' 1969 debut album classic "Whipping Post" was covered by Frank Zappa years after it was requested by a Finnish fan. The discussion of that recording, "Montana (Whipping Floss)," will come later. Zappa's version was drawn from three live versions plus Chad Wackerman's drum overdubs at UMRK. After Bobby Martin came into the band in 1981, he told Frank that he could sing "Whipping Post." As evidenced here, he certainly could. The band's version of "Whipping Post" became yet another platform for excellent Zappa solos.

The Zappa band's vocal version of "Whipping Post" in the fall of 1981 started out as a reggae number with Bobby Martin singing. The version of "Whipping Post" on "Halloween 81" shows its early arrangement. The 1982 band featured the song in more of an Allman Brothers style, but Zappa's guitar solos were done with reggae backing. The summer 1984 tour regularly played "Whipping Post," and they can be seen and heard on the video "Does Humor Belong In Music?". The guitar solo from "Whipping Post" in London (September 25) was called "That's Not Really Reggae" on the "Guitar" album. The best known FZ solo from the song was released first as "A Solo From Atlanta" on "The Guitar World According To Frank Zappa" and in edited form as the track "For Duane" on "Guitar." It came from an Atlanta, GA performance on November 25, 1984. Another live version from December 23, 1984 was released on the "Does Humor Belong In Music?" CD. On occasion, the song was quoted, as it was in 1974 and 1988. "Whipping Post" was also released on "Zappa '88: The Last U.S. Show."

"Planet Of My Dreams" closed this sampler with another song that Zappa wrote but did not play on. It was a number from FZ's sci-fi musical "Hunchentoot." "Planet Of My Dreams" came from a few sessions spanning a long period of time. George Duke's piano track came from December 1974, Patrick O'Hearn's bass was done in late 1976, and Chad Wackerman's drums and the vocals were tracked in the 1980s. Bob Harris sang the lead vocal, with his wife Thana, Ray White and Ike Willis backing him up.

* * *

DWEEZIL ZAPPA: Let's Talk About It/ Electric Hoedown (7" 45 rpm single)
Released August 22, 1986 as Barking Pumpkin B-74204

A-side
Let's Talk About It (3:56) (Dweezil Zappa) • Master #: B-74204A • STEREO
Recorded: Spring 1986 at UMRK, Los Angeles, CA
Personnel: Dweezil Zappa (guitars, backing vocals); Moon Zappa (lead vocal); Scott Thunes (bass); Chad Wackerman (drums)
Producer: Frank Zappa & Bob Stone
Engineer: Bob Stone

B-side
Electric Hoedown (3:24) (Dweezil Zappa) • Master #: B-74204B • STEREO
Recorded: Spring 1986 at UMRK, Los Angeles, CA
Personnel: Dweezil Zappa (guitars, arranger); Scott Thunes (bass, arranger); Chad Wackerman (drums, arranger)
Producer: Frank Zappa & Bob Stone
Engineer: Bob Stone

Dweezil Zappa's first album "Havin' A Bad Day" was co-produced by his father and engineer Bob Stone for Barking Pumpkin. The A-side is nine seconds shorter than its album appearance. The flip is the same as its album presentation. Frank's rhythm section helped Dweezil with the arrangements in addition to playing on the tracks. Moon sang the A-side, with the instrumental B-side arranged by Dweezil, Thunes, and Wackerman. The original Barking Pumpkin LP was reissued on CD by Rykodisc in 1987. The album has not since been reissued, nor has Dweezil's 1982 debut single "My Mother Is A Space Cadet"/ "Crunchy Water."

* * *

FRANK ZAPPA/ DWEEZIL ZAPPA: Sharleena/ MICHAEL SCIUTO: Grand Prize Stun Solo (6" 33 1/3 rpm flexidisc)
Released December 4, 1986 as Evatone Soundpage #28 (included with the January 1987 issue of Guitar Player Magazine)

A-side
Sharleena (6:50) (Frank Zappa) • Master #: 1013351AXS • STEREO
Recorded live on December 23, 1984 at Universal Amphitheatre, Los Angeles, CA
Personnel: Frank Zappa (lead guitar, vocal); Dweezil Zappa (lead guitar); Ike Willis (rhythm guitar, vocal); Ray White (rhythm guitar, vocal); Bobby Martin (keyboards, vocal); Allan Zavod (keyboards); Scott Thunes (bass); Chad Wackerman (drums)
Producer: Frank Zappa
Engineer: Mark Pinske

The first of FZ's two magazine flexidisc appearances was for Guitar Player. The disc contains an edit of "Sharleena" because the track reached the limit of what could be placed on a flexi. A longer version of the same mix can be found on "Stage, Vol. 3" and the "Stage Sampler." "Sharleena" featured Dweezil playing the initial guitar solo. Frank joined him later and the track faded on this portion. Brief mentions were made of the TV show "Battlestar Galactica" and Kool & The Gang's song "Jungle Boogie." The B-side was by aspiring guitarist Michael Sciuto.

* * *

FRANK ZAPPA: Black Page No. 1/ EVA-TONE INC.: Hear For Yourself How Sound Sells (6" 33 1/3 rpm flexidisc)
Released January 2, 1987 as Evatone Soundpage #29 (included with the February 1987 issue of Keyboard Magazine)

A-side
Black Page No. 1 (2:01) (Frank Zappa) • Master #: 1015501AXS • STEREO
Recorded: 1986 at UMRK, Los Angeles, CA
Personnel: Frank Zappa (composition on Synclavier)
Producer: Frank Zappa
Engineer: Bob Stone
Computer Assistant: Bob Rice

Zappa incorporated the Synclavier Digital Music System into his arsenal after seeing a demonstration of the Synclavier II at a 1982 trade show. The first released FZ album featuring the Synclavier was "Boulez Conducts Zappa: The Perfect Stranger," although Frank had been recording with the system since 1982. Zappa had recently released the "Jazz From Hell" album, which was Synclavier-based except for one live track ("St. Etienne"). The Synclavier arrangement of "Black Page No. 1" was derived from the sound samples used for many of the "Jazz From Hell" tracks, and it differed greatly from the vast number of released "Black Page" live performances from late 1976 to 1988.

Frank's role when using the Synclavier was solely as a creator of audio material. The only "performer" of the Zappa's works (including "Black Page No. 1") was the Synclavier system, which realized what Frank created with Bob Rice's extensive computer work with audio samples. The lead sheet for "Black Page No. 1" was included in the issue of Keyboard Magazine which contained the attached flexi. The B-side of the disc was meant to attract future advertisers by appearing on similar flexidiscs.

Other than its substandard presentation as part of the third volume of the "Beat The Boots III" download which is now out of circulation, this recording can only be obtained from the second-hand market. Also in the substandard department was a set of four 7" picture disc interview singles with Zappa that were issued in England on April 10, 1987 (Baktabak BAKPAK 1003).

* * *

FRANK ZAPPA: Peaches En Regalia – I'm Not Satisfied – Lucille Has Messed My Mind Up (3" CD single)
Released November 13, 1987 as Rykodisc RCD3-1001

Track 1
Peaches En Regalia (3:37) (Frank Zappa) • Master #: none • STEREO
see Peaches En Regalia/ Little Umbrellas

Track 2
I'm Not Satisfied (4:08) (Frank Zappa) • Master #: none • STEREO
Recorded: January 1968 at Apostolic Studios, New York, NY, and 1984 at UMRK, Los Angeles, CA (bass and drum overdubs)
Personnel: Ray Collins (lead vocals, backing vocals); Frank Zappa (acoustic guitar); Roy Estrada (backing vocals); Ian Underwood (organ, alto saxophone); Motorhead Sherwood (baritone saxophone, tambourine); Bunk Gardner (tenor saxophone); Jay Anderson (string bass; 1984 overdub); Arthur Barrow (electric bass; 1984 overdub); Chad Wackerman (drums; 1984 overdub)
Producer: Frank Zappa
Engineer: Dick Kunc (Apostolic); Bob Stone (UMRK)

Track 3
Lucille Has Messed My Mind Up (5:24) (Frank Zappa) • Master #: none • STEREO
see Joe's Garage (sampler)

Rykodisc wanted Frank Zappa to have the first commercially released 3-inch CD single, but they could not get it ready in time. The Delos International label issued a 17+ minute sampler of classical music in October 1987. So, Rykodisc had to settle for having the first pop CD single of the 3-inch variety. The intent of the $3.99 retail, 3-inch CD was to replace 7" vinyl singles with a single format that could hold 20 minutes.

This Ryko single came with cardboard packaging holding the disc at the bottom using a tab that would hold the disc in place. The very bottom of the packaging was perforated for those who wished to store the disc in a miniature sleeve. Of course, the wear and tear of repeatedly removing and replacing the disc would eventually leave the buyer with a disc that could no longer be connected to the packaging! The initial shipment of this CD to retailers was an overly aggressive 300,000 units.

The label wanted to start their singles slate with a sampler that would promote its ongoing rollout of the Frank Zappa catalog. The contents featured "Peaches En Regalia" from Zappa's "Hot Rats" remix, "I'm Not Satisfied" from the overdubbed "Cruising With Ruben & The Jets," and "Lucille Has Messed My Mind Up" from the first "Joe's Garage" volume. This was the first commercial single appearance for all three tracks, and in a way, "Peaches En Regalia" was finally given its first single release after its mysterious cancellation in 1969. None of the tracks on this single were unique, so there was no real incentive for people to buy this single if they bought the CDs that it promoted. To sum it up, it had no collector sex appeal.

* * *

FRANK ZAPPA: Sexual Harassment In The Workplace – Watermelon In Easter Hay (3" CD single)
Released November 14, 1988 as Rykodisc RCD3-1010

Track 1
Sexual Harassment In The Workplace (3:43) (Frank Zappa) • Master #: none • STEREO
Recorded live on December 12, 1981 (late show) at Fox Theater, San Diego, CA
Personnel: Frank Zappa (lead guitar – Hendrix Stratocaster); Ray White (rhythm guitar); Steve Vai (stunt guitar); Tommy Mars (keyboards); Bobby Martin (keyboards); Ed Mann (percussion); Scott Thunes (bass); Chad Wackerman (drums)
Producer: Frank Zappa
Engineer: Mark Pinske

Track 2
Watermelon In Easter Hay (4:03) (Frank Zappa) • Master #: none • STEREO
Recorded live on August 16, 1984 at Jones Beach Theater, Wantagh, NY
Personnel: Frank Zappa (lead guitar – custom Stratocaster); Ike Willis (rhythm guitar); Ray White (rhythm guitar); Bobby Martin (keyboards); Allan Zavod (keyboards); Scott Thunes (bass); Chad Wackerman (drums)
Producer: Frank Zappa
Engineer: Mark Pinske

Rykodisc's next brainstorm concerning the 3-inch CD format was to "surprise" fans with three FZ releases in that format. Having learned their lesson from the previous Zappa single and the eight 3" CD singles by other artists that followed, Rykodisc found it more cost effective to present two songs rather than three. The focus of this release was the FZ album "Guitar." Both tracks were directly from the album masters. "Sexual Harassment In The Workplace" is known to have been performed live only twice. It debuted during the late show of December 11, 1981. The version on this disc is from the second performance at the next evening's late concert. It also kicked off the "Guitar" album.

As most fans are aware, "Watermelon In Easter Hay" is one of Zappa's signature guitar works. The Jones Beach performance was just one of two known performances of the song during the first leg of the American tour. Jones Beach audience members (including myself) were delighted to receive a completely unexpected and ultimately classic performance.

* * *

FRANK ZAPPA: Zomby Woof – You Didn't Try To Call Me (3" CD single)
Released November 14, 1988 as Rykodisc RCD3-1011

Track 1
Zomby Woof (5:39) (Frank Zappa) • Master #: none • STEREO
Recorded live on July 7, 1982 at Parco Redecesio, Milan, Italy (incorrectly listed on packaging as July 6), and June 19, 1982 (late show) at Hammersmith Odeon, London, England (guitar solo only)
Personnel: Frank Zappa (lead guitar, backing vocals); Ray White (guitar, backing vocals); Steve Vai (stunt guitar); Tommy Mars (keyboards); Bobby Martin (lead vocal, keyboards, saxophone); Ed Mann (percussion); Scott Thunes (bass, backing vocals); Chad Wackerman (drums)
Producer: Frank Zappa
Engineer: Mark Pinske

Track 2
You Didn't Try To Call Me (3:39) (Frank Zappa) • Master #: none • STEREO
Recorded live on July 3, 1980 at Olympiahalle, Munich, Germany
Personnel: Frank Zappa (guitar, backing vocals); Ike Willis (guitar, lead vocal); Ray White (guitar, backing vocals); Tommy Mars (keyboards); Arthur Barrow (keyboards, bass); David Logeman (drums)
Producer: Frank Zappa
Engineer: Mick Glossop

The second of the three FZ CD singles from the fall of 1988 was drawn from "Stage, Vol. 1." "Zomby Woof" featured a quote from Jens Bodewalt Lampe's "Mysterioso Pizzicato." Zappa's first attempt at digital recording was "You Didn't Try To Call Me" from July 3, 1980. After all the bugs were worked out, Frank Zappa would embrace the world of digital recording. Once again, both tracks were exactly the same as the album masters.

* * *

FRANK ZAPPA: Montana (Whipping Floss) – Cheepnis (3" CD single)
Released November 14, 1988 as Rykodisc RCD3-1012

Track 1
Montana (Whipping Floss) (10:15) (Frank Zappa) • Master #: none • STEREO
Recorded live on September 22, 1974 (early show) at Kulttuuritalo, Helsinki, Finland
Personnel: Frank Zappa (lead guitar, lead vocal, arranger); Napoleon Murphy Brock (saxophone, backing vocals); George Duke (keyboards, backing vocals); Ruth Underwood (percussion); Tom Fowler (bass); Chester Thompson (drums)
Producer: Frank Zappa
Engineer: Jukka Teittinen

Track 2
Cheepnis (4:28) (Frank Zappa) • Master #: none • STEREO
Recorded live on September 22-23, 1974 at Kulttuuritalo, Helsinki, Finland
Personnel: Frank Zappa (lead guitar, backing vocals, arranger); Napoleon Murphy Brock (saxophone, lead vocal); George Duke (keyboards, backing vocals); Ruth Underwood (percussion); Tom Fowler (bass); Chester Thompson (drums)
Producer: Frank Zappa

Engineer: Jukka Teittinen

This was the last of the trio of 3-inch CD singles that Rykodisc issued at the same time. Both tracks came from "Stage, Vol. 2" and were precisely the same as their album masters. Just before performing "Montana" in Helsinki, Zappa was heckled by a guy, one Mr. Virtanen, that wanted to hear The Allman Brothers' "Whipping Post" instead. Not being an Allman Brothers consumer, Frank was caught not knowing the requested song. Zappa's inimitable ability to think on his feet led him to do some heckling himself by inserting numerous references to "Whipping Post" within the performance of "Montana." After Bobby Martin joined the band in 1981, he informed FZ at a rehearsal that he could sing the hell out of "Whipping Post." It took Zappa until April 29, 1988 to play "Whipping Post" at Jäähalli in Helsinki. Frank spotted Virtanen in the audience and delivered the song 13½ years later!

At the very end of "Montana," Napoleon Murphy Brock referred to "booger-bears." Similar references to boogers and booger-bears can also be found in "The Booger Man" ("Stage, Vol. 4" and the released bootleg "Beat The Boots III: Disc Five"), "Inca Roads" (numerous albums), "Florentine Pogen" (numerous albums), "RDNZL" ("Stage, Vol. 2"), "Cheepnis" ("Stage, Vol. 2 – see below), and "Smell My Beard" ("Stage, Vol. 4").

"Cheepnis" was drawn from two performances, but it is not known if the early and/or late show on September 22, 1974 were involved used because no audience tapes are known to exist for either performance. There is also no audience tape for the single show on the 23rd. The previous year's band performed the song as released on the "Halloween 73" set.

The 3" CD single experiment had run its course and was discontinued after this release. The manufacture of CD singles continued, but in standard (5") CD form. The rise of downloads has greatly diminished physical products such as CD singles, but collector's items are still produced to this day.

* * *

FRANK ZAPPA: Stairway To Heaven/ Bolero (12" 45 rpm single/ 5" CD single)
Released February 25, 1991 as Zappa 12FRANK 101 (12"; England) and Zappa FRANK CD 101 (CD single; England)
Both editions reissued February 22, 1993 with the same catalog numbers

<u>A-side (Track 1 on CD single)</u>
Stairway To Heaven (9:20) (Jimmy Page – Robert Plant) • Master #: none • STEREO
Recorded live on May 8, 1988 at Stadthalle, Vienna, Austria, June 6, 1988 at Palasport, Florence, Italy, and April 18, 1988 at Wembley Arena, London, England
Personnel: Frank Zappa (lead guitar, computer-synthesizer, arranger); Ike Willis (lead vocal, rhythm guitar, synthesizer); Mike Keneally (rhythm guitar, synthesizer, vocal); Bobby Martin (keyboards, lead vocal on last verse, backing vocals); Ed Mann (vibes, marimba, electronic percussion); Walt Fowler (trumpet, flugelhorn, synthesizer); Bruce Fowler (trombone); Paul Carman (alto saxophone, soprano saxophone, baritone saxophone); Albert Wing (tenor saxophone); Kurt McGettrick (baritone saxophone, bass saxophone, contrabass clarinet); Scott Thunes (electric bass, mini-Moog); Chad Wackerman (drums, electronic percussion); Senator Hawkins (sampled voice)
Producer: Frank Zappa
Engineer: Bob Stone (supervisor)

B-side (Track 2 on CD single)
Bolero (5:40) (Maurice Ravel) • Master #: none • STEREO
Recorded live on May 3, 1988 at The Ahoy, Rotterdam, Holland
Personnel: Frank Zappa (lead guitar, computer-synthesizer, arranger); Ike Willis (rhythm guitar, synthesizer); Mike Keneally (rhythm guitar, synthesizer, vocal); Bobby Martin (keyboards); Ed Mann (vibes, marimba, electronic percussion); Walt Fowler (trumpet, flugelhorn, synthesizer); Bruce Fowler (trombone); Paul Carman (alto saxophone, soprano saxophone); Albert Wing (tenor saxophone); Kurt McGettrick (piccolo, baritone saxophone); Scott Thunes (electric bass, mini-Moog); Chad Wackerman (drums, electronic percussion)
Producer: Frank Zappa
Engineer: Bob Stone (supervisor)

This unusual single was not given a US release. Both tracks originally appeared on the album "The Best Band You Never Heard In Your Life." The single reached #9 in Switzerland. "Stairway To Heaven" was given a quite unusual treatment by the band with its barrage of sampled voices and sounds. The band quoted the traditional "Tarantella Napoletana," John Walter Bratton and Jimmy Kennedy's "Teddy Bears' Picnic," Marvin Hatley's "Dance Of The Cuckoos" and Nelson Riddle's "The Untouchables." Ike Willis took the vocal lead. The opening 2:13 came from Vienna, with the next 6:08 coming from Florence, and the concluding 0:59 was derived from London. The horn section played the guitar solo part that Jimmy Page originally played on the Led Zeppelin recording. The 2010 bundle contained a Buffalo, NY version from March 9, 1988, while "Zappa '88: The Last U.S. Show" had a Towson, MD performance from exactly two weeks later.

Maurice Ravel's "Bolero" was performed with a reggae feel. A brief quote of The Knack's "My Sharona" was also worked in for good measure. "Bolero" was originally in the middle of Disc 1 of the album, where it segued into the next track "Zoot Allures." For this single, "Bolero" was presented in its complete form with audience response. This particular length is not available on any other release. On the back cover of the packaging, the left side has a photo of Ravel. The right side shows Zappa holding up John Godwin's book "This Baffling World."

"Bolero" was performed in Uniondale, NY on March 25, 1988, and it was released on "Zappa '88: The Last U.S. Show." It was also quoted within the tracks "We Are Doing Voter Registration Here" and "When The Lie's So Big." The latter was previously used in 2016 for the album "Frank Zappa For President." A previous quote of "Bolero" was made during the March 5, 1988 airing of "When The Lie's So Big" in Cleveland, OH.

* * *

FRANK ZAPPA: Bobby Brown/ I Have Been In You (7" 45 rpm single)
FRANK ZAPPA: Bobby Brown/ I Have Been In You – Dancin' Fool (12" 45 rpm single/ 5" CD single)
Released April 22, 1991 as Zappa INT 113.510 (7")/ INT 128.510 (12")/ INT 828.510 (CD single) (Germany)

A-side (7")/ A-side – Track 1 (12")/ Track 1 (CD single)
Bobby Brown (2:49) (Frank Zappa) • Master #: none • STEREO
see Bobby Brown/ Baby Snakes

B-side (7")/ B-side – Track 1 (12")/ Track 2 (CD single)
I Have Been In You (3:34) (Frank Zappa) • Master #: none • STEREO
Recorded live on January 25, 1978 at Hammersmith Odeon, London, England (basic tracks), and August 14, 15, 17 and 18, 1978 at The Village Recorders, Los Angeles, CA (vocal overdubs on the 14th and 15th; Tommy

Mars keyboard overdubs on the 17th and 18th)
Personnel: Frank Zappa (lead guitar, lead vocal); Adrian Belew (rhythm guitar); Tommy Mars (keyboards); Peter Wolf (keyboards); Patrick O'Hearn (bass); Terry Bozzio (drums); Ed Mann (percussion); Napoleon Murphy Brock (backing vocals); André Lewis (backing vocals); Randy Thornton (backing vocals); Davey Moire (backing vocals)
Producer: Frank Zappa
Engineer: Peter Henderson (Hammersmith Odeon); Joe Chiccarelli (The Village Recorders)

B-side – Track 2 (12")/ Track 3 (CD single)
Dancin' Fool (3:44) (Frank Zappa) • Master #: none • STEREO
see Sheik Yerbouti "Clean Cuts"

The original single of "Bobby Brown" hit #4 in Germany. This record surprisingly enjoyed further success, reaching #32 in its second go-around. Combined with the original release, "Bobby Brown" spent 50 weeks on the German singles chart. The labels for each format showed the title as "Bobby Brown Goes Down." All three tracks were the same as the "Sheik Yerbouti" album masters, and "Bobby Brown" had the Patrick O'Hearn "I knew you'd be surprised…" grout at its end (2:43-2:49). The same grout was used for "Broken Hearts Are For Assholes" on "Läther."

"I Have Been In You" made its single debut. It was faded to the point where it went into the next album track "Flakes." Frank Zappa visited Boston, MA radio station WBCN-FM on the night of October 19, 1977. Zappa brought along the album cover of the ill-fated "Läther" album, and he was asked if it could be a suitable cover for a Peter Frampton LP. Frampton followed up his enormously successful "Frampton Comes Alive!" with the studio album "I'm In You." The title song became a #2 hit. The song's name and message, combined with Peter Frampton's well-known looks, were suitable topics for FZ to deal with in its own classic way.

Zappa immediately came up with his response to Frampton, named "I Have Been In You." The song was premiered at the late show on October 20, 1977 at the Music Hall in Boston. The Halloween '77 performance of the song was released on "Halloween 77," as was the song's vamp for the world premiere of "Dancin' Fool" the night before. The rehearsal from October 30th was in the "Baby Snakes" film and 2012 soundtrack download. The edited intro of the Halloween night take was called "Is That Guy Kidding Or What?" in the film "Baby Snakes," the soundtrack download, and "Stage, Vol. 6." "Hammersmith Odeon" included the January 26, 1978 version of "I Have Been In You" from London, and "Stage, Vol. 6" also featured the October 29, 1978 gig from New York City. The song was rehearsed in the fall of 1980, but it was not performed on that tour.

For the "Sheik Yerbouti" version here, Zappa did the lead vocal with the usual album session quartet of backing vocalists: Brock, Lewis, Thornton, and Moire. Peter Frampton's sexual lyric connotations were straightforward, but Zappa's lyrics revealed a more intense pop star sexual encounter with multiple penetrations! Frampton was a good sport and did some radio spots for "Sheik Yerbouti" by speaking over "I Have Been In You," but they were not widely distributed. The album master of "Dancin' Fool" completed the single.

The Scandinavian release of this single on the Reel label came in all three formats. The 7" and CD single formats looked just like the German issues, but the Scandinavian 12" was packaged in a very simple blue-colored art sleeve. The respective Scandinavian catalog numbers for the 7", 12" and CD single were Reel REALSI 1, REALMA 1, and REALCDS 1.

* * *

FRANK ZAPPA: Valley Girl/ You Are What You Is (12" 45 rpm single/ 5" CD single)
Released August 9, 1993 as Zappa 12FRANK 102 (12") and CDFRANK 102 (CD single) (England)

<u>A-side (12")/ Track 1 (CD single)</u>
Valley Girl (4:50) (Frank Zappa – Moon Zappa) • Master #: none • STEREO
see Valley Girl/ No Not Now

<u>B-side (12")/ Track 2 (CD single)</u>
You Are What You Is (4:23) (Frank Zappa) • Master #: none • STEREO
see Special Clean Cuts Edition – You Are What You Is

The last single released during Frank Zappa's lifetime used a photo of Frank and Moon from 1991 on its front cover. It was an update of the 1982 picture sleeve photo. The back cover included the lyrics for "Valley Girl" along with Moon's notes to her father in 1982 and to fans dated May 15, 1991. Both recordings were the same as the album masters, except that "Valley Girl" was subjected to a quick fade.

* * *

POSTHUMOUS SINGLES

FRANK ZAPPA: Bobby Brown – Valley Girl/ The Torture Never Stops (12" 45 rpm single/ 5" CD single)
Released July 31, 1995 as Rykodisc 159.3094.0 (12")/ 159.3094.3 (CD single) (Germany)

<u>A-side – Track 1 (12")/ Track 1 (CD single)</u>
Bobby Brown (2:49) (Frank Zappa) • Master #: none • STEREO
see Bobby Brown/ Baby Snakes

<u>A-side – Track 2 (12")/ Track 2 (CD single)</u>
Valley Girl (4:50) (Frank Zappa – Moon Zappa) • Master #: none • STEREO
see Valley Girl/ No Not Now

<u>B-side – Track 1 (12")/ Track 3 (CD single)</u>
The Torture Never Stops (12:34) (Frank Zappa) • Master #: none • STEREO
Recorded live on December 29, 1976 at The Palladium, New York, NY
Personnel: Frank Zappa (conductor, lead guitar, lead vocal); Ray White (rhythm guitar, backing vocals); Eddie Jobson (keyboards, violin); Patrick O'Hearn (bass); Terry Bozzio (drums); Ruth Underwood (percussion, synthesizer); David Samuels (timpani); Mike Brecker or Lou Marini (flute)
Producer: Frank Zappa
Engineer: Bob Liftin

This single marked the third German single release of "Bobby Brown" and was Rykodisc's first opportunity to promote the "Strictly Commercial" compilation. The first two tracks were part of that release. The sleeve was very similar to the 1991 "Bobby Brown" reissue. "The Torture Never Stops" was from the live concerts that made up "Zappa In New York," but it did not appear on the original double LP or "Läther." It was reserved for CD editions of "Zappa In New York," the other album that this single promoted. "Bobby Brown" and "Valley Girl" were the same as the original album masters, but again, "Valley Girl" was quickly faded like the 1993 single. The studio version of "The Torture Never Stops" from "Zoot Allures" was overdubbed and retitled "The 'Torchum' Never Stops" on "Thing-Fish." "The Torture Never Stops" and the later "Dong Work For Yuda" mentioned an "iron sausage" in their lyrics.

The spartan packaging for the 12" was a black sleeve with an upper right corner sticker containing the titles and annotations. The CD single was packaged in a more professional form. The front covers of both editions listed the main track as "Bobby Brown," but the labels depicted the title as "Bobby Brown Goes Down." The album master with the ending grout was used. This time, "Bobby Brown" did not receive any German chart action.

"The Torture Never Stops" was premiered in rough form as "Why Doesn't Somebody Get Him A Pepsi?" during the spring 1975 tour with Captain Beefheart's vocals. That early version was on "Stage, Vol. 4" and "Cheep Thrills." The early 1976 lineup's more developed version of "Torture" can be heard on "FZ:OZ." The "recreational activities" recording from the "Zoot Allures" studio take was used in the background for the "Philly '76" version. "Beat The Boots II: Conceptual Continuity" had a Detroit, MI version from November 19, 1976. The expanded December 1976 lineup for the year-end New York City shows performed "The Torture Never Stops" on December 27 and 29. The version on the 29th – the version on this CD single – was inexplicably not included on the "Zappa In New York 40th Anniversary Deluxe Edition," which only had the December 27 performance.

Live performances of "The Torture Never Stops" through 1976 were very low-key. The song's intensity grew throughout live shows in 1977 with increasingly powerful FZ guitar solos. None of the early 1977 band's versions have been released, but six Halloween week versions were part of "Halloween 77." The first peak in Zappa's "Torture" solos was hit in early 1978. One of that era's solos was the aforementioned "Rat Tomago" on "Sheik Yerbouti." Two other full performances of "The Torture Never Stops" from February 1978 were released on "Stage, Vol. 1," the "Stage Sampler," and "Hammersmith Odeon."

The second peak in Frank Zappa's "Torture" solos took place during the fall of 1980. A full "Torture" performance from that band was included on "Buffalo." A solo from "Torture" called "Beat It With Your Fist" can be heard on "Return Of The Son Of Shut Up 'N Play Yer Guitar." Improvisations during "Torture" from the fall 1980 were issued as "The Jazz Discharge Party Hats" on "The Man From Utopia" and the second volume of Steve Vai's "Secret Jewel Box," and the improvs called "Tracy Is A Snob" and "Emperor Of Ohio" were on "Stage, Vol. 6."

The 1981 Halloween gig performance of "Torture" was in the video "The Torture Never Stops" and the CDs "Beat The Boots I: As An Am" and "Halloween 81." The song was quoted within "Tinsel Town Rebellion" during the last show of 1984 at Universal Amphitheater in L.A. on December 23. The 1988 band can be heard playing "Torture" (in two parts) on "The Best Band You Never Heard In Your Life" and "Zappa '88: The Last U.S. Show" (two versions). Solos from the 1988 tour were released on "Trance-Fusion" with the titles "Gorgo" and "After Dinner Smoker."

* * *

FRANK ZAPPA: I Don't Wanna Get Drafted – Dinah-Moe Humm – My Guitar Wants To Kill Your Mama
(5" CD single)
Released November 22, 1995 as Rykodisc REALCDS 4 (cardboard sleeve)/ REALCS 4 (jewel case) (Germany)

Track 1
I Don't Wanna Get Drafted (3:24) (Frank Zappa) • Master #: none • STEREO
see I Don't Wanna Get Drafted/ Ancient Armaments

Track 2
Dinah-Moe Humm (6:01) (Frank Zappa) • Master #: none • STEREO
Recorded: March 19, 1973 at Bolic Sound, Inglewood, CA
Personnel: Frank Zappa (lead vocal, guitar, arranger, conductor); George Duke (piano, synthesizer, clavinet); Tom Fowler (bass); Ralph Humphrey (drums); Ruth Underwood (percussion); Kin Vassy (backing vocals); Sal Marquez (backing vocals); The Ikettes – Tina Turner, Debbie Wilson, Linda "Lynn" Sims (backing vocals)
Producer: Frank Zappa
Engineer: Barry Keene

Track 3
My Guitar Wants To Kill Your Mama (3:31) (Frank Zappa) • Master #: none • STEREO
Recorded: February 1-7, 1969 at Criteria Studios, North Miami, FL (basic track), and August-September 1969 at T.T.G., Hollywood, CA (overdubs), and August-September 1969 at Whitney Studios, Glendale, CA (overdubs)
Personnel: Frank Zappa (lead vocal, acoustic guitar, electric guitar); Lowell George (rhythm guitar); Don Preston (keyboards); Ian Underwood (woodwinds); Bunk Gardner (woodwinds); Motorhead Sherwood (baritone saxophone); Buzz Gardner (trumpet); Roy Estrada (bass); Jimmy Carl Black (drums); Art Tripp (drums)
Producer: Frank Zappa
Engineer: Dick Kunc (Criteria & Whitney); Jack Hunt & Cliff Goldstein (T.T.G.)

This German CD single was packaged in jewel box or cardboard sleeve form with the same content. The sleeves have slightly different catalog numbers, but the discs for both editions are marked REALCDS 4. The main purpose of this single was to respectively promote the 1995 remastered CDs of "The Lost Episodes" and "Over-Nite Sensation" with the "Strictly Commercial" compilation. "I Don't Wanna Get Drafted" is the alternate mix on "The Lost Episodes," and "My Guitar Wants To Kill Your Mama" is the "Weasels Ripped My Flesh" version. Those songs have been discussed already, so we'll restrict this commentary to the track which makes its single debut – "Dinah-Moe Humm."

"Dinah-Moe Humm" was the notorious song in which Frank settled a bet between two sisters (Dinah and Dora) in which he could not get Dinah to achieve orgasm. Thanks to some zircon-encrusted tweezers, he did the business. The use of zircon was inspired by Blackouts keyboardist Terry Wimberly, who wore a zircon-encrusted ring while playing piano. Those same encrusted tweezers were also part of "Montana" and "The Poodle Lecture" which followed "Stink-Foot." Zappa accused Dinah of having cooties, which were also referenced in "Groupie Bang Bang," "Who Needs The Peace Corps?," "Our Bizarre Relationship," "Road Ladies," "The Clap," "What Will This Evening Bring Me This Morning?," and "Why Does It Hurt When I Pee?".

The "Over-Nite Sensation" master used here was repeated on "Understanding America." A remixed reconstruction of "Dinah-Moe Humm" was on "Have I Offended Someone?." The song was performed sparingly during the 1974 tour schedule. The first known live use of "Dinah-Moe Humm" was a quote during an improvisation at the D.A.R. Constitution (Washington, DC) early show on May 4, 1974. The 1976 band can be heard performing the song on "FZ:OZ," "Philly '76," and "Zappa In New York 40th Anniversary Deluxe Edition." Six Halloween 1977 versions were on "Halloween 77," with the Halloween night performance also in the "Baby Snakes" film, 1983 picture disc LP, and 2012 soundtrack download. The early 1978 lineup captured the tune on "Hammersmith Odeon," and the fall '78 band is evidenced on "Halloween." Nothing from the 1979-1981 bands has been released, and the song was not performed in 1982. A composite Chicago/ New York summer 1984 take of "Dinah-Moe Humm" was released on "Stage, Vol. 6," with the entire New York performance aired in the "Does Humor Belong In Music?" video.

* * *

THE TORNADOES: The Swag/ Raw-Hide (7" 45 rpm single)
Released February 15, 2000 as Sundazed S 149

A-side
The Swag (3:46) (Fred Link Wray, Sr. - Milton Grant) • Master #: none • MONO
Recorded: December 1962 at Pal Recording Studio, Cucamonga, CA
Personnel: James Norman "Roly" Sanders (lead guitar); Jesse Sanders (rhythm guitar); Gerald Sanders (bass); Leonard Delaney (drums)
Producer: Dave Aerni for Aertaun Productions
Engineer: Frank Zappa

B-side
Raw-Hide (1:50) (Fred Link Wray, Sr. - Milton Grant) • Master #: none • MONO
Recorded: December 1962 at Pal Recording Studio, Cucamonga, CA
Personnel: James Norman "Roly" Sanders (lead guitar); Jesse Sanders (rhythm guitar); Gerald Sanders (bass); Leonard Delaney (drums)
Producer: Dave Aerni for Aertaun Productions
Engineer: Frank Zappa

The first posthumous US Zappa-related single came from the first Tornadoes session that Frank engineered in December 1962. The band elected to cover two Link Wray & His Ray Men numbers: "The Swag" (the B-side of the 1958 landmark Cadence single "Rumble") and "Raw-Hide" (the flip of the 1959 Epic single "Dixie-Doodle"). Both were typical three-chord instrumentals that rose above the pack by Wray's outstanding guitar work. The Tornadoes had recently taken on George White as their saxophone and percussion guy, but he was not required for these tracks. Both sides exist only on a Pal acetate in group leader Gerald Sanders' possession.

As engineer, Frank Zappa got lead guitarist Roly Sanders to release his pent-up aggression on "The Swag" through both of its lengthy rapid strumming sections. In comparison, "Raw-Hide" was a more conventional instrumental with occasional stops. The band loved the tracks, but neither was considered singles material. They also were not included on their 1963 "Bustin' Surfboards" album.

Both titles were first released on July 27, 1999 on the CD "Beyond The Surf – The Best Of The Tornadoes" (Sundazed Music SC 11039) prior to this single. They sound best on the CD "The Charge Of The Tornadoes" (Crossfire Publications 9503-2; released July 3, 2006).

* * *

FRANK ZAPPA: Lumpy Money OMORP (5" CD-R promo sampler)
Released January 21, 2009 as Zappa (no #)

Track 1
Lumpy Gravy (Primordial): Mvt. I - Sink Trap (2:39) (Frank Zappa) • Master #: none • MONO
Recorded: February 13, 1967 and March 14-16, 1967 at Capitol Studios, Hollywood, CA
Personnel: The Abnuceals Emuukha Electric Symphony Orchestra – Sidney Sharp (contractor, violin); Robert H. Ross (copyist); Esther Roth (orchestra manager); John Guerin (drums); James Helms (guitar); Robert West (bass guitar); James Bond (bass); Kenneth Watson (timpani, mallets); Paul Smith (piano); Thomas Poole (percussion); Ted Nash (flute, bass flute, alto saxophone, clarinet, bass clarinet, contrabass clarinet); Jules Jacob (oboe, English horn, flute, piccolo, tenor sax); Johnny Rotella (flute, alto saxophone, bass saxophone, baritone saxophone, clarinet, E flat clarinet, E flat contrabass clarinet, bass clarinet, piccolo); John L. "Bunk" Gardner (flute, clarinet, baritone clarinet, bass clarinet, bassoon, bass saxophone, soprano saxophone, tenor saxophone, piccolo); Emil Radocchia (aka Emil Richards) (mallets, percussion, timpani, Latin); Gene P. Estes (mallets, percussion, timpani, Latin); James C. Zito (trumpet, flugelhorn, piccolo trumpet); Thomas J. Tedesco (guitar, bells, bongos); Kenneth Shroyer (tenor trombone, bass trombone, bass trumpet); Frank Capp (drums, Latin); Don Christlieb (bassoon, contrabassoon); Michael A. Lang (piano); John Balkin (bass); Alfred Viola (guitar); Dennis Budimir (guitar); Arthur E. Briegleb (French horn); George F. Price (French horn); Lyle Ritz (bass); Joan Steele (copyist); Robert M. Calderwood (copyist); Russell N. Brown (copyist); Vincent Bartold (copyist); Jack DuLong (copyist); Victor Feldman (timpani, Latin, percussion, mallets); Gene Cipriano (oboe, flute, bass flute, E flat clarinet); Charles Berghofer (bass); Lincoln Mayorga (piano); David A. Duke (French horn); Trefoni (Tony) Rizzi (guitar); Shelly Manne (drums); Leonard Malarsky (violin); William Kurasch (violin); Arnold Belnick (violin); Ralph Schaeffer (violin); Jerome A. Kessler (cello); Raymond J. Kelley (cello); Leonard Selic (viola); Joseph DiFiore (viola); Harry Hyams (viola); Philip Goldberg (viola); Joseph Saxon (cello); Jesse Erlich (cello); Tibor Zelig (violin); Harold Ayres (violin); Jerome J. Reisler (violin); Robert Ross (copyist); R.D. McMickle (copyist); John Donahue (copyist); Robert Calderwood (copyist); C.D. Goodwin (copyist); Russell N. Brown (copyist); Joan Steele (copyist); Alan Estes (timpani, mallets, percussion, Latin); Pete Jolly (piano); Lew McCreary (trombone); Vincent DeRosa (French horn); Richard Parisi (French horn); Arthur Maebe (French horn); Harold G. Bemko (cello); Alexander Koltun (violin); Bernard Kundell (violin); James Getzoff (violin)
Producer: Nick Venet
Engineer: Joe, Rex, Pete, Jim, Bob and Gary

Track 2
Absolutely Free (1968 Mono Mix) (3:26) (Frank Zappa) • Master #: none • MONO
Recorded: July 31-September 1967 at Mayfair Studios, New York, NY, and October 1967 at Apostolic Studios, New York, NY
Personnel: Frank Zappa (lead vocal, acoustic guitar, tambourine, marimba); Don Preston (piano); Ian Underwood (harpsichord); Euclid James Motorhead Sherwood (soprano saxophone, baritone saxophone); Bunk Gardner (woodwinds); Roy Estrada (bass); Billy Mundi (drums); Jimmy Carl Black (drums); Pamela Zarubica (Suzy Creamcheese vocal)
Producer: Frank Zappa
Executive Producer: Tom Wilson
Engineer: Gary Kellgren (Mayfair); Dick Kunc (Apostolic)

Track 3
Lumpy Gravy (Excerpt – 1984 UMRK Digital Remix) (3:01) (Frank Zappa) • Master #: none • MONO
Recorded: February 13, 1967 and March 14-16, 1967 at Capitol Studios, Hollywood, CA, and 1984 at UMRK,

Los Angeles, CA (bass and drum overdubs)
Personnel: same as Track 1, plus Arthur Barrow (bass); Chad Wackerman (drums)
Producer: Nick Venet (Capitol sessions); Frank Zappa (UMRK overdub recordings)
Engineer: Joe, Rex, Pete, Jim, Bob and Gary (Capitol); Bob Stone (UMRK)

Track 4
Lonely Little Girl - The Single (2:45) (Frank Zappa) • Master #: none • MONO
Recorded: July 27-September 1967 at Mayfair Studios, New York, NY and October 1967 at Apostolic Studios, New York, NY
Personnel: Frank Zappa (guitar [including guitar on "Love Of My Life" intro at the end of this track], piano, lead vocals, backing vocals, arranger, conductor); Ian Underwood (piano, woodwinds); Don Preston (keyboards); Euclid James Motorhead Sherwood (soprano saxophone, baritone saxophone); Bunk Gardner (woodwinds); Roy Estrada (bass, backing vocals); Billy Mundi (drums, vocals); Jimmy Carl Black (drums, trumpet, vocals); Dick Barber (snorks); Paul Buff (piano, drums, fuzz bass and saxophone on "Love Of My Life" intro at the end of this track)
Producer: Frank Zappa
Executive Producer: Tom Wilson
Engineer: Gary Kellgren (Mayfair); Dick Kunc (Apostolic)

Track 5
Section 8, Take 22 (2:39) (Frank Zappa) • Master #: none • STEREO
Recorded: March 14, 1967 at Capitol Studios, Hollywood, CA
Personnel: Frank Zappa (arranger); Sid Sharp (contractor, voice on countoff); Ted Nash (flute, bass flute, alto saxophone, contrabass clarinet); Jules Jacob (oboe, English horn, flute, piccolo, tenor saxophone); Johnny Rotella (flute, baritone saxophone, E flat contrabass clarinet, bass clarinet); John L. "Bunk" Gardner (flute, clarinet, bassoon, bass saxophone, soprano saxophone, tenor saxophone); Emil Radocchia (aka Emil Richards—mallets, percussion, tympani, Latin); Gene P. Estes (mallets, percussion, tympani, Latin); James C. Zito (trumpet, flugelhorn, piccolo trumpet); Thomas J. Tedesco (guitar, bells, bongos); Kenneth Shroyer (tenor trombone, bass trombone); Frank Capp (drums, Latin); Don Christlieb (bassoon, contra bassoon); Michael A. Lang (piano); John Balkin (bass); Alfred Viola (guitar); Robert West (bass guitar); Dennis Budimir (guitar); Arthur E. Briegleb (French horn); George F. Price (French horn); Lyle Ritz (bass), Joan Steele (copyist), Robert M. Calderwood (copyist), Russell N. Brown (copyist), Vincent Bartold (copyist), Jack DuLong (copyist); Nick Venet (spoken word)

Track 6
Concentration Moon (1968 Mono Mix) (2:22) (Frank Zappa) • Master #: none • MONO
Recorded: July 31-September 1967 at Mayfair Studios, New York, NY, and October 1967 at Apostolic Studios, New York, NY
Personnel: Frank Zappa (lead vocal, backing vocals, acoustic guitar, marimba); Ian Underwood (organ); Roy Estrada (bass, backing vocals); Billy Mundi (drums); Jimmy Carl Black (drums, voice); Gary Kellgren (voice)
Producer: Frank Zappa
Executive Producer: Tom Wilson
Engineer: Gary Kellgren (Mayfair); Dick Kunc (Apostolic)

Track 7
"What's Happening Of The Universe" (1:37) (Frank Zappa – David Silver) • Master #: none • MONO
Recorded: 1969 at WGBH-TV, Boston, MA

Personnel: Frank Zappa (voice); David Silver (voice)

Track 8
Mother People (1984 UMRK Digital Remix) (2:31) • Master #: none • STEREO
Recorded March 14-16, 1967 at Capitol Studios, Hollywood, CA (the "I Don't Know If I Can Go Through This Again" segment), July 26-September 1967 at Mayfair Studios, New York, NY and October 1967 at Apostolic Studios, New York, NY, and August 1983 at UMRK, Los Angeles (bass and drum overdubs)
Personnel: Frank Zappa (electric guitar, acoustic guitar, lead vocals, arranger, conductor); Ian Underwood (piano, woodwinds); Don Preston (keyboards); Euclid James Motorhead Sherwood (soprano saxophone, baritone saxophone); Bunk Gardner (woodwinds – see below); Roy Estrada (backing vocals); Billy Mundi (backing vocals); Jimmy Carl Black (trumpet, backing vocals); Dick Barber (snorks); Arthur Barrow (1983 bass overdubs); Chad Wackerman (1983 drum overdubs); The Abnuceals Emuukha Electric Symphony Orchestra on the "I Don't Know If I Can Go Through This Again" segment – Sidney Sharp (contractor, violin); Robert H. Ross (copyist); Esther Roth (orchestra manager); Robert West (bass guitar); James Bond (bass); Ted Nash (flute, bass flute, alto saxophone, clarinet, bass clarinet, contrabass clarinet); Jules Jacob (oboe, English horn, flute, piccolo, tenor saxophone); Johnny Rotella (flute, alto saxophone, bass saxophone, baritone saxophone, clarinet, E flat clarinet, E flat contrabass clarinet, bass clarinet, piccolo); John L. "Bunk" Gardner (flute, clarinet, baritone clarinet, bass clarinet, bassoon, bass saxophone, soprano saxophone, tenor saxophone, piccolo); Emil Radocchia (aka Emil Richards) (mallets, percussion, timpani, Latin); Gene P. Estes (mallets, percussion, timpani, Latin); James C. Zito (trumpet, flugelhorn, piccolo trumpet); Thomas J. Tedesco (guitar, bells, bongos); Kenneth Shroyer (tenor trombone, bass trombone, bass trumpet); Frank Capp (drums, Latin); Don Christlieb (bassoon, contrabassoon); Michael A. Lang (piano); John Balkin (bass); Alfred Viola (guitar); Dennis Budimir (guitar); Arthur E. Briegleb (French horn); George F. Price (French horn); Lyle Ritz (bass); Joan Steele (copyist); Robert M. Calderwood (copyist); Russell N. Brown (copyist); Vincent Bartold (copyist); Jack DuLong (copyist); Victor Feldman (timpani, Latin, percussion, mallets); Gene Cipriano (oboe, flute, bass flute, E flat clarinet); Charles Berghofer (bass); Lincoln Mayorga (piano); David A. Duke (French horn); Trefoni (Tony) Rizzi (guitar); Shelly Manne (drums); Leonard Malarsky (violin); William Kurasch (violin); Arnold Belnick (violin); Ralph Schaeffer (violin); Jerome A. Kessler (cello); Raymond J. Kelley (cello); Leonard Selic (viola); Joseph DiFiore (viola); Harry Hyams (viola); Philip Goldberg (viola); Joseph Saxon (cello); Jesse Erlich (cello); Tibor Zelig (violin); Harold Ayres (violin); Jerome J. Reisler (violin); Robert Ross (copyist); R.D. McMickle (copyist); John Donahue (copyist); Robert Calderwood (copyist); C.D. Goodwin (copyist); Russell N. Brown (copyist); Joan Steele (copyist); Alan Estes (timpani, mallets, percussion, Latin); Pete Jolly (piano); Lew McCreary (trombone); Vincent DeRosa (French horn); Richard Parisi (French horn); Arthur Maebe (French horn); Harold G. Bemko (cello); Alexander Koltun (violin); Bernard Kundell (violin); James Getzoff (violin)
Producer: Nick Venet ("I Don't Know If I Can Go Through This Again" segment only); Frank Zappa ("Mother People" original and overdub recordings)
Executive Producer: Tom Wilson ("Mother People" original recording)
Engineer: Joe, Rex, Pete, Jim, Bob and Gary (Capitol); Gary Kellgren (Mayfair); Dick Kunc (Apostolic); Bob Stone (UMRK)

Track 9
The Idiot Bastard Son (Instrumental) (2:48) (Frank Zappa) • Master #: none • STEREO
Recorded July 24-September 1967 at Mayfair Studios, New York, NY, and October 1967 at Apostolic Studios, New York, NY
Personnel: Frank Zappa (lead vocal, backing vocals, electric guitar, acoustic guitar); Bunk Gardner (alto flute, voice); Ian Underwood (clarinet); Don Preston (wah-wah clavinet, gong); Ray Collins (tambourine); Roy Estrada (bass); Billy Mundi (drums); Jimmy Carl Black (drums, voice); Motorhead Sherwood (voice); Gary

Kellgren (voice); other unknown backward voices
Producer: Frank Zappa
Executive Producer: Tom Wilson

Track 10
Flower Punk (1984 UMRK Digital Remix) (3:04) (Frank Zappa) • Master #: none • STEREO
Recorded July 26-September 1967 at Mayfair Studios, New York, NY and October 1967 at Apostolic Studios, New York, NY, and August 1983 at UMRK, Los Angeles, CA (bass and drum overdubs)
Personnel: Frank Zappa (electric guitar, lead vocal, clavinet, arranger, conductor); Ian Underwood (piano, woodwinds, voice); Don Preston (keyboards); Euclid James Motorhead Sherwood (soprano saxophone, baritone saxophone); Bunk Gardner (woodwinds); Roy Estrada (voice); Jimmy Carl Black (trumpet, voice); Dick Barber (snorks); Arthur Barrow (bass); Chad Wackerman (drums)
Producer: Frank Zappa
Executive Producer: Tom Wilson (original recording)
Engineer: Gary Kellgren (Mayfair); Dick Kunc (Apostolic); Bob Stone (UMRK)

Track 11
Creationism (1:11) (Frank Zappa) • Master #: none • STEREO
Recorded September 6, 1967 at Mayfair Studios, New York, NY
Personnel: Bunk Gardner (woodwinds); Ian Underwood (woodwinds); Don Preston (electric piano); Jimmy Carl Black (bass trumpet); Billy Mundi (timpani)
Producer: Frank Zappa
Engineer: Gary Kellgren

Track 12
Lumpy Gravy (Primordial): Mvt. IX - Teen-Age Grand Finale (3:30) (Frank Zappa) • Master #: none • MONO
Same recording dates, personnel, producer and engineers as Track 1

This 12-track CD-R sampler of "The Lumpy Money Project/Object" was bookended by the first and last movements of the original "Lumpy Gravy" album for Capitol presented in mono. As with the later 12" single, the studio chat preceding the first movement was omitted here. This disc includes the overdubbed "Lumpy Gravy" fragment that first appeared on "The Old Masters, Box One Sampler" promo LP.

The content of "Section 8, Take 22" was "King Kong." A 42-second piece of "Section 8" (from 0:05-0:47) was used on both the Capitol and Verve "Lumpy Gravy" albums, but the subsequent 1:52 was not. "Section 8" is part of the "Foamy Soaky" module of the Capitol album. The Verve album segment using "Section 8" was indexed as "King Kong." The "King Kong" bass line that Zappa used within Tommy Flanders' "Reputation" B-side was employed here. Zappa's arrangement also included the primary riff of the original "Transylvania Boogie" arrangement.

Two mono mixes from "We're Only In It For The Money" were presented: "Absolutely Free" and "Concentration Moon." The original single mix of "Lonely Little Girl," an instrumental version of "The Idiot Bastard Son" and "Creationism" were from the original "We're Only In It For The Money" sessions. The re-recorded version of "Money" with new bass and drum tracks was represented by "Mother People" and "Flower Punk." Part of the interview material on "Lumpy Money" was represented by David Silver's WGBH interview with Zappa.

The fact that this sampler was a CD-R was an admission that this type of promotional item did not need to involve the full expense of pressing up actual CDs for an archival release. This was the last Zappa-related sampler to be released. Even though the sampler presents no unique material, it is a pricey collectible.

* * *

FRANK ZAPPA: Penguin In Bondage/ The Little Known History Of The Mothers Of Invention (Mother's Day AAC digital download from zappa.com)
Released May 10, 2011 as Zappa Records (no #)

Track 1
Penguin In Bondage/ The Little Known History Of The Mothers Of Invention (26:02) (Frank Zappa) • Master #: none • STEREO
Recorded live on May 11-12, 1974 (late show on May 11) at Auditorium Theater, Chicago, IL
Personnel: Frank Zappa (lead guitar, vocals); George Duke (keyboards, vocals); Jeff Simmons (rhythm guitar, harmonica, vocals); Napoleon Murphy Brock (saxophone, backing vocals); Don Preston (synthesizer); Bruce Fowler (trombone); Walt Fowler (trumpet); Tom Fowler (bass); Ralph Humphrey (drums); Chester Thompson (drums)
Producer: Frank Zappa
Engineer: Bill Hennigh

This comprehensive track was performed by The Mothers, but was credited to Frank Zappa. It began just before midnight leading into Mother's Day, May 12, 1974. The tape reel was changed during the guitar solo after the 24-minute mark, so engineer Joe Travers patched in a piece to cover the changeover. During the time periods 1:31-1:34 and 6:51-7:35, the familiar "Penguin" version on "Roxy & Elsewhere" was used by Zappa.

As for the piece itself, it was an excellent performance which led into Zappa's nostalgic discussion about the history of The Mothers Of Invention. Meanwhile, the band laid down a relaxed groove. An extensive narrative of Paul Buff, the construction of his recording equipment and Frank's time with Buff at Pal in Cucamonga, CA followed. Zappa's conversation continued with how the MOI started, their early jobs under Herb Cohen's management, and their discovery by Verve producer Tom Wilson. Their infamous dealings with Verve/MGM and the recording of "Freak Out!" and "Absolutely Free" led into another guitar solo and the completion of the performance which faded out on a George Duke electric piano solo. This recording is currently unavailable.

"Penguin In Bondage" was regularly performed from August 1973 to May 1975, during the summer of 1978, and also the 1984 and 1988 touring cycles. Other versions of the song were released on "Road Tapes, Venue #2," "Halloween 73," the numerous "Roxy" film and audio releases, "Does Humor Belong In Music?," and "Beat The Boots III: Disc Five." "Road Tapes, Venue #2," "Halloween 73," numerous "Roxy" releases and "Stage, Vol. 2" also contained quotes of "Penguin In Bondage" within "Don't You Ever Wash That Thing?". "Beat The Boots II: At The Circus" used a quote of "Penguin In Bondage" within "Seal Call Fusion Music." Finally, the "Swaggart Version" of "Penguin" was released on "The Best Band You Never Heard In Your Life."

* * *

FRANK ZAPPA & THE MOTHERS OF INVENTION: Help I'm A Rock – It Can't Happen Here/ Who Are The Brain Police? – Who Are The Brain Police? (Basic Tracks) (12" 45 rpm red vinyl single)
Released July 4, 2013 as Barking Pumpkin BPR 1223

A-side
Help I'm A Rock – It Can't Happen Here (8:42) (Frank Zappa) • Master #: BPR 1223-A • STEREO
Recorded: March 12, 1966 at T.T.G. Studios, Hollywood, CA
Personnel: Frank Zappa (leader, arranger, copyist, piano solo, lead vocals, backing vocals); Ray Collins (backing vocals); Roy Estrada (bass, backing vocals); Jimmy Carl Black (drums, backing vocals); Gene Estes (tuned percussion); Kim Fowley (backing vocals); Jeannie Vassar (Suzy Creamcheese vocal); Benjamin Barrett (contractor); plus unidentified pianist, woodwind players, and numerous vocalists
Producer: Tom Wilson
Engineer: Ami Hadani & Tom Hidley

B-side – Track 1
Who Are The Brain Police? (3:24) (Frank Zappa) • Master #: BPR 1223-B • MONO
see Trouble Comin' Every Day/ Who Are The Brain Police?

B-side – Track 2
Who Are The Brain Police? (Basic Tracks) (3:42) (Frank Zappa) • Master #: BPR 1223-B • MONO
see Trouble Comin' Every Day/ Who Are The Brain Police?

The A-side of this 12" single consisted of the three-movement "Help I'm A Rock" stereo album track: "Okay To Tap Dance," "In Memoriam, Edgar Varèse," and "It Can't Happen Here." The title of the work came from a sign on a blue-painted rock that Zappa saw at teacher Phyllis Rubino's house. Zappa's work also conveniently referenced Paul Simon's recent song "I Am A Rock." Guitarist Elliot Ingber acted as an extra in Elvis Presley's 1962 film "Girls! Girls! Girls!". Later on, Ingber played "Help I'm A Rock" for Elvis, who ended up in the list of contributors for "Freak Out!". Zappa played the piano solo in the style of a Cecil Taylor, who was also mentioned in the contributing "Freak Out!" list. The single mixes of "It Can't Happen Here" and "Who Are The Brain Police" have been discussed earlier. The basic tracks of "Who Are The Brain Police?" were included on both editions of "The MOFO Project/Object" and were recorded on Zappa's mono recording unit while the multi-track at T.T.G. was running. This raw recording runs about 18 seconds longer than the finished mono master.

The A-side master is also featured on both "MOFO" editions, while the mono single master of "Who Are The Brain Police?" was included on "The MOFO Project/Object (fazedooh)" double CD but not the 4-CD edition.

* * *

FRANK ZAPPA: Don't Eat The Yellow Snow/ Down In De Dew (Record Store Day numbered 7" 45 rpm single)
Released April 19, 2014 as Barking Pumpkin BPR 1225

A-side
Don't Eat The Yellow Snow (3:26) (Frank Zappa) • Master #: none • STEREO
see Don't Eat The Yellow Snow/ Cosmik Debris

B-side
Down In De Dew (3:18) (Frank Zappa) • Master #: none • STEREO
Recorded: November 8, 1972 at Electric Lady Studios, New York, NY (drum track), and November 18, 1972 at Paramount Recording Studios, Los Angeles, CA (guitar and bass overdubs)
Personnel: Frank Zappa (guitars, bass); Jim Gordon (drums)
Producer: Frank Zappa
Engineer: Dave Whitman (Electric Lady); Kerry McNabb (Paramount)

The A-side of this Record Store Day 45 is a reissue of the 1974 single which was covered earlier. The flip is Zappa's alternate mix of "Down In De Dew." It was recorded at the same Jack Bruce/ Jim Gordon session as "Apostrophe (')," but Zappa stripped the rest of the track and built it up using the original Gordon drums. The original "Down In De Dew" mix on "Läther" and this mix contain different material from each other. This single mix was later used on "The Frank Zappa AAAFNRAA Birthday Bundle 21.12.2014" download and "The Crux Of The Biscuit." In terms of conceptual continuity, the last lyric of "Uncle Remus" is "down in the dew."

* * *

FRANK ZAPPA: Zoot Allures (1982)/ Cosmik Debris (1973) (Mother's Day 256kbps MP3 digital download from zappa.com)
Released May 10, 2014 as Barking Pumpkin ZPDD31/32

Track 1
Zoot Allures (1982) (6:12) (Frank Zappa) • Master #: none • STEREO
Recorded live on June 11, 1982 (late show) at Alte Oper, Frankfurt, Germany, and June 18-19, 1982 (early show on June 19) at Hammersmith Odeon, London, England
Personnel: Frank Zappa (guitar, vocals); Chad Wackerman (drums); Ed Mann (percussion); Tommy Mars (keyboards); Robert Martin (keyboards, tenor saxophone, vocals); Scott Thunes (bass, vocals); Steve Vai (guitar); Ray White (guitar, vocals)
Producer: Frank Zappa
Engineer: Mark Pinske

Track 2
Cosmik Debris (1973) (8:12) (Frank Zappa) • Master #: none • STEREO
Recorded live on August 23, 1973 (late show) at Finlandia-talo, Helsinki, Finland
Personnel: Frank Zappa (guitar, vocals); Ralph Humphrey (drums); George Duke (vocals); Bruce Fowler (trombone); Tom Fowler (bass); Jean-Luc Ponty (violin); Ian Underwood (bass clarinet, clarinet, flute, synthesizer); Ruth Underwood (percussion)
Producer: Frank Zappa
Engineer: Jukka Teittinen

"Zoot Allures" sounds crisp with excellent playing throughout. None of the edits are jarring, especially considering that this track is drawn from three shows. "Cosmik Debris," on the other hand, sounds like a roughly mixed guerrilla recording with overmodulated FZ vocals. It contains a very long and effective Zappa solo, and no other solos from George Duke and Ian Underwood, unlike this lineup's other performances. You had to grab this special Mother's Day release at the time. Both recordings are currently unavailable.

* * *

ESA-PEKKA SALONEN, CONDUCTOR – L.A. PHILHARMONIC: Overture (200 Motels)/ FRANK ZAPPA – THE ROYAL PHILHARMONIC ORCHESTRA – ELGAR HOWARTH, CONDUCTOR: What's The Name Of Your Group? (Record Store Day numbered 7" 45 rpm purple vinyl single)
Released April 18, 2015 as Barking Pumpkin BPR 1226

A-side
Overture (200 Motels) (2:18) (Frank Zappa) • Master #: none • STEREO
Recorded live on October 23, 2013 at Walt Disney Concert Hall, Los Angeles, CA
Personnel: Los Angeles Philharmonic, Esa-Pekka Salonen (conductor); Los Angeles Master Chorale; Michael Des Barres (Rance)
Producer: Frank Filipetti & Gail Zappa
Engineer: Frank Filipetti

B-side
What's The Name Of Your Group? (3:00) (Frank Zappa) • Master #: none • STEREO
Recorded live January 28-February 5, 1971 at Pinewood Studios, London, and April 1971 at Whitney Studios, Glendale, CA (overdubs)
Personnel: The Royal Philharmonic Orchestra – Elgar Howarth (conductor); Top Score Singers – David Van Asch (conductor); Phyllis Bryn-Julson (soprano); Classical Guitar Ensemble – John Williams (supervisor), Big Jim Sullivan, Timothy Walker
Producer: Frank Zappa
Engineer: Bob Auger (Pinewood); Barry Keene (Whitney)

"Overture" matches up exactly with "Semi-Fraudulent/Direct-From-Hollywood Overture" from the soundtrack of "Frank Zappa's 200 Motels." The first 1:05 of "Overture" uses the main theme of "Holiday In Berlin." The archival B-side was a previously unavailable recording. Numerous versions of the B-side turned up on the deluxe "200 Motels" set in December 2021. This take of "What's The Name Of Your Group?" was not in the film or soundtrack album. It was drawn from three segments of the composition "Dance Of The Rock & Roll Interviewers." The first 1:38 of "What's The Name…" can be traced to "Epilogue" on "Ahead Of Their Time," and the subsequent 1:22 involved a rearrangement of "A Pound For A Brown On The Bus."

* * *

FRANK ZAPPA: Pick Me, I'm Clean (Mother's Day 256kbps MP3 digital download from zappa.com)
Released May 10, 2015 as Barking Pumpkin ZPDD37

Track 1
Pick Me, I'm Clean (6:45) (Frank Zappa) • Master #: none • STEREO
Recorded live on July 3, 1980 at Olympiahalle, Munich, Germany
Personnel: Frank Zappa (guitar, vocals); David Logeman (drums); Arthur Barrow (bass); Tommy Mars (keyboards); Ray White (guitar, vocals); Ike Willis (guitar, vocals)
Producer: Frank Zappa
Engineer: Mark Pinske

This live nugget is the earliest released version we have of "Pick Me, I'm Clean." The song debuted during the North American tour covering March-May 1980. The more familiar "Tinsel Town Rebellion" version was drawn from three performances, but this recording came from just one location with a longer guitar solo section. Processed at maximum level throughout, this track is always on the edge of distorting. The track fades just before the band goes into "City Of Tiny Lites." The title of this song was mentioned in the lyrics of "Stick It Out" on "Joe's Garage." If you did not obtain this track around Mother's Day in 2015, you're out of luck. It is currently unavailable.

* * *

FRANK ZAPPA: Rollo/ Portland Improvisation (Record Store Day 10" 45 rpm clear vinyl single – gold numbered edition of 4,000 copies, although some copies are not numbered)
Released April 22, 2017 as Zappa/UME BPR 1230

A-side
Rollo > Includes: Rollo – The Rollo Interior Area – Rollo Goes Out (9:06) (Frank Zappa) • Master #: BPR 1230-A • STEREO
Recorded live on December 2, 1972 (early show) at Cowtown Ballroom, Kansas City, MO (NOTE: recording location on the single is incorrect)
Personnel: Frank Zappa (conductor, guitar, vocals); Malcolm McNab (trumpet); Gary Barone (trumpet); Tom Malone (tuba, saxophones, piccolo trumpet, trumpet); Earle Dumler (woodwinds); Glenn Ferris (trombone); Bruce Fowler (trombone); Tony Duran (slide guitar); Dave Parlato (bass); Jim Gordon (drums, steel drum)
Producer: Frank Zappa
Engineer: Barry Keene

B-side
Portland Improvisation (10:55) (Frank Zappa) • Master #: BPR 1230-B • STEREO
Recorded live on December 9, 1972 (late show) at Paramount Northwest Theatre, Portland, OR
Personnel: Frank Zappa (conductor, guitar, vocals); Malcolm McNab (trumpet); Gary Barone (trumpet); Tom Malone (tuba, saxes, piccolo trumpet, trumpet); Earle Dumler (woodwinds); Glenn Ferris (trombone); Bruce Fowler (trombone); Tony Duran (slide guitar); Dave Parlato (bass); Jim Gordon (drums, steel drum)
Producer: Frank Zappa
Engineer: Barry Keene

This Record Store Day single was recorded during the Petite Wazoo tour of the US which spanned October 27 – December 15, 1972. Both sides of the record are not available digitally. "Rollo" is taken entirely from the Kansas City performance, unlike its edit of Kansas City and an unknown location on the "Little Dots" CD. The module entitled "The Rollo Interior Area" was later worked into the "Saint Alfonzo's Pancake Breakfast" segment of the "Don't Eat The Yellow Snow" suite. The dog references continued with Zappa's short lyric set in "Rollo." Both sides were mixed by Zappa, with "Portland Improvisation" being an obviously edited performance that Zappa worked on at The Record Plant in Los Angeles in the mid-'80s. "Rollo" was mixed by Zappa at UMRK in the early 1980s.

Different arrangements of "Rollo" were performed by this lineup during the fall 1972 tour. The Abnuceals Emuukha Electric Symphony Orchestra performed the work in September 1975. That was released as part of the 40th anniversary edition of "Orchestral Favorites." Tommy Mars sang "Rollo" as the last segment of the five-part "Don't Eat The Yellow Snow" suite during the August-October 1978 European and US tour as well as the February-April 1979 European tour.

* * *

FRANK ZAPPA: Lumpy Gravy Primordial (Side One)/ Lumpy Gravy Primordial (Side Two) (Record Store Day 12" 45 rpm burgundy vinyl single)
Released April 21, 2018 as Zappa/UME BPR 1231

A-side
Lumpy Gravy Primordial (Side One) > I. Sink Trap (3:06); II. Gum Joy (3:44); III. Up & Down (1:52); IV: Local Butcher (2:33) (Total Time: 11:15) (Frank Zappa) • Master #: BPR 1231-A • MONO
Recorded: February 13, 1967 and March 14-16, 1967 at Capitol Studios, Hollywood, CA
Personnel: The Abnuceals Emuukha Electric Symphony Orchestra – Sidney Sharp (contractor, violin); Robert H. Ross (copyist); Esther Roth (orchestra manager); John Guerin (drums); James Helms (guitar); Robert West (bass guitar); James Bond (bass); Kenneth Watson (timpani, mallets); Paul Smith (piano); Thomas Poole (percussion); Ted Nash (flute, bass flute, alto saxophone, clarinet, bass clarinet, contrabass clarinet); Jules Jacob (oboe, English horn, flute, piccolo, tenor saxophone); Johnny Rotella (flute, alto saxophone, bass saxophone, baritone saxophone, clarinet, E flat clarinet, E flat contrabass clarinet, bass clarinet, piccolo); John L. "Bunk" Gardner (flute, clarinet, baritone clarinet, bass clarinet, bassoon, bass saxophone, soprano saxophone, tenor saxophone, piccolo); Emil Radocchia (aka Emil Richards) (mallets, percussion, timpani, Latin); Gene P. Estes (mallets, percussion, timpani, Latin); James C. Zito (trumpet, flugelhorn, piccolo trumpet); Thomas J. Tedesco (guitar, bells, bongos); Kenneth Shroyer (tenor trombone, bass trombone, bass trumpet); Frank Capp (drums, Latin); Don Christlieb (bassoon, contrabassoon); Michael A. Lang (piano); John Balkin (bass); Alfred Viola (guitar); Dennis Budimir (guitar); Arthur E. Briegleb (French horn); George F. Price (French horn); Lyle Ritz (bass); Joan Steele (copyist); Robert M. Calderwood (copyist); Russell N. Brown (copyist); Vincent Bartold (copyist); Jack DuLong (copyist); Victor Feldman (timpani, Latin, percussion, mallets); Gene Cipriano (oboe, flute, bass flute, E flat clarinet); Charles Berghofer (bass); Lincoln Mayorga (piano); David A. Duke (French horn); Trefoni (Tony) Rizzi (guitar); Shelly Manne (drums); Leonard Malarsky (violin); William Kurasch (violin); Arnold Belnick (violin); Ralph Schaeffer (violin); Jerome A. Kessler (cello); Raymond J. Kelley (cello); Leonard Selic (viola); Joseph DiFiore (viola); Harry Hyams (viola); Philip Goldberg (viola); Joseph Saxon (cello); Jesse Erlich (cello); Tibor Zelig (violin); Harold Ayres (violin); Jerome J. Reisler (violin); Robert Ross (copyist); R.D. McMickle (copyist); John Donahue (copyist); Robert Calderwood (copyist); C.D. Goodwin (copyist); Russell N. Brown (copyist); Joan Steele (copyist); Alan Estes (timpani, mallets, percussion, Latin); Pete Jolly (piano); Lew McCreary (trombone); Vincent DeRosa (French horn); Richard Parisi (French horn); Arthur Maebe (French horn); Harold G. Bemko (cello); Alexander Koltun (violin); Bernard Kundell (violin); James Getzoff (violin)
Producer: Nick Venet
Engineer: Joe, Rex, Pete, Jim, Bob and Gary

B-side
Lumpy Gravy Primordial (Side Two) > V. Gypsy Airs (1:41); VI. Hunchy Punchy (2:06); VII. Foamy Soaky (2:34); VIII. Let's Eat Out (1:48); IX. Teen-Age Grand Finale (3:29) (Total Time: 11:38) (Frank Zappa) • Master #: BPR 1231-B • MONO
same recording dates, personnel, producer and engineers as the A-side

Is this a single or an album? It is an extract of a larger release, so it should be considered a single. This 12" issue presents a mono master of the Capitol "Lumpy Gravy" album in 12" form. It was originally announced as a Black Friday release for November 24, 2017, but it was instead released on the following Record Store Day in April 2018. The "Primordial" single edition is the same as its presentation on "The Lumpy Money Project/Object" except that six seconds of studio chat prior to "Sink Trap" has been edited out. The "Sink Trap" portion of the Capitol "Lumpy Gravy" mono master differs from the Capitol stereo acetate in circulation.

The ongoing sequence of the differences is as follows:

1) This mix omits the "King Kong" segment (about 42 seconds in length) that was on the stereo Capitol acetate and the Verve LP edition.
2) The next 15-second segment appeared on the stereo "Lumpy Money" track "How Did That Get In Here?" and nowhere else.
3) A six-second fragment follows which is the same as the "Oh No" segment indexed as "Switching Girls" on recent CDs.
4) A two-second piece from both the stereo acetate and "How Did That Get In Here?" follows.
5) The rest of "Sink Trap" and the other segments on this "Primordial" master follow the stereo acetate.

In the conceptual continuity department, each "Primordial" track used the following indexed "Lumpy Gravy" CD segments and FZ themes (shown in parentheses):

<u>Side One</u>
"Sink Trap": "King Kong" (same title); "Switching Girls" ("Oh No"); "Oh No Again" ("Oh No"); "At The Gas Station" ("Oh No"). Outtake material appears on the "Lumpy Money" track "How Did That Get In Here?".

"Gum Joy": "Oh No" ("The World's Greatest Sinner," "Run Home Cues #2," same title); "At The Gas Station" ("Oh No"); "I Don't Know If I Can Go Through This Again" (same title). Outtake material appears on the "Lumpy Money" tracks "Unit 3A, Take 3," "How Did That Get In Here?," and "Unit 2, Take 9."

"Up & Down": "I Don't Know If I Can Go Through This Again" ("The World's Greatest Sinner," "Oh No," "A Pound For A Brown On The Bus"). Outtake material appears on the "Lumpy Money" track "N. Double A, AA."

"Local Butcher": "I Don't Know If I Can Go Through This Again" ("Envelops The Bath Tub," same title).

<u>Side Two</u>
"Gypsy Airs": "Envelops The Bath Tub" (same title).

"Hunchy Punchy": "Switching Girls" ("Oh No"); "Amen" (same title); "A Vicious Circle" (same title). Outtake material appears on the "Lumpy Money" track "How Did That Get In Here?".

"Foamy Soaky": "King Kong" (same title); "At The Gas Station" ("Oh No"); "Oh No Again" ("Oh No," "A Pound For A Brown On The Bus"); "Drums Are Too Noisy" (same title); "I Don't Know If I Can Go Through This Again" (same title). Outtake material appears on the "Lumpy Money" tracks "Section 8, Take 22," "N Double A, AA," and "How Did That Get In Here?".

"Let's Eat Out": "I Don't Know If I Can Go Through This Again" (same title – alternate take); "Kangaroos" (same title).

"Teen-Age Grand Finale": "Envelops The Bath Tub" (same title). Outtake material appears on the "Lumpy Money" track "How Did That Get In Here?".

* * *

FRANK ZAPPA: Peaches En Regalia (1969 Rhythm Track Mix) – Little Umbrellas (1969 Rhythm Track Mix)/ Peaches En Regalia (1969 Mono Single Master) – Little Umbrellas (1969 Mono Single Master)
(Black Friday 10" 45 rpm numbered picture disc single edition of 4,000 copies)
Released November 29, 2019 as Zappa/UME BPR 1234

A-side – Track 1
Peaches En Regalia (1969 Rhythm Track Mix) (4:14) (Frank Zappa) • Master #: none • STEREO
Recorded: July 28-29, 1969 at T.T.G. Studios, Hollywood, CA
Personnel: Ian Underwood (piano); Ron Selico (drums); Shuggie Otis (bass); Frank Zappa (voice on ending fade)
Producer: Frank Zappa
Engineer: Jack Hunt & Cliff Goldstein

A-side – Track 2
Little Umbrellas (1969 Rhythm Track Mix) (3:05) (Frank Zappa) • Master #: none • STEREO
Recorded: July 29, 1969 at T.T.G. Studios, Hollywood, CA
Personnel: Ian Underwood (piano); John Guerin (drums); Max Bennett (string bass)
Producer: Frank Zappa
Engineer: Jack Hunt & Cliff Goldstein

B-side – Track 1
Peaches En Regalia (1969 Mono Single Master) (3:30) (Frank Zappa) • Master #: none • MONO
see Peaches En Regalia/ Little Umbrellas

B-side – Track 2
Little Umbrellas (1969 Mono Single Master) (3:04) (Frank Zappa) • Master #: none • MONO
see Peaches En Regalia/ Little Umbrellas

The 50th anniversary of the release of "Hot Rats" was honored by the first official release of the intended single "Peaches En Regalia"/ "Little Umbrellas." This record was announced on October 8, 2019 for release on Black Friday with the mono single mixes of both tracks on side A and the rhythm track mixes on side B. The released running order reversed the sides. Even with the December 20, 2019 release of the 6-CD box set "The Hot Rats Sessions," we still do not know why this potentially commercial single was not originally issued. The box set did reveal that "Natasha" was the original title of "Little Umbrellas."

"The Hot Rats Sessions" includes multiple versions of "Peaches En Regalia" and "Little Umbrellas." The "Peaches" versions included on that set were the two on this single plus "Prototype," "Section 1, In Session," "Section 1, Master Take," two "Peaches Jam" parts (the unused second "Peaches" section), "Section 3, In Session," and "Section 3, Master Take." Concerning the "Little Umbrellas"-related versions, the box set featured "In Session" and "Master Take" editions of "Natasha" along with "Little Umbrellas" takes credited as "Cucamonga Version" (an acetate recorded at Pal Recording Studio in 1962 with saxophonist Mike Dineri, drummer/engineer Paul Buff, and FZ on guitar), "1969 Mix Outtake," and the two variations on this 10" single. To complete the picture, the box set track "Piano Music (Section 3)" quoted "Peaches En Regalia" and "Aybe Sea."

Both "1969 Rhythm Track Mix" editions on this 10" do not have the Zappa spoken intros available on their box set counterparts: "Can you still hear me? Can the machine hear me? Bingo bango bongo?" prior to "Peaches En Regalia," and "Watch me now! Hah!" prior to "Little Umbrellas." However, Frank can be heard at the very end of the "Peaches" rhythm track mix on this single, unlike the box set, which is unnecessarily faded early.

At 2:35.2 of the "Peaches En Regalia" single mix, there is a digital error which repeats an organ note for about a tenth of a second. The rhythm track mix of "Little Umbrellas" has a wobbly right channel which starts at the 1:20 mark. Both defects appear on this single and the box set presentations of the tracks.

* * *

FRANK ZAPPA: The Zappa Movie Official Soundtrack EP! - Exclusive Backer Reward Edition (purple splashed transparent vinyl numbered 12" 45 rpm single)
Released November 6, 2020 as Zappa EES-002

A-side – Track 1
"The Full Impact" (1:00) (Frank Zappa) • Master #: none • MONO
Recorded: summer 1967 at WRVR-FM Studios, New York, NY
Personnel: Frank Zappa (voice)
Producer: Frank Zappa
Engineer: unknown

A-side – Track 2
Rawgah (3:32) (Frank Zappa) • Master #: none • MONO
Recorded: July 1966 at T.T.G. Studios, Hollywood, CA
Personnel: Frank Zappa (guitars, basses); John Guerin (drums)
Producer: Frank Zappa
Engineer: Ami Hadani & Tom Hidley

A-side – Track 3
Watermelon In Easter Hay (3:30) (Frank Zappa) • Master #: none • STEREO
Recorded live on November 17, 1981 at The Ritz, New York, NY
Personnel: Frank Zappa (guitar); Steve Vai (sitar); Robert Martin (keyboards); Tommy Mars (keyboards); Ed Mann (percussion); Ray White (guitar); Scott Thunes (bass); Chad Wackerman (drums)
Producer: Frank Zappa
Engineer: Mark Pinske

B-side – Track 1
Vault Of Imaginary Diseases (5:26) (Frank Zappa) • Master #: none • STEREO
Recorded live on March 24, 1973 at Sports Arena, San Diego, CA
Personnel: Frank Zappa (narration); George Duke (keyboards); Jean-Luc Ponty (violin); Ian Underwood (woodwinds); Bruce Fowler (trombone); Sal Marquez (trumpet); Tom Fowler (bass); Ruth Underwood (percussion); Ralph Humphrey (drums); Don Preston (synthesizer)
Producer: Frank Zappa
Engineer: Barry Keene

B-side – Track 2
Brutality (Maniac Mix) (4:34) (Frank Zappa) • Master #: none • STEREO
Recorded: 1985 at UMRK, Los Angeles, CA

Personnel: Frank Zappa (Synclavier)
Producer: Frank Zappa
Engineer: Bob Stone

Available to only some Kickstarter backers of Alex Winter's "Zappa" film, this color-splashed 12" started out with a summer 1967 interview segment from New York City's long-gone WRVR-FM in which Frank discussed that The Mothers Of Invention were playing ragas before groups like The Byrds. Matty Biberfeld was the WRVR interviewer that was edited out of the interview segment presented here. The subsequent track "Rawgah" is proof of Zappa's statement. A small soundbite from "Rawgah" can be heard at the end of "Are You Hung Up?" on "We're Only In It For The Money." The version of "Watermelon In Easter Hay" came from the legendary Ritz concert in November 1981. Don Preston was the guest synthesist on "Vault Of Imaginary Diseases," whose Zappa-narrated themes would be embellished on "Stink-Foot" and "Suicide Chump." The last track came from the "Resolver + Brutality" cassette. None of these tracks were used in the finished cut of Alex Winter's film, so they are exclusive to this release.

* * *

FRANK ZAPPA: A Very Zappa Birthday (digital download EP in numerous formats)
Released December 21, 2020 as Zappa/UME (no #)

Track 1
Fembot In A Wet T-Shirt (4:44) (Frank Zappa) • Master #: none • STEREO
see Joe's Garage 12" promo sampler

Track 2
Valley Girl (4:50) (Frank Zappa) • Master #: none • STEREO
see Valley Girl (Dutch single)

Track 3
Stink-Foot (7:39) (Frank Zappa) • Master #: none • STEREO
Recorded live on February 20, 1988 at Orpheum Theater, Boston, MA, February 23, 1988 at Mid-Hudson Civic Center, Poughkeepsie, NY, and May 4, 1988 at The Ahoy, Rotterdam, Netherlands
Personnel: Frank Zappa (lead guitar, synthesizer, vocal); Ike Willis (rhythm guitar, synthesizer, vocal); Mike Keneally (rhythm guitar, synthesizer, vocal); Bobby Martin (keyboards, vocal); Ed Mann (vibes, marimba, electronic percussion); Walt Fowler (trumpet, flugelhorn, synthesizer); Bruce Fowler (trombone); Paul Carman (alto saxophone, soprano saxophone, baritone saxophone); Albert Wing (tenor saxophone); Kurt McGettrick (baritone saxophone, contrabass clarinet); Scott Thunes (electric bass, Minimoog); Chad Wackerman (drums, electronic percussion)
Producer: Frank Zappa
Engineer: Bob Stone

Track 4
Dirty Love (2:58) (Frank Zappa) • Master #: none • STEREO
Recorded March 19, 1973 (basic tracks) and May 31, 1973 (vocal overdubs) at Bolic Sound, Inglewood, CA
Personnel: Frank Zappa (guitar, arranger, conductor, vocals); Ralph Humphrey (drums); George Duke (keyboards); Tom Fowler (bass); The Ikettes – Tina Turner, Debbie Wilson, Linda "Lynn" Sims (backing vocals)
Producer: Frank Zappa

Engineer: Barry Keene

Track 5
Watermelon In Easter Hay (5:59) (Frank Zappa) • Master #: none • STEREO
Recorded live on February 24, 1978 at Rhein-Neckar Stadion, Eppelheim, Germany
Personnel: Frank Zappa (lead guitar, voice); Terry Bozzio (drums); Patrick O'Hearn (bass); Tommy Mars (keyboards); Peter Wolf (keyboards); Ed Mann (percussion); Adrian Belew (rhythm guitar)
Producer: Frank Zappa
Engineer: Davey Moire

Track 6
I'm The Slime (3:34) (Frank Zappa) • Master #: none • STEREO
see I'm The Slime/ Montana

This is a collection of previously released material that most fans already have. The only unusual selections are "Stink-Foot" from "Make A Jazz Noise Here" and "Watermelon In Easter Hay" from "Frank Zappa Plays The Music Of Frank Zappa." "Stink-Foot" was played during each 1974-1988 rock band touring year. This particular version included quotes from "Dragnet" and "Dickie's Such An Asshole" and was the latest released version of the song. "Stink-Foot" was on "Apostrophe (')," and the KCET-TV version was later included on both the audio and video editions of "The Dub Room Special!" and "A Token Of His Extreme." The other released live version from 1974 was recorded in Helsinki, Finland and was on "Stage, Vol. 2." During the January 1976 Australian tour, "Stink-Foot" was paired with "The Poodle Lecture" and was released on "FZ:OZ," and the fall tour of that year linked the two works on the albums "Philly '76" and "Beat The Boots II: Conceptual Continuity." The October 30, 1977 performances of "Stink-Foot" and "The Poodle Lecture" were issued on the film/soundtrack releases of "Baby Snakes (The Movie)" as well as the "Halloween 77" box set. "The Poodle Lecture" was also extracted on "Stage, Vol. 6." The Halloween 1978 version of "Stink-Foot" was included in the 2003 album "Halloween."

After the debut of "Dirty Love" on "Over-Nite Sensation," live versions from 1976 were on "FZ:OZ," "Philly '76," and "Beat The Boots II: Conceptual Continuity." Like "Stink-Foot," the October 30, 1977 take of "Dirty Love" ended up on "Halloween 77." The European tour of February-April 1979 also featured "Dirty Love," and of those dates, the February 18 version ended up on "Stage, Vol. 6."

www.ingramcontent.com/pod-product-compliance
Lightning Source LLC
Chambersburg PA
CBHW080849020526
44118CB00037B/2322